# THE THOUGHT OF
# REINHOLD NIEBUHR

# THE THOUGHT OF

# REINHOLD NIEBUHR

GORDON HARLAND

*New York · OXFORD UNIVERSITY PRESS · 1960*

CHARLES SCRIBNER'S SONS GRANTED PERMISSION TO REPRINT PASSAGES FROM *The Children of Light and the Children of Darkness* by Reinhold Niebuhr, copyright 1944 by Charles Scribner's Sons; *Faith and History* by Reinhold Niebuhr, copyright 1949 by Charles Scribner's Sons; *The Irony of American History* by Reinhold Niebuhr, copyright 1952 by Charles Scribner's Sons; *Moral Man and Immoral Society* by Reinhold Niebuhr, copyright 1932 by Charles Scribner's Sons; *The Nature and Destiny of Man* (Vol. I) by Reinhold Niebuhr, copyright 1941 by Charles Scribner's Sons; *The Nature and Destiny of Man* (Vol. II) by Reinhold Niebuhr, copyright 1943 by Charles Scribner's Sons; *Christian Faith and Social Action* by Reinhold Niebuhr, (edited by John Hutchison) copyright 1953 by Charles Scribner's Sons; *Beyond Tragedy* by Reinhold Niebuhr; *Christianity and Power Politics* by Reinhold Niebuhr; *Discerning the Signs of the Times* by Reinhold Niebuhr; *Christian Realism and Political Problems* by Reinhold Niebuhr; copyright 1953 by Reinhold Niebuhr; *The Self and Dramas of History* by Reinhold Niebuhr, copyright 1955 by Reinhold Niebuhr.

TO RUTH

Reinhold Niebuhr's thought and work have been dominated throughout by one persistent concern. He has sought to clarify the insights and resources of Christian faith in such a way that they may be savingly related to the structures, dynamics, and decisions of large social groups.

It is an immense task, beset by countless problems and pitfalls. The greatest problem, however, inheres in the very nature of Christianity itself, as its history abundantly reveals. The heart of the Christian revelation is *Agape*—heedless, sacrificial, sin-bearing love. But how can a social ethic be derived from *agape*? A social ethic demands prudent, discriminate judgments, not heedless sacrifice of self. What meaningful relationship can *agape* have to the struggles of power upon which the securing and maintaining of justice are necessarily dependent? What relevance can such a faith have to the policy of nations when the first responsibility of the leaders of nations is to maintain national security and further the national interest?

The very possibility of a Christian social ethic is dependent upon a clear and honest facing of such questions. To blunt the radicality of the Christian norm, or to minimize the peculiar problems and dynamics of collective life, can serve only to obscure the genius of Christianity and to spread confusion into social analysis. And that has happened, perhaps especially in the period in which Niebuhr has done his work. The result has been that the task of clarifying the relation between Christian faith and social responsibility has been complicated by the necessity to disclose the inadequacy of a wide variety of Christian and "secular" approaches to the problem. Thus in order to get the dimensions of the real problem before us, to bring the question into clear focus, a good deal of Niebuhr's work has necessarily involved a polemic against those views of man and history, as well as distortions and dilutions of Christian faith, which prevented the problem being seen with clarity and wholeness.

Niebuhr is a Protestant theologian, and not the least of his claims upon our gratitude is that he spoke again the Reformation understanding with such insight and power to a generation of Americans who had almost completely forgotten its peculiar perspective. Niebuhr's apprehension of the meaning of the Gospel is in direct line with that of the Great Reformers. That is not to say that the Reformation is, for Niebuhr, without defect. Its most glaring defect is precisely at the point of his own passionate concern, the relation between *agape* and the necessity, demand, and conditions for securing social justice. Thus both the achievement and the failure of the Reformation define the direction and character of Niebuhr's task. Indeed, nowhere has he more clearly outlined his own life work than in the following passage. "Reformation insights", he says, "must be related to the whole range of human experience more 'dialectically' than the Reformation succeeded in doing. The 'yes' and 'no' of its dialectical affirmations: that the Christian is 'justus et peccator,' 'both sinner and righteous'; that history fulfills and negates the Kingdom of God; that grace is continuous with, and in contradiction to, nature; that Christ is what we ought to be and also what we cannot be; that the power of God is in us and that the power of God is against us in judgment and mercy; that all these affirmations which are but varied forms of the one central paradox of the relation of the Gospel to history must be applied to the experiences of life from top to bottom."[1]

Nothing less than this is the task which Niebuhr has set himself, and the degree to which he has succeeded is the measure of his achievement. The whole work, however, serves the one concern— to relate redemptively Christian faith and social responsibility, *agape* and the struggle for social justice.

It is hoped that this present inquiry will do something to dispel the still widespread impression that Niebuhr is obsessed with sin, and consequently unduly pessimistic in his social analysis and outlook. Niebuhr's admirers and detractors, have both contributed to the perpetuation of this notion. Holtan P. Odegard states categorically, "The central, overwhelming idea for Reinhold Niebuhr is sin." [2] Sin is "the fundamental principle upon which his interpretations are based." [3] Niebuhr is even said to have "faith in sin." [4] Hans Hofmann, who is certainly not lacking in appreciation of Niebuhr, says with almost equal bluntness, "Sin is Niebuhr's central concern." [5] Perhaps the general impression was best articulated by Whitney J. Oates, when he remarked that despite Niebuhr's "profound sense of the comprehensiveness of Christianity," he has been guilty of overemphasizing sin in his reaction to modern sentimental versions of Christian faith. "Yet another imbalance in its turn tends to vitiate Niebuhr's position. Planted squarely as he is in the prophetic tradition, he has concentrated too exclusively on the fallen state of man, or to put it somewhat facetiously, has been so busy rehabilitating sin as a fact of man's nature that other and equally important aspects of Christianity suffer from underemphasis." [6]

It is not our purpose to debate such judgments here, though their validity may be tested throughout the present inquiry. It is sufficient to say that Niebuhr's penetrating analysis of sin is but part of his total task of illuminating what is involved in relating Christian insight creatively to the social task. This, not sin, is Niebuhr's central concern.

Indeed, Niebuhr's influence as a Christian apologist has been due in large measure to the richness with which he has shown the social significance of the Christian understanding and experience of grace. This has not been generally recognized. It has seemed wise therefore to devote a full chapter (Chap. 5) to a discussion of his understanding of the positive resources of Christian faith for the social task.

The centrality of Christology in Niebuhr's thought is clear and of the highest importance. A full treatment of Niebuhr's Christology has not, however, been undertaken in this study. Paul Lehmann's splendid essay on "The Christology of Reinhold Niebuhr" in *Reinhold Niebuhr: His Religious, Social and Political Thought* is so accurate and penetrating as to render further exposition unnecessary.

The focus of this presentation of Niebuhr's thought is the relation between love and justice, but the aim and purpose of the book is to expound and interpret his thought as a whole. It is not an inquiry into the evolution of Niebuhr's thinking. It deals with his mature thought, indicating those changes and striking continuities only when it appears useful to do so.

Inasmuch as Niebuhr's thought has been forged in daily encounter with the shattering events of our age, wide use has been made of his almost countless articles and editorials as well as of his published books. Impressive as the books are, nothing is more exciting or instructive than to see Reinhold Niebuhr week in and week out, year in and year out, wrestling to speak the prophetic and clarifying word of Christian understanding in the midst of the momentous events and decisions of the past three decades.

This book is divided into two Parts. Part I delineates the structure of Niebuhr's theological ethic and Part II carries this forward by analyzing Niebuhr's views on a number of issues, movements, and events pertaining to politics, economics, war, and race. The division into two parts has been made to facilitate the handling of such a vast amount of material. It will be clear from the discussion that this division in no way suggests that Niebuhr's theological reflections and political analyses lack organic relation. On the contrary, his theological and political thought form one consistent whole.

Niebuhr's latest book, *The Structure of Nations and Empires,* appeared after this manuscript was completed. This book ought to be consulted by any reader wishing to pursue Niebuhr's political philosophy which I have endeavored to analyze in Chapter 6.

It is a pleasure to be able to express my indebtedness to a number of people. Dean S.R. Hopper of the Graduate School and Dean

B.W. Anderson of the School of Theology of Drew University have consistently shown me their interest and encouragement. My greatest debt is to three friends and colleagues, Will Herberg, George Kelsey, and John Dillenberger. While writing this book, I greatly enjoyed and profited from numerous conversations with them concerning the theological and political issues facing us today.

My wife and Miss Sherry Pierpont have typed the various manuscripts and helped in preparing the index.

I am grateful for the assistance provided by a grant from The Humanities Research Council of Canada and Drew University's William S. Pilling Traveling Fellowship.

*G.H.*

*Drew University, Madison, New Jersey*
*Christmas 1959*

# Acknowledgments

The author wishes to thank the following publishers for permission to reprint selections from their publications:

The Antioch Press for a passage from *Sin and Science* by Holtan P. Odegard; Harper and Brothers for passages from *Goals of Economic Life,* edited by A.D.Ward; *The Organizational Revolution* by K. Boulding; *Faith and Ethics* edited by Paul Ramsey; *God's Grace and Man's Hope* by D.D. Williams; *Justice and the Social Order* by E.Brunner; and *Man's Disorder and God's Design;* Doubleday and Company for passages from Reinhold Niebuhr's essay in *Religion and Freedom of Thought* by Perry Miller, Robert L. Calhoun, Nathan M. Pusey, and Reinhold Niebuhr. Copyright 1954 by The Union Theological Seminary; Henry Holt and Company for a passage from *The Limits of Foreign Policy* by C.B.Marshall; The University of Chicago Press for a passage from *Natural Right and History* by Leo Strauss, copyright 1953 by the University of Chicago; The Macmillan Company for passages from *Reinhold Niebuhr: His Religious, Social, and Political Thought* edited by Kegley and Bretall.

In addition, the author wishes to thank the following magazines for permission to quote:

*Christianity and Crisis, The New Leader,* and *The Christian Century.*

# Contents

PART ONE

## One

# THE NORM OF LOVE

Reinhold Niebuhr has frequently remarked that he is not a theologian. Whether we accept this genial self-depreciation will depend on the meaning we assign to the word. Certainly, as Paul Lehmann has put it, "Niebuhr is not writing systematic theology. But he is writing theological ethics. And what he demonstrates is that when Christian doctrine is considered in relation to ethics, the insights expressed in the doctrine take on reality and meaning and the concerns of ethics are given foundation and direction."[1] The world he knows so well and which he has analyzed so perceptively, has always been viewed by him from the perspective of the revelation in Christ. Niebuhr's thinking is thoroughly Christocentric. And if profound and continuous reflection on the meaning of the Christ event for man and history is the mark of the theologian then assuredly Niebuhr is a theologian. Be that as it may, the Christocentric character of Niebuhr's thought is of paramount significance for his ethics. His concern is ever to show how the *agape* of the Cross illumines the whole meaning of our existence and provides both insight and resource for the responsible living of our life. At the Cross we discern that love which is the norm, the law of human life.

Simply to say this is to be confronted with a number of questions that lead us at once into the heart of Niebuhr's thought. What does Niebuhr mean by the love which is the law of life? Throughout the years he has been involved in continuous controversy over this matter and thus has had ample opportunity to state and clarify his thought. We can best get his understanding before us by asking him two questions: (1) What is the nature of the norm? and (2) What is the source of the norm? When we have secured our answers to these questions, we shall then be able to inquire how he understands the relationship of the norm to the decisions and structures of our historical existence.

## 1. THE NATURE OF THE NORM

In a word, the norm of life is love—sacrificial, heedless, uncalculating love. "The law of his [i.e. man's] nature is love, a harmonious relation of life to life in obedience to the divine centre and source of his life." [2] It is the love that "seeketh not its own," but sacrificially and spontaneously seeks ever the neighbor's good. It is the *agape* of the Cross which, as someone has said, Paul in Corinthians did not so much think up as copy down.

This understanding has certainly not gone unchallenged. Niebuhr has had continually to define and defend his understanding, especially against three other positions: (1) those who believe that the concept of mutual love is more meaningful and relevant; (2) the proponents of natural law; and (3) those who are impatient with all norms and who conceive self-interest as "normative." It is only as we see Niebuhr's position in relation to these that the full dimensions of his concept of sacrificial love as the norm of life can be uncovered. At this point it will be most profitable for us to note his debate with those who contend that the concept of "mutual love" more fully interprets the meaning of Christian love.

This debate began early. In 1933, in a critical discussion of *Moral Man and Immoral Society*, George A. Coe joined the debate with Niebuhr at this very point. It is the transcendent character of the norm of sacrificial love that disturbs Coe as much as Niebuhr's loss of "confidence in human nature." Thus we find Coe writing:

> It is characteristic of his [i.e. Niebuhr's] mind to "go the limit" with an ideal, but also to "go the limit" with disappointment when it is

obstructed. He is both intellectually and emotionally attracted towards absolutes, but often his absolutes turn out, Hegel-wise, to contain their own opposites. His treatment of the Christian law of love is an instance. As it is formulated by Jesus it requires me to love myself as I love my neighbor, to do as I would be done by, hence to calculate and plan, to take circumstances into account (my own and others'), and to balance probabilities against one another, all in the interest of a common good in which I am to share. Niebuhr first turns this complex of acts that are relative into an absolute. He identifies Christian love with absolute disinterestedness, an utter giving of oneself without weighing the consequences to anyone—a process that would spoil any voluntary beneficiaries of it.[3]

This sacrificial and "disinterested" love which Niebuhr "mistakenly calls Christian," continues Coe, "if it existed, would be a nuisance. But he thinks it sublime, and therefore regards as inescapable tragedy the fact that it won't work."[4]

Niebuhr's formulation of the dialectical relations between *agape* and mutual love, *agape* and justice, has acquired both refinement and enrichment since 1933. However, his reply to Coe in the same issue of *The Christian Century* embodies much of his present position and is an instance of the continuity of his thought. Niebuhr replies to this particular criticism in this way:

In dealing with the inner ethical problem there will always be a place for the Christian law of love. Dr. Coe thinks I interpret it in terms too pure and that I should be satisfied with the ideal of mutual love and forget the idea of disinterested love, which he thinks is a nuisance and which I regard as sublime. That interpretation seems to me to evade the whole profundity of the moral problem. It is precisely because mutual love has the root of selfishness in it that it lends itself so readily to a justification of egoism if it does not stand under the scrutiny of the higher ideal of disinterested or sacrificial love. I do not regard it as a "tragedy that this love won't work." It does work as an ideal which constantly reminds us of the alloy of egoism in every mutual relation and saves us from the hypocrisy of believing that we are unselfish when we affirm the interest of another in order that he may affirm our interest. This ideal is absolutely necessary for the preservation of the highest inner check upon egoism. It fails to work only when it is assumed that an inner check upon egoism is enough.[5]

Niebuhr has discarded such terms as "ideal" and "inner check"; but, as we have already indicated, it is the same basic position expressed here which has gained subsequent clarification and elaboration. This may be seen most clearly in a consideration of his "debate" with Daniel D. Williams, which was joined with the publication of the latter's Rauschenbusch Lectures, *God's Grace and Man's Hope*, and continued in the second volume of *The Library of Living Theology* devoted to Niebuhr's thought. This friendly controversy is of sufficient significance, both for the importance of the issue and for placing Niebuhr's position in clear relief, to merit some consideration.

Williams is concerned to uphold the reality of God's redemptive work within history, and this concern motivates both his criticism of Niebuhr and his own attempt at a positive statement. It is his conviction that the reality of God's redemptive work is missed both in liberalism and neo-orthodoxy.

> Liberalism has no place for redemption because it does not see the need for it. It conceived the emergence of man from sin and the overcoming of evil as primarily a problem of creation, the making of the new man and the new world. Neo-orthodoxy recognizes the need for redemption; but it has never made an adequate place for the real possibility of redemption as transformation of our human existence, hence it postpones redemption to another realm. These statements may be too sweeping, but I believe they are essentially just.[6]

From this general view of neo-orthodoxy, Williams discerns three specific weaknesses. They are: (1) "Neo-orthodoxy's treatment of the doctrine of original sin has led to a distorted version of the natural life of man." (2) "In the second place, neo-orthodoxy has its own metaphysics in which time and process are dealt with in such a way that the element of connected development in Christian experience must be denied." (3) God's power in action is not properly delineated, for "some break with sin in fact as well as in principle is possible or else the whole of Christian experience is a delusion."[7]

Niebuhr is included under this general label of neo-orthodoxy and the criticisms above are leveled quite specifically in his direction. From this general standpoint, Williams proceeds to attack Niebuhr's *formulation* of the meaning of *agape* and the nature of its relationship to mutual love. The essence of Williams's criticism is that mutuality is the substance of love, that it is the "order" which "the love of God intends," and therefore it is "not a denial of Christian love to intend my own good in the service of the Kingdom."[8] The tension between sacrificial love and mutual love in Niebuhr's thought is thus overcome in Williams by making the sacrificial aspect a subordinate feature of the will to true community. The heart of William's criticism is thus directed at Niebuhr's distinction between sacrificial and mutual love in the interests of upholding the reality of God's redemptive work in history or the growth of more mature and inclusive community.

It is frequently a disconcerting experience to read Williams's criticism of Niebuhr. Williams has appropriated a good measure of Niebuhr's thought into his own and he often expounds Niebuhr fairly and sympathetically. One could not ask for a brief statement that better entered into the spirit and structure of Niebuhr's thought than the following:

> By asserting the paradoxical relationship of sacrificial and mutual love he holds them together without identifying them. The Christian Gospel becomes a support of the human struggle for the good, a prophetic criticism of the spirit of that struggle, and a final assertion that man receives from God the forgiveness which enables him both to know and to accept his limitations.[9]

When Williams turns from exposition to criticism, however, Niebuhr's position undergoes a corresponding distortion. Instead of a distinction between sacrificial and mutual love in which they are still held together, Williams asserts three pages later in his book that this distinction is raised "to the level of a metaphysical dualism."[10] That this is not merely loose phrasing would appear from the fact that seven years later he reiterates the same charge. Niebuhr's distinction, he asserts, "leaves the Christian caught between two worlds which have two differing ultimate norms, and therefore distraught and divided in all ethical decision."[11] We shall make it clear: Niebuhr nowhere separates sacrificial love and mutual love, *agape* and justice, in such a manner as to have "a metaphysical dualism" or to leave man with "two ultimate norms." In both intent and formulation, his thought is clearly and consistently directed against any such effort.

Niebuhr has, I think, seen everything that is at stake in this controversy and in his reply to Williams has stated the issue and the heart of his own position with great clarity. He writes:

> The relation between sacrificial love and mutual love contains the issue of the relation between the eschatological and the historical in a nutshell. Love, heedless of the self, must be the initiator of any reciprocal love. Otherwise the calculation of mutual advantages makes love impossible. But heedless love usually wins a response of love. That is a symbol of the moral content of history. But this response cannot be guaranteed, as modern thought sought erroneously to guarantee it. That is symbolic of the "tragic" dimension of history and a proof that the meaning of life always transcends the fulfillments of meaning in history. That is why Christian faith is "eschatological" and has a touch of "otherworldliness," which one cannot eliminate by trying to contain all facets in the processes of history.[12]

This understanding of the relation between sacrificial and mutual love requires some elaboration. It is necessary to discuss it in fuller detail because the whole structure of Niebuhr's ethics revolves about the dialectical relation of *agape* to the relative achievements of man in history. This is why Niebuhr always spends so much time delineating this relation. This is also the reason why the really serious criticisms of his position become focused in this area. *Agape* as heedless, sacrificial love and its relation to the need for discriminate judgment and resolute action form the keystone of the entire structure. A more careful analysis of how Niebuhr

conceives the relation between sacrificial and mutual love is therefore necessary.

We may begin by looking at the relationship from the standpoint
of mutual love. Mutual love needs sacrificial love in order to remain
mutual love. Without it, mutual love will remain neither mutual
nor love. "If mutual love is not constantly replenished by impulses
of grace in which there are no calculations of mutual advantages,
mutual relations degenerate first to the cool calculation of such
advantages and finally to resentment over the inevitable lack of
complete reciprocity in all actual relations." [13]

For this reason self-realization, even though it be through devotion to the greatest common good, cannot be the conscious end
of our action, as Williams contends. Niebuhr has insisted on this
with notable consistency. In his first great work he says: "The paradox of the moral life consists in this: that the highest mutuality is
achieved where mutual advantages are not consciously sought as
the fruit of love. For love is purest where it desires no returns for
itself; and it is most potent where it is purest." [14] In the Gifford
Lectures he says bluntly: "Mutuality is not a possible achievement
if it is made the intention and goal of any action." [15] And in one of
his later writings he asserts again: "For the kind of self-giving
which has self-realization as its result must not have self-realization as its conscious end; otherwise the self by calculating its
enlargement will not escape from itself completely enough to be
enlarged." [16]

This is the nub of the problem. We shall have more to say about
it when we consider Niebuhr's understanding of the self. It will be
sufficient at this point to note his criticism of Erich Fromm contained in his lengthy and important review of Fromm's *Man For
Himself*. Niebuhr agrees with Fromm's strictures against a moralistic legalism and with his clear recognition of the limitations of a
sense of duty for providing the needed ethical resource. Niebuhr's
criticism is centered on Fromm's failure to measure the fact that
the "real problem of the self is that it seeks to contain itself as free
spirit within itself as contingent existence." In a word, the love of

the neighbor is not just the result of a "phenomenon of abundance" of the self which first loves itself. Our ability to love is not simply the overflow of a vital self-love. On the contrary, "Whatever spiritual wealth the self has within itself is the by-product of its relations, affections and responsibilities, of its concern for life beyond itself."[17] The advocates of "self-love" thus fail to understand the nature and dimensions of the self's relations just as grievously as do the legalists. Niebuhr puts this memorably:

> The psychiatric proponents of self-love are afraid that such an impoverished life will be presented with the false cure of the law to be unselfish. Actually both admonitions, that the self ought to love itself and that the self ought to love others, are spiritually impotent. An insecure and impoverished self is not made secure by the admonition to be concerned for itself; for an excessive concern for its security is the cause of its impoverishment. Nor is it made secure by the admonition to love others because that is precisely what it can not do because of its anxiety about itself. That is why a profound religion has always insisted that the self can not be cured by law but only by grace; and also why the profoundest forms of the Christian faith regard this preoccupation as not fully curable and therefore as requiring another kind of grace: that of forgiveness.[18]

Mutual love thus cannot be the conscious end of our actions. Sacrificial love is needed to save mutual love from degenerating into a prudent calculation of the self's interests. As we have already seen, this does not mean a radical separation between sacrificial and mutual love. They are not divided by any neat line.[19]

Viewed from a more positive perspective, Niebuhr sees sacrificial love as having "a threefold relation of transcendence" to the norms of mutuality.

We have already sufficiently discussed the first, and the following quotation succinctly states the relation: "Sacrificial love (*agape*) completes the incompleteness of mutual love (*eros*), for the latter is always arrested by reason of the fact that it seeks to relate life to life from the standpoint of the self and for the sake of the self's own happiness."[20]

Niebuhr defines the second relation as "a transcendent perfection which clarifies obscurities of history and defines the limits of what is possible in historic development."[21] That is to say, the sacrificial love of the Cross illumines both the nature of our historical situation and the character of our decisions, and it reveals that the ultimate norm of our life is not a simple possibility of history. The norm of sacrificial love is the love of the Cross. It enters history to be crucified. It is not a strategy of historical success. Sacrificial love remains truly sacrificial. It is relevant to all history but it is not *directly* applicable as historical strategy. In a word, it "defines the limits of what is possible in historical development." We shall have a good deal more to say about this at later points of our study, but here we must consider what has come to be regarded as one of Niebuhr's more notorious statements, because the validity of his construing the norm of life as sacrificial love is at stake.

Niebuhr has been saying that the sacrificial love of the Cross is not a simple historical possibility, which utopians are under the illusion it is, and that the final justification of the way of *agape* can never be derived from history. He then makes this statement:

> Since this possibility does not exist, it is not even right to insist that every action of the Christian must conform to *agape*, rather than to the norms of relative justice and mutual love by which life is maintained and conflicting interests are arbitrated in history. For as soon as the life and interest of others than the agent are involved in an action or policy, the sacrifice of those interests ceases to be "self-sacrifice." It may actually become an unjust betrayal of their interests.[22]

Williams quotes this passage (leaving off, it may be noted, the important qualifying phrase "since this possibility does not exist") and then pounces on it with the declaration: "This example reveals what is mistaken in Niebuhr's doctrine."[23] Paul Ramsey also quotes this passage and says that "Pondering this paragraph will suggest its own revision and improvement..."[24] Perhaps. But there are certain things that ought to be said about this statement. First, it is set in a highly polemical context. And if the critics of this passage would quote the one remaining sentence of the paragraph, the reader would know exactly both the context of the passage and its real meaning. The sentence is: "Failure to understand this simple fact and this paradoxical relation between individual and collective action has resulted in the unholy alliance between Christian perfectionism and cowardly counsels of political expediency in dealing with tyrants in our own day."[25] Specifically Niebuhr means the alliance between Christian pacifism and political isolationism.

Second, Niebuhr has not here chosen a second "ultimate norm" to be preferred in this situation to the norm of *agape*. There is only one ultimate norm in Niebuhr for both individuals and groups, and that is *agape*. What he is saying is that *agape* is not a simple historical possibility. It is related to history dialectically through the norms of relative justice and mutuality. Moreover, if we realize that *agape* "defines the limits of what is possible in historic development" we will be saved from the evils that always attend our viewing it as a simple historical possibility.

Third, when he says that "it is not even right to insist that every action must conform to *agape*" he is not saying that *agape* has ceased to be the norm. What he is saying is this: No action or decision *can simply conform to agape*. To insist that they can is to fail to understand *both the tragic dimension of history and the transcendent character of agape*. The norm of *agape* ever stands in judgment upon even our best efforts and achievements. Failure clearly to recognize this results in ethical confusion.

This leads us directly to the third "relation of transcendence" of sacrificial love to the norms of mutuality. "The Cross", he says, "represents a perfection which contradicts the false pretensions of virtue in history and which reveals the contrast between man's sinful self-assertion and the divine *agape*."[26] Every form of historical reality contains some admixture of sin. For this reason, no matter what may be the attainments of man in achieving structures of justice or relationships of mutual love, he will always stand in need of forgiveness. It is the "good news" of the Gospel that this forgiveness is available to us through the sacrificial love of

Him who "emptied Himself," sought nothing for Himself, but freely gave Himself for the unworthy.

The relationship between *agape* and mutual love is a thoroughly dialectical relation. *Agape* completes the incompleteness of mutual love, it clarifies the historical possibilities and limitations of mutuality, and it contradicts all our achievements of love and justice insofar as they contain an admixture of sin. And *agape*—heedless, undiscriminating, sacrificial love—is the norm, the law of life.

## 2. THE SOURCE OF THE NORM

The centrality of Christology in Niebuhr's thought is clear and unmistakable. This is somewhat remarkable in one whose major task has been focused on the Christian view of man to the extent that he is not infrequently (though not very wisely) referred to as an "anthropologian," and perhaps especially in one who has contributed so notably to political and social analysis. This may be one of the surprising things about Niebuhr, but there is no gainsaying the fact that it is precisely because his social, political, and ethical inquiries are Christologically controlled, and indeed a working out of the meaning of Christology in ever wider realms of experience, that Niebuhr's thought has gained for Christianity a new relevance in surprising quarters in our time. As Paul Lehmann has observed, "What is important . . . is that the pivotal position in a discussion of the Christian view of man should be given to the specific connection between man and the person and work of Christ. The traditional theological distinction between the work of Christ 'for us' (*pro nobis*) and the work of Christ 'in us' (*in nobis*) is the crucial point in Niebuhr's exposition of Christian anthropology." [27] Niebuhr's accounts of the person and work of Christ, of the doctrines of Incarnation and Atonement, are the perspective from which he views man in history. Even when analyzing the latest political event, Niebuhr's thought is never far from the vantage point of the Cross.

Thus when we ask the question of the *source* of the norm, it would seem natural just to answer, "The Cross." The answer would not be wrong. But it would be much too simple. It would be too simple because the relationship of *agape* to the very constitution of selfhood constitutes one of the most interesting and important aspects of Niebuhr's thought. Moreover, this relationship is decisive for a proper consideration of the source of the norm.

Niebuhr's starting point is that man can understand himself only from a vantage point beyond himself. "To understand himself truly means to begin with a faith that he is understood from beyond himself, that he is known and loved of God and must find himself in terms of obedience to the divine will."[28] This is the relationship of faith. The important thing to stress here is that in this relationship, which is the presupposition of profound self-knowledge, man is not submitting himself to an authority or law alien to his own being. This relationship, which is established and maintained by grace, is the precondition of authentic freedom and hence of true selfhood. We see the real nature of the norm of life in the Cross precisely because it is there that we see our own essential nature, true manhood. In a word, the norm of *agape* revealed by Christ on the Cross, far from being something alien and heteronomously imposed, is rather the clarification of the norm given by the nature of our own selfhood. Niebuhr states this explicitly:

> The fact is that the revelation of the "Cross of Christ" does not superimpose, but merely clarifies, the truth about man's situation when ultimately considered. The situation which is clarified by the Christian faith can be validated by common experience. It is that the self is bound to destroy itself by seeking itself too narrowly, that it must forget itself to realize itself, but that this self-forgetfulness can not be induced by the calculation that a more ultimate form of self-realization will flow from the forgetfulness. The ethic of the Cross therefore clarifies, but does not create, a norm which is given by the very constitution of selfhood.[29]

This assertion that the Cross clarifies but does not create a norm which is given with the very constitution of selfhood requires further discussion, because it is a statement which raises a host of questions. In particular it requires that we understand what he means by the terms "essential" and "existential" man. Niebuhr has given us in the first volume of *The Nature and Destiny of Man* a profound discussion of this which is immediately relevant to our concern to locate the source of the norm of life. We cannot hope to indicate the richness of his thought on this matter, but we must seek to bring his position into focus.

Niebuhr begins by observing the universality of the conflict between what man is and what he ought to be. "The good I would do and do not" expresses the situation of all men.

> No man, however deeply involved in sin, is able to regard the misery of sin as normal. Some memory of a previous condition of blessedness seems to linger in his soul; some echo of the law which he has violated seems to resound in his conscience. Every effort to give the habits of sin the appearance of normality betrays something of the frenzy of an uneasy conscience. The contrast between what man is truly and essentially and what he has become is apparent even to those who do not understand that this contrast is to be found in every human being and has its seat in the will of man himself.[30]

Two ideas basic to Niebuhr's thought are laid down in this quotation: (1) Existential man has some knowledge of the law of his life and some awareness of the fact that he has broken it, and (2) existential man is not the source of the norm. Sin cannot be given the appearance of normality without betraying "something of the frenzy of an uneasy conscience."

What then is the source of the "ought" which man experiences and which reveals the depth of the contradiction within the self? We have said that it is not a law alien to his being and yet that it transcends the empirical, existential self. Niebuhr answers that the "ought" is the claim of man's essential nature upon him. "This sense of obligation is," he writes, "the claim which the essential nature of man makes upon him in his sinful state." [31]

In what does the essential nature of man consist? To that inevitable question Niebuhr has fortunately given us a very succinct answer.

> The essential nature of man contains two elements; and there are correspondingly two elements in the original perfection of man. To the essential nature of man belong, on the one hand, all his natural endowments, and determinations, his physical and social impulses, his sexual and racial differentiations, in short his character as a creature imbedded in the natural order. On the other hand, his essential nature also includes the freedom of his spirit, his transcendence over natural process and finally his self-transcendence.[32]

The two elements of man's essential nature are his finiteness and his freedom. Moreover, these two elements cannot, as it were, be laid side by side. The freedom of man is able to qualify the natural functions of man. "The freedom of man contains the capacity of transcending nature so that the self in the unity of its freedom and finiteness contains a bewildering degree of mixtures of spiritual freedom and natural necessity."[33] In thus describing the essential nature of man as finite freedom, Niebuhr necessarily resists any attempt to discuss man's essential nature in definite terms as though it were a fixed and static possession. Indeed, only the "theological virtues" of faith, hope, and love are dynamic enough to characterize the freedom of the self in the full dimensions of its relations. We shall shortly discuss in more detail the content of "original righteousness" or the law of man's essential nature in the terms of faith, hope, and love. At this point it will be sufficient to see why Niebuhr regards *agape* as the norm of man who is both finite and free. He answers in the same terms we have been using.

> The law of love is the final law for man in his condition of finiteness and freedom because man in his freedom is unable to make himself in his finiteness his own end. The self is too great to be contained within itself in its smallness. The Gospel observation that "whoso seeketh to gain his life will lose it" is thus not some impossible rule imposed upon life by Scriptural fiat. It describes the actual situation of the self, which destroys itself by seeking itself

too immediately. The true self dies if the contingent self tries too desperately to live.[34]

Thus far we have established two things. We have located the source of the norm in man's essential nature and we have seen that *agape* is the virtue corresponding to man's essential nature. If we now ask in what manner man experiences his essential nature and apprehends its law we open up another facet of Niebuhr's understanding. How then does man experience his essential nature?

We have been using such terms as *requirement, obligation, claim,* and *law of life.* Therein is the whole point. Our essential nature is experienced as a law and as a claim *because we experience it not as a possession but as a lack.* This is perfectly expressed in the commandment "Thou shalt love." "Here something is commanded and demanded. That means law. But what is commanded is a state of heart and mind, a harmony between the soul and God ('Thou shalt love the Lord thy God'), a harmony within the soul ('with all thy heart, and all thy soul, and all thy mind') and a harmony between the self and the neighbour ('thy neighbour as thyself') which, if attained, would exclude all commandment."[35] Man's essential nature is therefore not an immanent possession of the historical self. It is apprehended by virtue of the self's capacity for self-transcendence as that which it lacks but which is nevertheless the law of its being. The consciousness of "original righteousness" thus is placed "in a moment of the self which transcends history, though not outside of the self which is in history."[36] The existential self is aware of its essential nature, but it experiences it as lack rather than possession, and therefore as law and consequently only in a fragmentary and distorted fashion.

Niebuhr expounds the relationship of this "original righteousness" to existential, sinful man by way of a quite remarkable exegesis of the story of the rich young ruler. His own summary is most pertinent to our inquiry.

The explicit and implicit views of human nature which this story yields, may be summarized as follows: (a) Man as sinner is not unmindful of the ultimate requirements of his nature as free spirit. He knows that any particular historical concretion of law is not enough. (b) He is not fully conscious of the nature of these ultimate requirements, and (c) he is not ready to meet these requirements once they are defined. These three propositions give an accurate account of the typical relation of "original righteousness" to man as sinner (Matt. 22:37–39).[37]

We stated above that the content of our essential nature could not be described as something fixed and static or located in any particular part of man's being, that its content could be described only in the dynamic terms of faith, hope, and love, because these terms alone are appropriate to man as man-in-relation. We need now to say more about these terms and how Niebuhr sees them as the terms which alone can properly characterize the law for man in his freedom.

His procedure is to take Jesus' summary of the law with its three terms and consider them with the Pauline triad of faith, hope, and love. The first requirement, "Thou shalt love the Lord thy God," is basic and corresponds to faith and hope "in which obedience is transcended by love, trust and confidence."[38] "Faith in the providence of God is a necessity of freedom because, without it, the anxiety of freedom tempts man to seek a self-sufficiency and self-mastery incompatible with his dependence upon forces which he does not control."[39] Hope is closely integrated with faith, indeed it "is faith with regard to the future."[40] One is here reminded of that remarkable passage in Calvin's *Institutes* on the relation between faith and hope. "Hope is no other," says Calvin, "than an expectation of those things which faith has believed to be truly promised by God. Thus faith believes the veracity of God, hope expects the manifestation of it in due time; faith believes him to be our Father, hope expects him always to act towards us in this character; faith believes that eternal life is given to us, hope expects it one day to be revealed; faith is the foundation on which hope rests, hope nourishes and sustains faith. . . ."[41]

The second requirement "is that of a complete inner accord

within the soul"[42] as expressed in the words "with all thy heart and with all thy soul and all thy mind." Sinful man knows that this inner accord is required of him just as surely as the fact that he knows that he does nothing with all his heart and soul and mind.

The third requirement, expressed in the words "Thou shalt love thy neighbor as thyself," means "the perfect accord of life with life and will with will."[43] Love between man and man is the final requirement of all human relations, the final obligation laid upon us by our essential nature. It transcends all the schemes of justice we are able to contrive. Only in love is the uniqueness of the other known and "both the uniformities and the differences of nature, which bind men together and separate them, are transcended."[44] Love is the ultimate requirement of human freedom.

We began this discussion of the source of the norm by emphasizing the centrality of Christology in Niebuhr's thought. Perhaps now the question will be raised as to the propriety of this, inasmuch as we have located the source of the norm and indicated the terms of its content without any specific reference to the revelation of the Cross. We have proceeded from the recognition of the universal conflict in man, through an analysis of man's consciousness of his essential nature as law, and we have shown how Niebuhr expounds this by way of commandment and parable. The question of how crucial a role is played by the revelation of the Cross in the matter of the source of the norm is inevitable.

It must be said clearly and vigorously that the Cross is not now brought in as an extra to be added to the knowledge derived from existential analysis. Niebuhr has no layer-cake conception of theology. On the contrary, the revelation of the Cross has been a presupposition of the entire analysis. Niebuhr's whole concern in proceeding as he has done is to show that the norm of *agape* revealed in the Cross is not an alien norm imposed in external, authoritarian fashion. On the contrary, he is seeking to show that the *agape* of the Cross is verily the law of man's true nature. In this sense the Cross "clarifies, but does not create, a norm which is given by the very constitution of selfhood." But the Cross does clarify. Indeed one wonders if the word clarify is strong enough to bear the weight of meaning Niebuhr intends for it. For the clarification involves a radical transformation of all the conceptions of existential man. In the crucified Christ we see our own essential nature. "He is what I am essentially, and therefore what I ought to be." [45] But what I cannot be. For at the Cross we learn also the depth of our own self-contradiction and hear, for the first time, our true name pronounced: Sinner, beloved of God.

At the Cross, we who thought ourselves to be lovers learn what love really is. All this and more must be borne by the word clarify. However, it is the theonomous nature of the law of life that Niebuhr is asserting with such insight and power. He in whom we see *agape* is Very Man as well as Very God. Therefore, we must say that the law of love is clarified but not created by the Cross, or as he has recently expressed it, it is "an old law and a new law." [46]

Niebuhr's answer to our question regarding the source of the norm may now be stated in this fashion: the source is our own essential nature which is clearly apprehended in the relationship of faith with Him who through the *agape* of the Cross reveals Himself as Very Man. Our essential nature, which we experience not as a possession, but as a lack, and as a law which we ought to fullfill but cannot, is actualized in Christ in whom the law which constitutes our being is fulfilled.

This, of course, is not all that is revealed at the Cross. There God discloses Himself and we learn the nature of the reality which bears the world. We learn also, as we have said, the depth of our own sin. We have revealed to us not only the law of life but also the depth of that "other law in our members." When we learn these two things and how properly to think them together we begin to see how the norm is relevant to our daily life. *Agape* is no simple historical possibility and yet it is relevant to every historical situation. It must be related to historical reality dialectically through the effort to achieve justice.

*Two*

# LOVE AND JUSTICE

Reinhold Niebuhr's entire thought has been motivated by one passionate concern. That concern has been so to understand and present the historic Christian faith that its insights and resources might bring illumination and healing to the frightening problems and perplexities of our age. It is our conviction that this has been not only his motivating concern but also his most distinctive achievement. It is significant that the judgment "No man has had as much influence as a preacher in this generation; no preacher has had as much influence in the secular world"[1] was spoken not by an admiring fellow-theologian but by a distinguished historian. If one word had to be chosen to indicate the character of Niebuhr's work and achievement, that word would have to be "relevance."

Nothing is perhaps more remarkable, or instructive, about Niebuhr's celebrated relevance than the fact that he achieved it by setting himself against the whole current of American theology and preaching, which was so intent upon being *directly* relevant that it was actually irrelevant. Much of the latter was concerned so exclusively about the "situation" to which its message was addressed that it became itself part of the situation. It could not mediate redemption because it lacked a sufficiently transcendent vantage point from which to speak its word of judgment. In its passion for relevance it diluted the faith. It is only when we see Niebuhr in such a context that we can begin to measure the greatness of his achievement. No one can understand him who does not see that his social relevance goes hand in hand with his religious profundity. Instead of diluting the faith to seek a spurious relevance, Niebuhr achieved relevance by throwing the "scandal" and "offence" of the Gospel into bold relief. But here again it was the way in which he did it that measures his stature. A vertebrate Christian gospel in all its distinctiveness was set over against our culture, but set over against it in such a way that it was again related to it, and related redemptively. The relationship is one of tension, but just therein consists its reality and significance.

> The ethical fruitfulness of various types of religion is determined by the quality of their tension between the historical and the transcendent. This quality is measured by two considerations: The degree to which the transcendent truly transcends every value and achievement of history, so that no relative value of historical achievement may become the basis of moral complacency; and the degree to which the transcendent remains in organic contact with the historical, so that no degree of tension may rob the historical of its significance.[2]

Motivated by such a concern, it was inevitable that Niebuhr should become involved in a series of polemical dialogues on a variety of fronts as he sought to speak with prophetic voice to the issues of the day. This continuous engagement with the realities of daily events and the consequent debates with what he considered to be inadequate, sentimental, or untenable positions did much to bring his distinctive position to clear and firm expression. This fact dictates our procedure in this chapter. We shall first outline the relation of love and justice in Niebuhr's thought and then attempt to show more clearly the character of his position by a brief consideration of some of the major controversies in which he has been involved.

## 1. RELATION BETWEEN LOVE AND JUSTICE

Just as we were faced with the necessity of clearly stating what Niebuhr understands by Love as the norm of life, so here we are confronted immediately with the definitional problem as concerns justice. What is Niebuhr's understanding of the meaning and relations of the term justice?

Emil Brunner has recently raised this question in pointed fashion. He feels that Niebuhr's failure to give a clear definition of justice means that he lacks an "adequate concept of justice." Brunner writes: "Always he was concerned for human dignity and for justice. All the more surprising is it, therefore, that Reinhold Niebuhr has never worked out a clear concept of justice whereby the difference between the demands of justice and those of the supreme ethical norm of love might be understood."[3] Brunner continues his demand by saying that it is necessary for Niebuhr "to make clear what justice is as distinguished from love and in what relation justice stands to love, the sovereign norm for Christian ethics."[4] Phrased in that way, I find the question quite incredible because the relation between love and justice, being at the heart of Niebuhr's thought, informs his whole work and is reiterated over and over again. On the other hand the question is perhaps not so surprising, because the difference between Brunner and Niebuhr at this point is one of the important differences between theologians otherwise of remarkably similar approach. Niebuhr does not *define* justice, but that does not mean that he does not have a clearly articulated concept of justice. Niebuhr does not define justice because it has no independent basis. Justice is not a definable entity in itself. Justice is a relational term in Niebuhr, it is the relative embodiment of *agape* in the structures of society.

What then is the relation between *agape* and justice? The first thing to be said is that they cannot be simply identified. *Agape* is transcendent, heedless, and sacrificial. Justice is historical, discriminating, and concerned with balancing interests and claims. Love and justice are never simply the same thing. But if they must be distinguished, they cannot be torn asunder. Justice is the relative social embodiment of love and as such it is an approximation of love. Justice is love finding a relatively complete expression in the world. The terms are not interchangeable. But justice is never something apart from, or independent of, love and pertaining to another realm.

The relationship is dialectical. Love is both the fulfillment and the negation of justice. This position is reiterated time and again. One quotation will put his understanding clearly before us.

> Love is . . . the end term of any system of morals. It is the moral requirement in which all schemes of justice are fulfilled and negated. They are fulfilled because the obligation of life to life is more fully met in love than is possible in any scheme of equity and justice. They are negated because love makes an end of the nicely calculated less and more of structures of justice. It does not carefully arbitrate between the needs of the self and of the other, since it meets the needs of the other without concern for the self.[5]

*Love demands justice.* For justice is not alien to love, it is love making its way in the world. Love thus prompts us to seek ever wider and more inclusive structures of justice. One simply cannot say that he is concerned that love may be expressed but not concerned with politics, economics, laws, and customs. To be unconcerned for the achievement of more equal justice is to deny the claims of love. Justice is the embodiment of love in complex human relations.

*Love negates justice.* For love always transcends justice. This is true for our ideas of justice as well as for historical structures of justice. Justice is discriminating, it must always calculate and weigh conflicting interests. Love transcends the calculation of more and less and does not reward according to deserts. Thus every structure and every idea of justice stand under the higher judgment of love. Justice, to remain justice, can thus never be complacent, because the norm is not in itself but in *agape.* "There is no justice, even in a sinful world, which can be regarded as finally normative. The higher possibilities of love, which is at once the fulfillment and the negation of justice, always hover over every system of justice."[6] Thus love is not only "the source of the norms of justice" but also the "ultimate perspective by which their limitations are discovered."[7]

*Love fulfills justice.* Only love can illumine and meet the special need. "A sense of justice may prompt men to organize legal systems of unemployment insurance through which a general sense of obligation toward the needy neighbour is expressed. But no such system can leave the self satisfied when it faces particular needs among those who are the beneficiaries of such minimal schemes of justice."[8] Love fulfills justice also because love alone can meet the other in his uniqueness and freedom. "The other has special needs and requirements which cannot be satisfied by general rules of equity."[9] Love fulfills justice because *agape* is redemptive. Properly to expound this dimension of the relation between love and justice would lead us into the doctrine of the Atonement. We shall discuss that later. Mention of it here will serve, however, to indicate the vital organic relation between Niebuhr's social and political thought and the ultimate reaches of his theological reflections. At this point in our inquiry it will be sufficient to note that laws of justice, taking, as they must, sinful self-interest for granted, seek to establish equitable divisions between competing interests. "They are, therefore, always in danger of throwing the aura of moral sanctity upon the sinful self-interest which they take for granted. They must consequently stand under the criticism of the law of love."[10] But the love which stands over justice in criticism and negation is also able to redeem. *Agape,* which demands that we ever seek justice, which judges and finds wanting our highest achievements, also redeems and thereby fulfills what remains incomplete and distorted by sin.

Love demands, negates, and fulfills justice. Thus, although love and justice are not the same they do not exist apart from each other; when they are sought apart from each other, each is destroyed.

Justice without love ceases to be justice. "Any justice which is only justice soon degenerates into something less than justice."[11] Thus as mutual love needs *agape* to keep it from degenerating into a calculation of interests, so "Justice," as Niebuhr once so cryptically put it, "without love is merely the balance of power."[12]

Love without justice ceases to be love. It becomes a vague sentimentalism that fails to come to grips with the realities of existence. Or it issues in a perverse lovelessness by refusing mistakenly, in the name of love, to deal realistically and courageously with the fact of power upon which the securing and the maintaining of justice depend. Or it becomes corrupted by being defined in terms of attitudes, and love is thereby restricted to personal relations and exercises of philanthropy, and thus the universal kingship of the Lord of the Cross is reduced to a pleasant deed transacted in a corner.

Love and justice must never be sharply separated, though they must always be clearly distinguished. They exist together in a dialectical relation of tension. The character and significance of Niebuhr's thought will become clearer, I trust, when seen against other positions he has opposed. But first it would be instructive to explore yet more fully the relations between love and justice.

Niebuhr has sought to clarify this complex relation by considering it in two dimensions. The first dimension pertains to the rules and laws of justice while the second is concerned with the historical structures of justice. Obviously the contradiction between love and the structures of justice is greater than that between love and the principles of justice. We shall consider the relation between love and the "rules and laws" of justice first.

Rules and laws of justice bear a positive relation to love inasmuch as they are instruments of brotherhood. Niebuhr has himself given such a succinct summary of this positive relation that we ought to allow him to speak it for himself.

> Systems and principles of justice are the servants and instruments of the spirit of brotherhood in so far as they extend the sense of obligation towards the other, (a) from an immediately felt obligation, prompted by obvious need, to a continued obligation expressed in fixed principles of mutual support; (b) from a simple relation between a self and one "other" to the complex relations of the self and the "others"; and (c) finally from the obligations, discerned by the individual self, to the wider obligations which the community defines from its more impartial perspective. These communal definitions evolve slowly in custom and in law. They all contain some

higher elements of disinterestedness, which would not be possible to the individual self.[13]

In these three ways then, rules of justice extend the sense of obligation and provide the supporting framework necessary for love. This is evident in even the most intimate of social groups. "Even the love within a family avails itself of customs and usages which stereotype given adjustments between various members of the family in such a way that each action need not be oriented by a fresh calculation of competing interests."[14]

However, the rules of justice bear a negative as well as a positive relation to love. They are the necessary instruments of love in a sinful world but even as instruments of love they contradict the meaning of love. "The fence and the boundary line are the symbols of the spirit of justice. They set the limits upon each man's interest to prevent one from taking advantage of the other. A harmony achieved through justice is therefore only an approximation of brotherhood."[15]

The negative relation becomes even more clear when we estimate the thoroughly contingent character of the rules of justice. To say this is, of course, to bring Niebuhr at once into conflict with both Marxist and Catholic social theory. The Marxist is able to discern the ideological taint in all theories but his own. The Catholic recognizes the contingent character of "positive" law but not of "natural" law. We shall discuss Niebuhr's criticism of natural law theories in the course of this chapter. Here it will be sufficient to note that Niebuhr's claim that the rules as well as the structures of justice are contingent is a direct challenge to this fundamental Catholic distinction. Rules of justice are the product of social processes in which partial perspectives are being continually challenged and more inclusive ones attained. The rules of justice are thus themselves contingent upon the health of particular societies. There is no universal reason or completely impartial perspective in history. Even our highest principles of justice bear the limitations of the historical situation and the taint of self-interest. Love both fulfills and negates our principles of justice.

The positive relation of principles of justice to the ideal of brotherhood makes an indeterminate approximation of love in the realm of justice possible. The negative relation means that all historic conceptions of justice will embody some elements which contradict the law of love. The interests of a class, the viewpoint of a nation, the prejudices of an age and the illusions of a culture are consciously and unconsciously insinuated into the norms by which men regulate their common life. They are intended to give one group an advantage over another. Or if that is not their intention, it is at least the unvarying consequence.[16]

The positive and negative relations between love and justice are more apparent when we consider the historical structures of justice. For here we deal primarily with the fact of power which both organizes and balances the vitalities of history. The equivocal relation is thus much more obvious and yet it is fundamentally the same as that which exists between love and the rules of justice. The political, economic, and social structures of justice are the necessary expressions of love, but they contain elements of injustice which stand in contradiction to love; they thus stand under the possibility of higher realizations of love, and in the end must be both supplemented and redeemed by the grace of *agape*.

Let us now return to Brunner's insistence that "one is duty-bound to say exactly what this 'justice' is as distinguished from love."[17] The answer is that Niebuhr cannot and will not. To do so would be to destroy or at least obscure the real nature of justice. Justice cannot be properly *thought* apart from love. Because justice always exists in a dynamic relation between *agape* and the uniqueness of concrete historical situations one can never say "exactly" what justice is apart from either *agape* or the situation. For Niebuhr, as John Bennett has said in his valuable essay, "justice must always be thought of in dynamic terms" and "love can always raise justice to new heights."[18] This is not only one of the most distinctive aspects of Niebuhr's thought, it is also, I believe, the key to the relevance of his theology to the perplexing issues of our communal life. This claim can be tested only throughout the course of our inquiry. However, something of its immense social importance will become clear as we consider certain other positions with which he has been in debate.

## 2. NIEBUHR'S CRITICISM OF NATURAL LAW

Our age is experiencing a renewed interest in natural law. This is due in large part to the catastrophic events of our time and the inability of prevailing philosophies to provide adequate insight or resource to cope with the terrible realities of this era. There is a very great truth in the recognition that all our values are relative and historically and culturally conditioned, which we overlook at our peril. But if what we call right and wrong, good and evil, true and false are *only* the product of a particular culture, possessing validity only in that context, then we are left with no basis upon which to resist Nazism or Communism with anything like an unqualified "No." Faced with the unheard of atrocities of the demonic movements of our time, the question of whether the distinction between right and wrong has any basis in reality has become a most urgent intellectual and social question. The need for some trans-cultural standard has become imperative, and consequently the old tradition of natural law has entered into the contemporary ethical and political discussion with fresh significance and vitality. An excellent example of this resurgent interest in natural law, as well as a notable contribution to the ongoing discussion, is given us in Leo Strauss's *Natural Right and History*. Taking as his point of departure the bankruptcy of so much contemporary social science in providing us with a basis for discriminating between "legitimate and illegitimate, just and unjust, objectives," Strauss vividly describes the situation into which natural law theories have leaped with such new meaning. Strauss writes:

> According to our social science, we can be or become wise in all matters of secondary importance, but we have to be resigned to utter ignorance in the most important respect: we cannot have any

knowledge regarding the ultimate principles of our choices, i.e. regarding their soundness or unsoundness; our ultimate principles have no other support than our arbitrary and hence blind preference. We are then in the position of beings who are sane and sober when engaged in trivial business and who gamble like mad men when confronted with serious issues—retail sanity and wholesale madness. If our principles have no other support than our blind preferences, everything a man is willing to dare will be permissible. The contemporary rejection of natural right leads to nihilism—nay, it is identical with nihilism.[19]

It is not our concern here to discuss the contribution which Strauss has made. His concern is not to revitalize the Catholic theory of natural law, but insofar as his own position is clear, it would appear that he would prefer to cut back behind it to the classical tradition. In any event, the notable contribution of his work lies in his subtle history of the idea. Our concern here is simply to note the fact that natural law has gained a fresh respectability in our day. When this is coupled with the resurgent power of neo-Thomism we are able to see still another aspect of the significance of Niebuhr in contemporary ethical, and especially political, thought. Niebuhr has always been a forceful critic of natural law and, as is everywhere evident, he has had a profound influence upon recent political thought. In a word, Niebuhr's thought provides an alternative to both positivist relativism and natural law in the contemporary political discussion.

We have already noted that Niebuhr challenges the traditional Catholic distinction between the contingency of "positive" or "civil" law and the finality and universality of "natural" law. Moreover, what we have seen of how Niebuhr views the relation between love and justice, essential and existential man, of how the law of love is the law for man in his finiteness and freedom—but that he knows this law as a lack rather than as a possession—serves to prepare us for the criticisms he will make of Catholic natural law theories. Our task now is to show more explicitly the criticisms he makes and why he makes them.

The natural law of Catholic moral theory is defined as the

participation of the rational creature in the eternal law. Correlated with this is the view of the Fall as that which robbed man of a *donum superadditum* but left him with an essentially intact nature. Fallen man lacks the capacity of faith, hope, and love or, in other words, that relationship of communion with God wherein he is delivered from the anxieties, fears, and sins that attend his estrangement from God. The fallen man is thus an incomplete man, requiring the infusion of sacramental grace to restore, in part at least, the supernatural virtues lost in the Fall. However, man's capacity for natural justice is not seriously impaired. Man's reason is capable of discerning the permanent structure of human existence and of deriving in a "necessary" or logical manner the more or less detailed requirements of the natural law from the primary proposition that "good is to be done and promoted and evil is to be avoided."

Niebuhr's criticism of Catholic moral theory is focused on the question of natural law and proceeds from his quite fundamentally different view of man. Niebuhr acknowledges that there "is indeed a permanent structure of human personality,"[20] but this is not nearly so fixed and immutable as Catholic law supposes. Or to put it more precisely, the immutable characteristics of man are the characteristics of *human* nature rather than of nature, and this means that they are indefinitely qualified by the indeterminate freedom of man. Man is not simply nature and spirit but a creature who has his being at the juncture of nature and spirit.

> There is not much that is absolutely immutable in the structure of human nature except its animal basis, man's freedom to transmute this nature in varying degrees, and the unity of the natural and spiritual in all the various transmutations and transfigurations of the original "nature." Man's social nature is derived from both his natural gregariousness and from the requirements of his spiritual nature. . . . The most immediate limitations of man as a creature of nature are immutable; but any particular historic expression of them is mutable.[21]

The indeterminate character of human freedom and the endless variety of unique historical occasions thus make it much more difficult to be so sure about what ought to be done and not done than is supposed by a law based upon the fixed structures of nature.

If Catholic thought fails to do justice to the manner in which man's freedom qualifies the expression of the immutable character-istics of man's nature, it also fails, by virtue of its view of the Fall, to do justice to the positive character of the sinful element in all definitions and realizations of justice. The Catholic view that the reason is not seriously impaired by the Fall is the basis for its undue confidence in reason as the source of law.[22] This means that the historically conditioned perspective of reason is given a universality and sanctity it does not possess. This in turn is the basis for the amazing assurance with which Catholic moralists are able to define justice and injustice in every concrete situation. This is no small matter, because it leads to an error involving immense social consequences. It means that religious absolutes are con-stantly insinuated into historically contingent moral judgments.

> Thus the whole imposing structure of Thomistic ethics is, in one of its aspects, no more than a religious sanctification of the relativities of the feudal social system as it flowered in the thirteenth century. The confusion between ultimate religious perspectives and relative historical ones in Catholic thought accounts for the fury and self-righteousness into which Catholicism is betrayed when it defends feudal types of civilization in contemporary history as in Spain for instance.[23]

Man's reason is historical rather than universal and therefore his definitions of justice are limited; man's reason is the reason of sin-ful man and therefore all "statements and definitions of justice are corrupted by even the most rational men through the fact that the definition is coloured by interest."[24] Natural law theories thus fail to do justice to ever new historical occasions and configurations on the one hand, and provide the basis for the absolutizing of relative historical judgments and situations on the other.

Still further, and indeed fundamentally, all this means that natural law theories make impossible the proper relating of love to justice. Justice is defined independently of love, while love is added to justice as that which completes justice. But we have argued that it is precisely this way of conceiving the matter which ultimately destroys both justice and love. "There is no possibility of giving any rational definition of a just relation between man and man or nation and nation short of a complete love in which each life affirms the interests of the other. Every effort to give a definition of justice short of this perfect love invariably introduces contingent factors, conditions of time and place, into the definition."[25] And what of the norm of love? *Agape* is removed to the realm of a "counsel of perfection" which is certainly relevant to the ascetic in his pilgrimage but not to the market place. Thus a layer-cake relation is substituted for the dialectical relation and justice thereby loses the redeeming power of a living relation with love, and love ceases to have its due relation to the whole of life.

## 3. NIEBUHR AND CONTEMPORARY EUROPEAN THEOLOGY

We have previously remarked that the task Niebuhr has set himself is that of relating Reformation insights to the whole gamut of experience more dialectically than he believes the Reformation itself succeeded in doing. This concern provides an illuminating entrance into some of the discussions which he has carried on with the most celebrated leaders of contemporary European theology. Niebuhr owes a great deal to European "dialectical" theology, although to regard him simply as its American voice would be palpably ridiculous. Something of the difference in tone and structure of say Brunner or Barth and Niebuhr can be understood by the difference of their historical and cultural contexts and traditions. There are, however, certain differences that are real and consequential and of particular significance for our inquiry. It is indeed in his disagreements with the "dialectical" theologians that the real dialectical character of Niebuhr's understanding of the relation of love and justice is clearly shown.

We may begin by noting some differences between Niebuhr and Emil Brunner. Nothing should obscure the closeness of much of their thought and concerns. Both the close affinity and the difference are acknowledged by Niebuhr in these words: "I may say that Brunner's whole theological position is close to mine and that it is one to which I am more indebted than any other. I say this though in recent years our respective treatment of the ethical problem has diverged rather widely, through his increasing adoption, and my increasing rejection, of the concept of 'Natural Law.' "[26] We have already touched on this difference but we need now to state it more clearly.

The manner in which Brunner derives the concept of justice from the "order of creation" indicates at once a different procedure and habit of thought from that which we find in Niebuhr. "The Christian conception of justice," writes Brunner, "is . . . determined by the conception of God's order of creation. What corresponds to the Creator's ordinance is just—to that ordinance which bestows on every creature, with its being, the law of its being and its relationship to other creatures. The 'primal order' to which every one refers in using the words 'just' or 'unjust,' the 'due' which is rendered to each man, is the order of creation, which is the will of the Creator made manifest."[27] Niebuhr finds this concept of the "order of creation" dubious for the same reason that he cannot accept natural law. "The difficulty with this concept is that human freedom alters and transmutes the 'given' facts of creation so much that no human institutions can be judged purely by the criterion of fixed principles of 'creation.' "[28]

Brunner is emphatic that the law of justice is given by one and the same God who gives the law of love for He who is our Creator is also our Redeemer. Nevertheless justice and love are radically different. Justice and love are also clearly distinguished in Niebuhr, as we have seen. But the manner in which the difference between love and justice is conceived is the measure of the divergence be-

tween Brunner and Niebuhr. For Brunner the law of justice is
that "by which earthly systems are framed" and the law of love
is "for our relations with our fellow men."[29] "Justice belongs to
the world of systems, not to the world of persons. . . .Yet in its own
place, justice is supreme. Within the system as such there can be
nothing higher, for love knows nought of systems."[30] Love can
operate in systems only " 'between the lines' " through the "meshes
of the systems."[31] Love begins where justice ends: "The real gift
of love only begins where justice has already been done, for it is
that which is beyond justice."[32] Therefore the "obligations of justice can be fulfilled because they are distinct, but love is never
fulfilled. . . ."[33]

Niebuhr would never formulate the relationship in that way.
For Brunner the demand of justice is fixed. "The demand of justice
can be satisfied."[34] Love begins where this ends. It is indeed not
improper to regard love in this way as a work of supererogation.[35]
For Niebuhr the demands of justice are never fixed, nor can they
be satisfied, for they are in the end the demands of love. Justice
in Brunner is given a different rootage in the order of creation and
thus the dialectical relation between *agape* and justice, if not
broken, is at least badly obscured.

To be sure, Brunner does not consistently use the language of
a radical separation of love and justice. In many places he appears
to conceive the relation in the same way as does Niebuhr. He
writes, for example, "Justice is nothing but that form of love which
has currency in the world of institutions, that materialization of
love which is necessary as long as men live in institutions. That is
why love is always just too, but justice is not always love."[36] Or
again, "Justice derives from love; still it is not love in itself, but
different from love. The unity of origin does not remove the distinction in content, just as the distinction in content does not
remove the unity of origin."[37] All that comes very close to
Niebuhr's understanding of the relation. But the difference brought
out earlier remains.

Niebuhr's criticism, in general terms, may be put thus: Brunner, in deriving his concept of justice from the "order of creation," has separated it too radically from the one ultimate norm of *agape*, with the result that the concept of justice is given a fixity which it does not possess and the full relevance of *agape* to our ideas of justice and to the social and political task is obscured.

Thus Brunner comes dangerously close to asserting different norms for the social and personal realms of experience. Justice is the norm for social structures, "the world of systems" that knows nothing of love, while love is the norm for "personal relations" which is operative in the social realm only through the "meshes of the system." Moreover it is the realm of personal relations that is held to be decisive. Brunner says explicitly: "At a time when all the emphasis is laid upon quantitative thinking, upon work 'on a large scale,' on external changes, it is supremely necessary to emphasize the truth that what is decisive always takes place in the realm of personal relations, and not in the 'political' sphere, save where we are concerned with preserving the whole order from a general breakdown."[38] Leaving aside the nice question as to the point at which a statesman might consider that he was concerned with "preserving the whole order from a general breakdown" and when he was engaged in less important business, this statement clearly points up the fact that Brunner views the political task as "a matter of secondary importance."[39] This is the consequence of his too radical separation between justice and love and his deriving these norms from different sources. Well might Niebuhr assert that "Brunner is in great error when he interprets an act of personal kindness as more 'Christian' than a statesmanlike scheme in the interest of justice. Brunner's dictum that love 'never seeks great things' is capricious. It separates love too completely from the realm of justice. . . ."[40] I do not think that Brunner intends this but his formulation of the relation between love and justice, informed as it is by his excessive fear of legalism, leads him inevitably to it. Paul Ramsey's query is therefore not improper, "What man nurtured in the Bible can be content with love effective only through the interstitial spaces?"[41] *Agape* must not be confined to the love expressed through personal relations. It is relevant to the whole of life through justice and in this way justice achieves its dynamic character.

One could not discuss Niebuhr's relation to contemporary European theology without some mention of his views on the thought of Karl Barth. Here again, the divergence is held within a large area of agreement and the differences are discussed in an atmosphere of friendly respect. Karl Barth is the most eminent Protestant theologian of our time and one of the most powerful and exciting theologians of any century. Nothing should obscure the fact that Niebuhr's criticism is always held within the context of profound respect and gratitude for the leadership Barth has exercised in our time. Nevertheless, Niebuhr has felt it necessary to voice one criticism consistently across the past three decades. That criticism deals with the very center of our inquiry—the relationship of God's kingdom to the kingdoms of the world, of the absolute norm to the relative decisions and proximate solutions of our day by day political life.

In the early 'thirties, Niebuhr's criticisms continually revolved about one point—that Barth viewed life from such an exclusively "transcendent" or "eschatological" perspective that the "nicely calculated less or more" of political justice received altogether too little concern and attention. Barthian theology failed, Niebuhr argued on numerous occasions, to provide discriminating guidance for the making of political and social decisions, or even properly to support the significance of exercising such discrimination.[42]

This criticism may seem to be singularly inappropriate and misinformed when we think of the clear-cut stand Barth was to take against Nazism and the tremendous intellectual and moral leadership he gave to the Church in its life and death struggle with Hitler. Niebuhr, who saw so clearly and so quickly the real meaning of Hitlerism, has never been unmindful of the debt that Christendom owes to Barth for the leadership of that hour. But even when in the deepest agreement with Barth politically, Niebuhr was not happy with the relationship Barth drew between the demands of the Gospel and the necessary political action. Niebuhr made this perfectly clear in his comments on the letter Barth wrote to Hromadka after the Munich debacle. In the course of that letter Barth had said: "Every Czech soldier who will then fight and suffer will fight and suffer for all of us and—I say this without reserve—also for the church of Jesus Christ which in the midst of such Hitlers and Mussolinis will either decline into ridicule or will be wiped out." Niebuhr agreed completely with Barth on the meaning of Nazism, and also that it must be resolutely withstood. But the difference was right here in the relationship of the Gospel to our relatively good causes and so Niebuhr comments, "We agree neither with Barth's previous separation of the Gospel from fateful political and historical decisions which we as men must make, nor yet with his present identification of the Czech soldier with the liberty of the church of Christ."[43] Barth does not, Niebuhr claims, see the relationship between the gospel and the world, between love and justice in sufficiently dialectical fashion. "Here again Barth, the exponent of dialectical theology, has proved himself to be not sufficiently dialectical. In all the years before the crisis his 'no' to the problem of culture and civilization was too unreserved, and in the hour of crisis his 'yes' is too unreserved."[44]

This is the nub of Niebuhr's criticism of Barth. This was brought out clearly in the exchange between Niebuhr and Barth after the Amsterdam conference, which was published in *The Christian Century*. This exchange was initiated by Niebuhr in a reply to Barth's Amsterdam address which has been published under the title of "No Christian Marshall Plan." God's design, Barth contended was not to be discerned from man's disorder nor to be confused with all our schemes of social salvation. The design of God is no Christian Marshall Plan. In his reply, teasingly entitled, "We are Men and Not God," Niebuhr, although of course agreeing that Barth's thought is a welcome antidote to all types of moralism, expresses his criticisms of Barth's whole approach. It is, Niebuhr says, "a very 'undialectical' gospel in which the 'yes' of the divine

mercy has completely cancelled out the 'no' of the divine judgment,"[45] a gospel more fitted for resisting tyranny when it is full
blown than for illuminating the less dramatic issues that make for
social health. It is a theology that forgoes the apologetic task and
as such can all too readily become the source of cultural obscurantism. "We are embarrassed about our correction," Niebuhr
admits, "because we cannot deny that this 'Continental' theology
outlines the final pinnacle of the Christian faith and hope with
fidelity to the Scriptures. Yet it requires correction, because it has
obscured the foothills where human life must be lived."[46] The
struggle for justice is a *Christian* responsibility and therefore the
"possibilities as well as the limits of every scheme of justice must
be explored."[47]

Barth replied that Niebuhr's blows had missed the mark because they were aimed at a caricature. Barth regarded this as an
indication of the depth of the problem of communication when one
so distinguished and sympathetic as Niebuhr could so misunder-
stand. The real division between "Continental" and "Anglo-Saxon"
theology is "the different attitude to the Bible, from which we
take our start."[48] Anglo-Saxon theology lacks mystery and interest
because it does not sufficiently plumb the specifically biblical dimension of such themes as God's free choice in grace and judgment,
Creation, Reconciliation, the Kingdom, Sanctification, and the
Congregation—regarded as events, not principles.

Niebuhr acknowledges that Barth has here focused attention on
a real difference in approach and certainly it is a point at which
much "Anglo-Saxon" thought is in grave error. Nevertheless right
at this point which Barth had selected—and it is a point of great
strength in Barth—Niebuhr again feels the weakness of an "undialectical" theology. An exegesis that eschews commerce with
the wisdom of the world possesses its own great perils. Barth has
assuredly performed a remarkable work of reformation on the basis
of a profound biblical theology, but the manner in which he seeks
to preserve the purity of the gospel, Niebuhr believes must be
called into serious question.

Yet it is, I hope, not too presumptuous to say that there are many in the Anglo-Saxon world whose gratitude for Barth's profound interpretations of our biblical faith will yet not beguile them into accepting his method of preserving the purity of that faith from corruption. They believe that it easily leads to two errors. One is the introduction of irrelevant standards of the good, when the Christian life requires a great deal of freedom from every kind of law and tradition, including the kind which is woven together from proof-texts. The other is that it fails to provide sufficient criteria of judgment and impulse to decisive action in the moments of life when a historic evil sneaks into the world upon the back of some unobtrusive error which when fully conceived may produce a monstrous evil.[49]

For an example of the need to regard, to enter into conversation with, and to learn from the wisdom of the world even in the task of understanding the biblical message, Niebuhr refers to Barth's exegesis of the Genesis phrase "male and female created he them." Barth's whole treatment of the doctrine of creation calls forth Niebuhr's admiration, but he raises the question as to why the Church across the ages did not see, as Barth so clearly sees, that this phrase "male and female created he them" cannot be squared with the notion that only a man can be a priest because only a man can represent a male Christ. Has not the "secular" experience contributed to the opening of the implications of the biblical text?

> When, therefore, we expound the word of Genesis, "male and female created he them," it behooves us not to take a prestidigitator's delight in pulling rabbits out of a hat which every previous exegete regarded merely as a hat. We ought rather to admit contritely that we understand the full implication of the scriptural word that God created both man and woman in his design of the human person because we are heirs of a spiritual history which includes a secular revolt against religion. . . . It is not the first nor the last time that a facet of the full truth in Christ has been clarified and restored by heresy after being obscured by orthodoxy. There are certain insights about the political order which come to us in the same way from modern secularism, despite its libertarian or equalitarian illusions.[50]

The dialogue with the world is necessary not only for the sake of the world, but also for understanding the Gospel of Him who died and rose again for the world. Cultural disciplines must be taken seriously, not only to understand the limits of their schemes of rational coherence and not only for the purpose of seeing the full relevance of the Christian message, but also for apprehending the real meaning of the message itself.[51]

It is Niebuhr's conviction that it is Barth's failure to enter into a vital engagement with the world and his insistence on "viewing this troubled globe from a religious airplane"[52] that has led him into serious mistakes in political judgment. We have already noted Niebuhr's criticism of Barth's undialectical theology in the period of Hitler's rise to power and again at the time of Munich. Since the war Barth's "neutralism" suggests a reversion to his position of the pre-Nazi period. In this respect the position Barth adopted regarding Communism, especially in Hungary, has brought forth Niebuhr's vigorous criticism. In a review of Barth's collection of essays *Against the Stream,* and with particular reference to the pieces dealing with Hungary, Niebuhr concludes:

> In short these essays reveal political naïveté, posing in the guise of theological sophistication, together with a consequent incapacity to make any prudent or sensible political and moral judgments. The whole performance prompts revulsion against every pretension to derive detailed political judgments from ultimate theological propositions. When a man lacks ordinary common sense in reacting against evil, no theological sophistication will help him. He may even, as Barth, think that the distinction of moment for Christians is that the Nazis tried to corrupt Christianity while communism only tries to kill it.[53]

After the heroic rebellion of the Hungarians against the Russian tyranny in the autumn of 1956, Niebuhr returned to this question of Barth's theology and his political judgments in an article published in *The Christian Century* entitled "Why Is Barth Silent on Hungary?" In this article Niebuhr seeks to show what he considers to be the defects in Barth's "confidently held theological frame of reference, and also in the lower political frame of reference." [54] The first defect Niebuhr believes to be that Barth is too consistently "eschatological" for the "nicely calculated less and more" that makes all the difference in our political decisions. The second defect "is his extreme pragmatism which disavows all moral principles," [55] which deprives him of the guidance of the instructive, though inexact, analogies of history. For these reasons Niebuhr agrees with the rather common charge that Barth's approach is designed for the Church of the Catacombs. "The description is accurate: Barth's view makes no provision for discriminating judgments both because of its strong eschatological emphasis and because of the absence of principles and structures of value." [56] One wonders whether such phrases as "too consistently eschatological" and "strong eschatological emphasis" are the happiest ways Niebuhr could find for pointing his criticism. It would perhaps have been better to use the term "undialectical," because the burden of his critique is the obscuration of the dialectical relation between love and justice with the consequence that the illumination and the resources of *agape* are not properly brought to bear on the complex problems of relative decisions, and also with the result that political judgments are informed more by impulse than by profound political reflection. In a word, Niebuhr criticizes Barth for a theologism that issues in confused political guidance. If one is going to make political judgments from the vantage point of theological prestige he must take the political disciplines seriously. If one is going rigorously to reject natural law theories, he is obliged to show how the norm of *agape* is related to the necessity for making discriminating political judgments.

## 4. CONFLICT WITH LIBERAL MORALISM

Undoubtedly the most crucial struggle in which Niebuhr has been engaged has been with the prevailing moralism of modern culture in general and American religion in particular. The liberal moralism, which in America reached its peak in the 'twenties and 'thirties, and which continues largely to inform the American religious outlook, constitutes the immediate context of most of Niebuhr's polemical writings. Indeed it is no exaggeration to say that it has been out of this conflict that Niebuhr's thought has acquired its particular cast and peculiar power—the rare combination of religious profundity and political realism.

The prevailing moralism derived its strong crusading social zeal from the heritage of the social gospel. On the whole it was marked, however, by vagueness and sentimentality. General exhortations to righteousness, peace, love, self-sacrifice, and social concord failing to dip down low enough to encounter any concrete situation or specific evil, often managed to go nicely above the heads of dutiful Sunday listeners and readers of the religious press. This was alternated by getting very specific about particular issues but in such a sentimental fashion that more often than not the spokesmen of religion were, and remain, sources of social confusion rather than light. I do not think it need be argued that this combination of vague exhortation and sentimental solutions of complex problems was, and remains, very widespread in the American Church. One need only to peruse the religious periodicals and the popular religious books of the 'twenties and 'thirties (and still today!) to be persuaded of this.

From the earliest days of his writings, Niebuhr's religious profundity and social realism recoiled from this presentation of the gospel and approach to serious social issues. As his own thought gained toughness and clarity, his profound dissatisfaction turned into an all out assault upon the sentimental optimism of the day. Niebuhr quickly gained the reputation—and it is one that has stuck —of being a pessimist. The words optimist and pessimist are utterly irrelevant for judging his work or that of any other theologian, but the point to be seen is that this tag was derived not from what he wrote but from the context in which he wrote.

Niebuhr here was engaged in no sham battle. The whole ethos of American Christianity was, and generally remains, against him.

It was no sham battle also by virtue of the greatness of the issues. We need refer here only to the position of much of the American religious press at the outbreak of World War II to sense the appalling confusion that had been introduced into the American scene by a sentimental, religious moralism. For sentimentalism is never a small matter. It is a dry rot, destructive of both moral fiber and intellectual perception.

The root of the sentimentality of the prevailing outlook was the conception that love is a simple historical possibility. If only more people would live by the law of love, then the nasty business of "power politics" could be dispensed with, co-operation would supersede the need for coercion, class struggles would cease, and international peace would reign.

> The moralistic utopianism of the liberal Church has been expressed in various forms. Liberal theologians sometimes go to the length of decrying all forms of politics as contrary to [the] Christian spirit of love. Sometimes they deprecate only coercive politics without asking themselves the question whether any political order has ever existed without coercion. Sometimes, with greater realism, they merely declare all forms of violent coercion to be incompatible with the Christian ethic.[57]

It is not our purpose at this point to seek to show the justness of this general description. That will become evident when, later in our inquiry, we discuss the pacifist issue. Our point here is simply to indicate that Niebuhr's criticism served to reveal how irrelevant the liberal Church's attempt at being directly relevant had become because of its assumption that love was a simple historical possibility. Moreover, one does not have to return to 1935 to know how the following biting description fits all too frequently the resolutions committee of almost any Church conference.

> The sum total of the liberal Church's effort to apply the law of love to politics without qualification is really a curious medley of hopes and regrets. The Church declares that men ought to live by the law of love and that nations as well as individuals ought to obey it; that neither individuals nor nations do; that nations do so less

than individuals; but that the Church must insist upon it; that, unfortunately, the Church which is to insist upon the law has not kept
it itself; but that it has sometimes tried and must try more desperately; that the realization of the law is not in immediate prospect,
but the Christian must continue to hope. These appeals to the moral
will and this effort to support the moral will by desperate hopes are
politically as unrealistic as they are religiously superficial. If the
liberal Church had had less moral idealism and more religious
realism its approach to the political problem would have been less
inept and fatuous. Liberal solutions of the social problem never take
the permanent difference between man's collective behavior and
the moral ideals of an individual life into consideration. Very few
seem to recognize that even in the individual there is a law in his
members which wars against the law that is in his mind.[58]

There are three main reasons for the sentimentality of such
moralism. The first is that it is unaware of the depth and power of
sin. It does not understand the real condition of man, that he is a
creature involved in a contradiction with the will of God and thus
in a profound self-contradiction. Thus, as Niebuhr puts it in a reply
to G. G. Atkins, "It is not moral complacency of which liberal
Christianity stands convicted but moral superficiality."[59] "What
is lacking," he says elsewhere, "is the realization that even the best
human will in the world has the corruption of sin in it."[60] Such
moralism fails utterly to meet the deepest needs of the individual
soul in its pilgrimage, and equally to be deplored is its failure to
read the historical situation so as to provide the proper basis for
justice and order. It is this superficial reading of the human condition, this tacit assumption that men do not fulfill the law of love because they have not heard it often enough or clearly enough, that
leads moralism into such a sentimental approach to social issues.

If moralism fails to plumb the depth of man's sin, it does so
because it has failed to delineate the religious heights disclosed
in the gospel. "Our whole difficulty in American Protestantism,"
Niebuhr writes, "is in having so long regarded Christianity as
synonymous with the simple command to love God and our fellow
men, that we have forgotten that the Christian religion is really

a great deal more than this." [61] Faced with the desperate human cry "Who will deliver me from the body of this death?" the Christian message declares "that the divine mercy revealed in Christ is on the one hand a power which overcomes the contradiction between what we are and what we ought to be, and on the other hand a pledge of forgiveness for this sinful element which is never completely overcome short of the culmination of history. Only such a faith can disclose the actual facts of human existence. It alone can uncover the facts because it alone has answers for the facts which are disclosed." [62]

It is this failure to discern either the depths of man's plight or the manner in which *agape* transcends all our ideas and achievements of the good that leads to the third manifestation of sentimentalism—the lack of political and social realism. Failure to measure the depth of man's sinfulness and the atoning work of Christ is what lies at the basis of the inability of liberal moralism to come to grips with the realities of our corporate life.

> This is why all moralistic preaching which does not reveal the religious heights which stand over every specific moral ideal of justice is also so incapable of coming to terms with the political realities of our existence. It always substitutes ideals of love for the political necessities of justice. It wants people of changed heart to grant their fellow men love so that their fellow men will not have to demand justice. It always suggests that the brutal realities of politics are necessary only because people haven't heard and been charmed by the ideal of love. It does not realize that if all men professed Christ and even if they understood his gospel so well that they felt under the tension of the commandment, "Thou shalt love thy neighbor as thyself," the fact of sin would still make political and economic coercion for the establishment of justice necessary. Moralistic preaching which makes love a substitute for justice merely increases the moral confusion of our day. [63]

It is to be noted again that it was because Niebuhr challenged the efficacy of this simple moralism that he acquired the reputation for being a pessimist. But what must be asserted in the strongest possible terms is this: Niebuhr challenges this moralism not in order to give voice to the realism of a Worldly Wiseman but in order to clarify the situation to the end that the illumination and resource of biblical faith might be brought to bear. This is the motivation of all his polemical writings.

Perhaps no one failed more dismally to get inside Niebuhr's thought while engaged in serious debate with him than C.C. Morrison, then editor of *The Christian Century*. In an Editorial Conversation, Morrison attacked Niebuhr's position that the law of love is no simple historical possibility. He chose to do it in a very inept fashion, but it was the sort of argument to which American liberal Protestantism had long since grown accustomed. Morrison wrote: "What follows from the impracticability of the law of love is that Christians must take up the task of making a world in which the law of love *shall be* practicable. To set about the making of such a world is itself the highest form of practicing the law of love." [64] There you have it. In those two sentences by the editor of this popular and influential journal we see the stubborn persistence of this simple moralism that informed *The Christian Century*'s approach to the social and political issues of the critical years of the 'thirties. Morrison had said, "The Christian ideal of love is an attainable ideal, that is the truth which Christianity must attain or cease to be Christian." It was as simple as that, and to fail to affirm this credo meant that one had somehow forsaken the Christian message and hope to trumpet a disillusioned and worldly pessimism.

John Ferguson has recently put forth essentially this same moralistic position, though with much greater scholarship, urbanity, and theological insight. Ferguson makes the same mistake as Williams in lumping Brunner and Niebuhr together at the point where they are in sharpest disagreement. His own position is summarized in three statements. (1) The term justice is misleading and it would therefore clarify thinking to abandon it since "The Christian knows no principle of absolute morality save love, and that as revealed in Jesus Christ." [65] Niebuhr would agree with the latter statement. (2) "Secondly, there is no justification for accepting a different

moral standard as applicable to relationships between groups
from that of individual relationships."[66] Niebuhr would again
agree: *agape* is the only ultimate norm for all life. (3) "Thirdly,
the Christian's prime task is to bear witness unflinchingly to this
higher principle. He is not called upon to accept a second-best in
the name of expediency. If love and 'justice' are in conflict he will
choose love, whatever the cost."[67] What Ferguson apparently does
not see is that it is precisely here that the problem lies. Ferguson
assumes that love is a simple historical possibility and therefore to
seek justice is to be guided by a second, inferior, and independent
norm. Whereas our real situation is that "to choose" love is to seek
justice, for failure to seek justice is to lose love, knowing all the
while that justice is something less than love, *not because justice
is a secondary choice but because love is not a simple historical
possibility. Agape transcends its own relative embodiment in justice.* In other words the real ethical question begins for Niebuhr
at the point where Ferguson breaks off. *Agape* is the norm—the
real question is how it is related to our daily decisions and social
structures when it is itself not a simple historical possibility. Although the cruder aspects of utopianism have been clearly shed
in people like Ferguson, the root idea that the law of love can be
realized in history remains. Niebuhr's answer to this is succinctly
put: "The Christian utopians think they can dispense with all
structures and rules of justice simply by fulfilling the law of love.
They do not realize that the law of love stands on the edge of history and not in history, that it represents an ultimate and not an
immediate possibility."[68] Being the ultimate possibility and the
law of all life, *agape* is perpetually relevant to every historical
situation, but can be related thereto only dialectically through
justice.

Our foregoing discussion has been a descriptive account of a
few of the major debates in which Niebuhr has been engaged regarding the relation of the Christian norm of love and the struggle
for justice. The discussion has been carried on to the end that the
nature and relevance of Niebuhr's thought might secure greater

clarity, indicating the context in which it was forged as well. It is clear that he has certain affinities with these positions against which he has so resolutely contended. But it is certainly obvious that he is no mere eclectic. The distinctive character of his thought lies precisely in this understanding of the nature of the relation between love and justice. Having thus reviewed his criticisms of other significant Christian positions, we can round out our discussion by stating briefly how Niebuhr himself conceives the significance of reason, power, and the regulative principles of equality and liberty for the task of securing justice under the norm of love.

## 5. REASON, POWER, AND JUSTICE

It is sometimes said that Niebuhr pays insufficient attention to the significance of reason in the achieving of justice. Certainly it is true that he sees both the motivation to do justice and the norm of justice as rooted in religious faith, but this in no way means that he underestimates the significance of reason. Indeed, he never fails to point out and emphasize the necessity and positive role of reason. "Faith can no more dispense with reason in dealing with the details of a social ethic than it can dispense with logic in elaborating a total world view, or with science in analyzing the detailed facts of human experience."[69] Or again, "The will to do justice ultimately has a religious root and no rational reason can be given why a man ought to be just, unless it be the prudential one that injustice will finally destroy its beneficiaries as well as its victim. . . . But all this does not change the fact that life in Christian, non-Christian and in mixed societies is partially ordered by insights which are derived from man's tentative capacity to transcend his own interests and to consider the interests of others. Those insights are on the whole derived from his reason."[70]

But, we ask, what is to be said of the contribution of reason in a more specific sense? In our discussion above on the "rules and laws of justice,"[71] it is to be observed that the rational element is constitutive in each of them. Niebuhr himself states this in his discussion of these rules and laws.

> An immediately felt obligation towards obvious need may be prompted by the emotion of pity. But a continued sense of obligation rests upon and expresses itself in rational calculations of the needs of others as compared with our own interests. A relation between the self and one other may be partly ecstatic; and in any case the calculation of relative interests may be reduced to a minimum. But as soon as a third person is introduced into the relation even the most perfect love requires a rational estimate of conflicting needs and interests.[72]

The first great contribution of reason then is in delineating the principles of justice whereby our sense of obligation is widened. But this is not all. Reason also plays a significant role in the awakening of the conscience to the existence of social evil, and for the undermining of the reverence and pretension from which great inequities derive sanction and support.

> The force of reason makes for justice, not only by placing inner restraints upon the desires of the self in the interest of social harmony, but by judging the claims and assertions of individuals from the perspective of the total community. An irrational society accepts injustice because it does not analyse the pretensions made by the powerful and privileged groups of society. Even that portion of society which suffers most from injustice may hold the power responsible for it, in reverence. A growing rationality in society destroys the uncritical acceptance of injustice. It may destroy the morale of dominant groups by making them more conscious of the hollowness of their pretensions, so that they will be unable to assert their interests and protect their special privileges with the same degree of self-deception. It may furthermore destroy their social prestige in the community by revealing the relation between their special privileges and the misery of the underprivileged. It may also make those who suffer from injustice more conscious of their rights in society and persuade them to assert their rights more energetically.[73]

These few references ought to be sufficient to show that the rational contribution to social ethics is far from being neglected in Niebuhr.

However the limitations of reason are such that he must reject all purely rational ethics.

Reason does not transcend the particular interests of the self nearly so much as rationalists generally suppose. It too is conditioned by history and tainted by sin. "When will our modern rationalists learn," Niebuhr writes in a discussion of Stuart Chase, "that men are not logical, not because they do not know logic but because they are capable of standing outside, rather than inside a system of logic, and thus making it the servant of their interests?" [74] Reason is not the source of virtue and consequently can be the obedient servant of the self in the pursuit of its own interests as much as anything else. Reason then is limited by the fact that it can provide neither adequate motivation nor a pure enough norm for truly responsible living.

Since reason is always to some extent the servant of interest in a social situation, it is altogether naïve to suppose that justice can be secured by rational persuasion alone. The corruption of interest means that power must be challenged by power.

Perhaps there is no point at which Niebuhr's realism stands in such marked contrast with the thought of most theologians (and indeed even some political thinkers) as here in his profound grasp of the significance and nature of power and its relation to the struggle for justice.

The social effort to secure justice is never simply a matter of reason and morality. It certainly is not simply a question of morality against power as all the banal talk about setting love and morality against "power politics" would suggest. All politics is power politics. The task of securing justice is a never-ending political task. It is therefore always involved in a contest of power.

American Protestantism has long been reluctant to take the measure of this rather obvious fact. It has thus failed not only to come to terms with the elementary facts of social existence, it has also introduced confusion into the situation by failing to acknowledge and measure the significance of the fact that even the most moral of men are power seekers, and that this is even more

true of groups than of individuals. Or, as we have previously emphasized, it has failed because it lacked both political realism and
religious depth.

The consequence of this has been that the religiously sensitized
social conscience has most frequently found expression in philanthropy rather than basic social criticism. "Philanthropy," as
Niebuhr has remarked, "is usually a generous concession of power
to weakness. It usually does not touch the equilibrium of social
power and it is therefore something less than justice. It becomes
corrupted into an enemy of justice as soon as the next step is taken
and it is used by the powerful to beguile the weak from challenging
the basic equilibrium of justice." [75]

The struggle for justice can thus never be dissociated from efforts
to secure a more equal distribution of power in society. Disproportionate power is always irresponsible power and thus the source
of injustice. Not a little then of the task of securing justice must
assume the form of increasing the power of those social groups
which suffer most from the existing disproportion. "Justice is
basically dependent upon a balance of power." [76] This, of course,
raises the whole question of the "balancer" of power, which on the
domestic scene in a technical society means the whole complex
question of the role of government in the managing of effective
equilibria of power. We shall postpone consideration of this question of basic political and economic philosophy to a later point in
our study. Our concern here is simply to emphasize that the question of justice must never be made a moral question divorced from
the realities and use of power, the necessity for a balance of power,
and of an organizing center which can redress radical disproportions of power without itself becoming the source of a new
tyrannical power.

Power is thus the instrument of both good and evil. It is not in
itself evil. Niebuhr is explicit about this: "But power cannot be
evil of itself, unless life itself be regarded as evil. For life is
power. Life is never pure form or reason. It is inherently dynamic. Even the purest 'reason' is power. According to the Christian

faith perfect power and goodness are united only in God."[77]

To acknowledge that justice is dependent upon a balance of power which always possesses the potential of overt conflict is to recognize just how precarious is any achieved social harmony. And modern technology and mass communication serve only to exaggerate the tentativity of any such achievement. Moreover, a structure of justice based upon a balance of power is certainly very different from brotherhood, "a community of love."

It is right here, however, that the structure of Niebuhr's thought possesses its relevance. *Agape* is heedless, self-sacrificing; justice is discriminating, concerned with interests. Justice is further dependent upon power, upon an effective balance of the power of parties contending for their respective interests. The Christian then must hold clearly in view the norm of love and the power of self-love, the law of life and the other law in our members. All this becomes focused on the question of how we view the use of power. Consequently the real structure of our theological thinking will usually be quickly delineated when we confront concretely the question of power. Niebuhr's own views have been put with great clarity.

> For to understand the law of love as a final imperative, but not to know about the persistence of the power of self-love in all of life but particularly in the collective relations of mankind, results in an idealistic ethic with no relevance to the hard realities of life. To know about the power of self-love but not to know that its power does not make it normative is to dispense with ethical standards and fall into cynicism. But to know both the law of love as the final standard and the law of self-love as a persistent force is to enable Christians to have a foundation for a pragmatic ethic in which power and self-interest are used, beguiled, harnessed and deflected for the ultimate end of establishing the highest and most inclusive possible community of justice and order. This is the very heart of the problem of Christian politics: the readiness to use power and interest in the service of an end dictated by love and yet an absence of complacency about the evil inherent in them. No definitions or structures of justice can prevent these forces from getting out of hand if they are not handled with a sense of their peril.[78]

Justice is not an independent norm. It is the relative social embodiment of love which always stands under the criticism and the higher possibilities of love. Justice is dependent upon power, specifically upon the balance and diffusion of power. Although reason provides neither the norm nor the basic motivation for justice, it plays an immensely significant role in the securing of justice. Can we now go further in speaking of the principles of justice? Niebuhr does. Although he cannot embrace a rationalistic egalitarianism, still from within his framework of Christian thought he insists that equality is a principle ingredient of justice. Every higher justice is always a more equal justice.

Because equality is the mark of any "higher justice," Niebuhr sometimes suggests that it occupies a medial position between justice and love. He expresses this in a number of ways. He describes equality as "a rational, political version of the law of love" which shares with love "the quality of transcendence." [79] And elsewhere, "Equality as a pinnacle of the ideal of justice implicitly points towards love as the final norm of justice; for equal justice is the approximation of brotherhood under the conditions of sin." [80] Or, again most specifically, "Equality stands in a medial position between love and justice. If the obligation to love the neighbor as the self is to be reduced to rational calculation, the only guarantee of the fulfillment of the obligation is a grant to the neighbor which equals what the self claims for itself. Thus equality is love in terms of logic. But it is no longer love in the ecstatic dimension. For the principle of equality allows and requires that the self insist upon its own rights and interests in competition with the rights and interests of the other. Therefore equal justice is on the one hand the law of love in rational form and on the other hand something less than the law of love." [81]

Now what does this add up to? It would be a mistake to form the image in our minds of a nicely tiered hierarchy of values stemming from vitality, through justice and equality to sacrificial love. Niebuhr simply doesn't work with such static images. He is saying that equality is a *regulative* principle of justice inasmuch as when love is embodied in history in structures of justice, those structures are distinguished by a greater measure of equality.

Equality is a regulative principle of justice but it is not a constitutive principle. Justice can ultimately be described only with reference to *agape* and the concrete situation. Equality cannot be elevated to the constitutive principle of justice without disaster because, important as it is, our very ideas of equality betray their ideological taint. This is one of the basic errors of Marxism. Not only does it fail to do justice to the necessary inequality of function in any society, it also introduces an absolute character into the relativity of its perspective on equality, thus forming the solid basis for self-righteous fury and tyranny.

Moreover the very nature of the self, to say nothing of the larger community, demands that equality not be the sole regulative principle of justice. Just as there is a dialectical relation between *agape* and justice, so there is a continuous tension between equality and liberty as the two regulative principles of justice. Every higher justice is a more equal justice. However, equality without liberty strikes at the very nature of our humanity. The "one unanimous and harmonious ant-heap" of the Grand Inquisitor is not a state of justice. *Agape* alone is the norm for man in his finite freedom. Equality therefore is only a regulative and not a constitutive principle of justice; it must ever be held in tension with liberty.

An interesting shift in emphasis has here occurred in Niebuhr's thought with the passing years. Niebuhr was never unmindful of the significance and necessity of liberty. But the shedding of the remnants of his abstract idealism, and his increasing knowledge of the monstrous tyranny derived from the illusions of communist idealism, have formed the context for an increased emphasis upon liberty as well as equality as the two regulative principles of justice. In his Oxford conference paper Niebuhr could write: "The question . . . arises whether there is any regulative principle by which the merits of these partial achievements in justice may be judged. The answer is that there is only one such principle, the principle of equality." [82] In later writings the two principles are always held in tension. For example: "Gradually . . . a rational analysis of all the permanent and the contingent factors in a social situation will reveal liberty and equality to be the regulative principles of justice . . ." [83]

It is obvious, of course, that liberty and equality are principles in tension with each other. The tragedy of modern history has been that instead of existing together in tension they have been torn asunder. Both, as Niebuhr points out, were considered to be "self-evident" by the Enlightenment, but liberty has been the war cry of the middle classes and equality that of the industrial classes. "These preferences were the occasion for the civil war which rent the unity of most Western societies. The preference for each value by the respective class was advanced the more fanatically because it was supposed to be rationally justified. Yet each preference was ideologically motivated." [84] It is indeed ironic that so much of our history has been, and remains, a fierce conflict between those who, making liberty the constitutive instead of a regulative principle, insist that it will inevitably lead to equality; while those who exalt equality to an absolute norm hold out the promise of restoring man to the freedom of his essential nature.

Both liberty and equality are regulative principles of justice. A more just order grants man liberty within a framework of increasing equality. But neither is an absolute social norm, neither is a constitutive principle of justice. Both are expressions of love finding embodiment in the ideas and structures of justice, and in turn expressing within justice something of the tension between love and justice.

*Three*

# LOVE, JUSTICE, AND THE SELF

As he sought to bring the insight of the Christian faith to bear upon the social issues of our day, Niebuhr everywhere found himself confronted with deep-seated habits of thought which made inevitable erroneous estimates of human nature. This remains a profound cultural problem. Nothing has so distinguished the modern era as its phenomenal conquest of nature. The remarkable achievements of the scientific method in increasing our understanding of, and mastery over, nature have frequently led us to the disastrous assumption that man is to be understood (and controlled) through the extension of the same method. The fabulous scientific achievements of our age have beguiled us into assuming that man too is to be understood as a part of nature. This development reached its climax at the precise moment in history when our very technical achievements have made the problems of human togetherness of such immense importance that the survival of civilization depends upon our realistic and imaginative grappling with them. But our culture is not well equipped to deal with specifically human problems, especially on such a large scale, just insofar as our achievements in mastering nature lead us to assume that man is to be understood as a piece of nature and the problems of human community are capable of being solved by the same method. "We thus confront the ironic fact that a culture, intent upon understanding nature and boasting of ever more impressive achievements in the 'conquest' of nature, has become involved in ever more serious misunderstandings of human nature, of the self and its uniqueness, and in its dramatic-historical environment."[1]

In order to speak meaningfully and persuasively to his age, Niebuhr was thus led to a rich study of the history of thought in the Western world. His method is typological in the sense that he speaks about idealism and naturalism rather than giving detailed analyses of particular idealists and naturalists. This has the result that he is usually something less than just to the special nuances of particular thinkers. However, few possess his capacity to penetrate to the core of the thought of a movement or tradition. The operative concepts are grasped with great clarity. Niebuhr knows as well as anyone that the inhabitants of Athens do not always say the same thing, anymore than do those who dwell in Jerusalem. But there is a tradition which has powerfully shaped our culture which is properly identified as Hellenic and another equally significant, which is properly labeled Hebraic. These traditions are the two great components of our culture. Western culture is, he says, "unique in human history in that it draws upon two different sources for its conceptions of meaning, the Hebraic and the Hellenic. Each of these sources has the capacity to do justice to one of the dimensions of meaning and is defective in comprehending the other, but the two together comprehend both natural and historical reality more adequately than any other culture." [2]

It is not our purpose here either to report or assess his delineation of the nature and history of these two great traditions. Our purpose is simply to indicate wherein he sees these two traditions diverging in their approach to the question of the self. One quotation will suffice to show his general approach.

> It is commonly asserted that we have our religion, and possibly our ethics, from the Hebraic side, and our philosophy from the Hellenic side, of our heritage. This generalization is, broadly speaking, correct, but it does not point accurately to the peculiar virtues and defects of each part of our heritage. It does not do justice to the fact that there is a yearning after the ultimate in the Hellenic, as in the Hebraic culture; and that there are ethical and religious concepts in both. But the Hellenic is defective in understanding the self and its dramas because it tries to understand both rationally

and ontologically. The Hebraic, on the other hand, is defective in analyzing any permanent structure in the flow of temporal events. For the one history is made into another dimension of nature; and for the other nature is subsumed under history. Both nature and history are understood as standing under a divine sovereignty, rather than as subject to self-explanatory laws. Thus the one culture misunderstands human selves and their history, where freedom is more apparent than laws. The other misunderstands nature because it is primarily to be understood in terms of analyzable laws.[3]

The greatest problem of the modern age is the problem of human community. We need desperately to have every resource of understanding that will bring light and healing to the question of man, his freedom, and his history. It is just these questions with which the Hebraic, or Christian, tradition (for when Christianity "is true to itself, it is Hebraic rather than Hellenic"[4]) deals most profoundly. However, it is also precisely this side of our culture which has been progressively relegated to the status of superstition, with the onward march of science and the progressive viewing of man as a part of nature. Thus we can see why Niebuhr has been increasingly compelled in his apologetic task to deal with the problems of the self and history.

## 1. THE DIALOGIC LIFE OF THE SELF

The uniqueness of man in Western culture is usually indicated by the metaphor drawn from the Hebraic tradition made "in the image of God." Frequently the content has been supplied by the Hellenic, and construed as man's reason. But the "image of God" is a relational term, describing man's position, his position "before God." The uniqueness of man can thus best be described by drawing out the content of his "dialogic life" to use the rich and meaningful phrase of Martin Buber. Man's dialogic life is a triadic relation. "The self is a creature which is in constant dialogue with itself, with its neighbors, and with God, according to the biblical viewpoint."[5]

Man is a creature engaged in a continuous internal dialogue; he is constantly talking to himself. The self glories and pities, accuses and excuses, condemns and defends itself. But this internal dialogue must not be understood in such a way as to jeopardize the unity of the self. "The fact is that there are not two distinct selves in this internal dialogue. There are merely two foci of the same self."[6] This dialogue may be described and discussed in terms of the will and the conscience, both of which "are two levels of the transcendence of the self over itself."[7] Of even greater interest and significance is the relation of the self to its "parts" or "functions," or the relations between body, soul, and spirit. In discussing this, Niebuhr makes a very interesting use of Charles Lindbergh's account of his epoch-making flight across the Atlantic in which he describes in memorable, non-academic terms, the internal dialogue as he fought against fear and fatigue.[8] There is an internal relation between the self and the body. One does not speak of "my body" as he does of "my car." "The self is 'soul' insofar as it has an experience of the unity."[9] But the self is not a particular self merely because it is in a particular body. The self transcends the body and can take a relatively objective view of it. Thus although there is an internal experience of the organic unity between the self and the body, the self possesses a unity and freedom that transcends the body. This is what we call "spirit." The self is spirit in its freedom, and awareness of its freedom, over its functions of mind and body. If we are to penetrate the mystery of the self we must do justice both to the organic unity of the self and its functions, and the freedom and transcendence of the self over its functions, of its spatial and non-spatial dimensions. In this complex relation the internal dialogue is set.

Man has his being in relationships. The truly significant is what happens between man and man. The self is thus in constant dialogue with others. It is not enough to describe these dialogues as those of a "social animal" inasmuch as they "move above the level of social cohesion which may be observed objectively."[10] There are certain conditions attending the dialogue with others

which Niebuhr discusses and which we can briefly summarize.
(1) "The self faces the other self as a mystery which can never be
fully penetrated."[11] (2) "The self sees the other as an instrument
for its purposes and as a completion for its incompleteness."[12] (3)
"The self can not be truly fulfilled if it is not drawn out of itself
into the life of the other."[13] Here again we see the necessity of
*agape* for the structure of mutuality. (4) "The self recognizes the
other as the limit of its expansiveness . . . There must therefore be
an element of reservation and reverence for the other in even the
most mutual relations."[14] (5) "The uniqueness of the individuals
which enter into any dialogic relation makes each one of these
relations highly unique, however general may be the natural basis
of the relation."[15] (6) "While the self is a unique center of life it is
indeterminately 'open' to other selves."[16] (7) "The pattern of these
dialogues is conditioned by historic factors."[17]

The third dimension of man's dialogic life is the dialogue of the
self with God. This dialogue reveals the self in search of ultimate
meaning. Both the dialogue of the self with itself and that of the
self with others point beyond themselves to this dimension. This
search takes many different forms, but Niebuhr feels that they may
be placed under three general categories. The first may be described as the idolatrous attempt to establish the ultimate significance of the self, individually as in romantic or existentialist
thought or in the assertion of the significance of the collective self.
Whether the latter is expressed in primitive religions or contemporary nationalism, statism, or communistic messianism we see
that it "corresponds to a perennial desire in the human heart to
eat one's cake and have it, too; to subordinate the finite self to
something greater than it but not so great that the self may not
participate in the exaltation of the finite value."[18] The second
response is that of mysticism which he described as the "heroic
effort to transcend all finite values and systems of meaning, including the self as particular existence, and to arrive at universality
and 'unconditioned' being."[19] The third alternative embraces the
biblical faiths of Judaism and Christianity. "These faiths interpret

the self's experience with the ultimate in the final reaches of its self-awareness as a dialogue with God."[20] In this dialogue man is convicted not for his finiteness but for his sin, and he is convicted by a love that has the power not only to convict but also to uphold and redeem. In this dialogue he learns that the attempts to seek the fulfillment of the self from the standpoint of the self are both idolatrous and self-defeating; that the self can find fulfillment only when centered in God; and that this can be found not when self-fulfillment is sought as the conscious end, but the glory of God only. For the Christian the encounter or dialogue with God finds its norm and form in the revelation in Jesus Christ. Here we learn the meaning of true selfhood and the nature of the relationship which characterizes it. The dialogic life of the self is thus the clue to the "nature" of the self. And the ultimate dimension of the self's dialogic life, the dialogue with God, is the point where the self finds its ultimate meaning, the relationship which is the sustaining "ground" of its life. It is precisely this dialogic life of the self which the Hebraic tradition both assumes and illuminates, and which the Hellenic obscures or destroys. "The self is not related to God by sharing its reason with God and finding a point of identity with the divine through the rational faculty. The self is related to God in repentance, faith, and commitment. All these forms of relation imply a certain degree of existential discontinuity with God. The self is always a creature, conscious of its finiteness, and equally conscious of its pretension in not admitting its finiteness. Insofar as it becomes conscious of its pretensions it is capable of repentance and a new life. The encounter with God is in short a dramatic one."[21]

## 2. THE SELF AND ITS FUNCTIONS

The peculiar problems and perils of the present age have conspired to provide the eternal question of authentic individuality or selfhood with an urgent social context. This cryng social need thus lends passion and urgency to the perennial task of the Christian apologist to hold clearly before the world the unique dimension of human freedom. It is Niebuhr's passionate conviction that nothing must be allowed to obscure the capacity of the self to transcend all the natural, social, and rational coherences through which it is provisionally defined and expressed. To do so is to corrode the foundation of true individuality, to lay the framework for the loss of selfhood at the precise moment in history when the real nature of the self's freedom is not only the perennial human concern but an utter social necessity.

The first question to be faced is the relation between individuality and particularity. Niebuhr answers succinctly: "Individuality is a fruit of both nature and spirit." [22] "Genuine individuality, embodying both discreteness and uniqueness, is a characteristic of human life. It must consequently be regarded as the product of spirit as well as of nature. Nature supplies particularity but the freedom of the spirit is the cause of real individuality. Man, unlike animal existence, not only has a centre but he has a centre beyond himself." [23] The life of man is thus lived in the tension between his creaturely particularity and his capacity for self-transcendence in which inheres his uniqueness. If we are properly to discern the nature and basis of individuality, both of these must be clearly held together.

Niebuhr sees a fairly consistent denial of the significance of selfhood in the naturalistic tradition through its failure properly to assess the dimension of man's freedom over his functions, and the significance of this self-transcendence for understanding the real nature of the relationship between this freedom and the organic unity of the self with the vitalities of nature.

It is not our purpose to report on Niebuhr's tracing of this tradition. One example may be taken from our own time. It is, admittedly, an example of a rather crude naturalism but not less significant on that account for revealing the operative assumptions of a significant portion of our culture. We refer to the Kinsey report. Our concern is not to debate Kinsey's findings. Whether we agree with them or not, his report undoubtedly has revealed a good deal about the sex mores of America. Our concern is with the assumptions which informed the inquiry and which insinuate themselves into its evaluations. It is this aspect of the question which has attracted Niebuhr's attention.

> The report assumes that the modern revolt against sexual disciplines is primarily due to the inadequacy of the standards established by the "Judeo-Christian" tradition, and that more adequate standards will be achieved by defining "normal" behavior through a statistical study of actual behavior. The first proposition is not altogether wrong. Neither Catholicism nor Protestantism has ever completely realized the ideal of relating sexual life sacramentally to the whole of personality and to the whole of a loyal community of persons in the family partnership.

> But the second proposition of the Kinsey report proves how much more grievously modern secularism errs in dealing with these issues. If the Christian faith has failed to bring the tumultuous stuff of the sexual life under adequate discipline or sublimation, the philosophy behind the Kinsey report proposes to solve the problem, simply by ignoring all deeper aspects of human existence. Sexual drives are analyzed as if they were merely biological impulses and "sexual objects" are discussed as if "impulses" had to find their "objects" without the overarching of personality in each case.

> Even more dangerous is the assumption that new norms can be created by a statistical study of the actual sex practices of the day. Here we have the modern sociological approach to the problem of norms reduced to its final absurdity. A learned doctor, reviewing the Kinsey report asks the relevant question, whether the fact that most people have colds in the winter establishes the cold as "normative." [24]

In a later article, Niebuhr comes to grips with the root fallacy in this whole approach. It is the failure to deal with the personal dimension because the self is dealt with as a piece of nature. The radical freedom of the person "makes for the uniqueness of the individual about which nature knows nothing." [25] This is as we have said, a crude and extreme form of naturalism. The fact, how-

ever, that it could pose as being truly scientific reveals the degree
to which ideas that obscure the real dimension of man's uniqueness
are powerfully operative in our culture. Moreover, although this
example does not at all do justice to the rich insights of the great
tradition of naturalism, it does serve forcibly to point up the loss
of the self in naturalism.

Idealism exalts the dimension of selfhood obscured in naturalism.
But it just as surely loses the self in the end.

> This self of idealistic rationalism is both less and more than
> the real self. It is less in the sense explained by Kierkegaard:
> "The paradox of faith is this that the individual is higher than
> the universal, that the individual determines his relation to the
> universal by his relation to the absolute, not his relation to the
> absolute by his relation to the universal." In idealism the true
> self is that reason which relates the self to the universal. But since
> the true self in idealistic thought is neither more nor less than this
> universal reason, the actual self is really absorbed in the universal.
> The actual self is, however, less, as well as more, than reason;
> because every self is a unity of thought and life in which thought
> remains in organic unity with all the organic processes of finite
> existence.[26]

The tendency of all idealism to identify reason and spirit thus
obscures both the radical freedom of the self over all its functions
and the perils of this freedom. For these reasons neither the
grandeur nor the misery of man is sufficiently plumbed. The perennial overtone of rationalistic idealism is always mysticism in which,
in its most consistent forms, the particular self is absorbed in an
undifferentiated unity of being.

The debate between naturalism and idealism in modern culture
has been, in its latter stages, further complicated by the rebellion
of romanticism against rationalism in both its naturalistic and
idealistic forms. This romantic revolt has received many different
expressions—the vitalism of Nietzsche's will to power, the revolt
against the dishonest pretension of reason by a Marx, the challenge
to the claim of reason to be the organizing principle of life as in

Bergson.[27] Certainly the romantic protest has, in its various expressions, been the bearer of profound insights into the human situation. However, it too has failed properly to delineate the relationship between the structure of selfhood and the freedom of the self over its structure. Niebuhr expresses his basic criticism in these words:

> Its error consists not so much in reducing . . . vitality to bio-mechanical proportions as bourgeois naturalism tends to do. Its basic error lies in its effort to ascribe to the realm of the biological and the organic what is clearly a compound of nature and spirit, of biological impulse and rational and spiritual freedom. Man is never a simple two-layer affair who can be understood from the standpoint of the bottom layer, should efforts to understand him from the standpoint of the top layer fail. If rationalism tends to depreciate the significance, power, inherent order and unity of biological impulse, romanticism tends to appreciate these without recognizing that human nature knows no animal impulse in its pure form.[28]

Romanticism is, nevertheless, a revolt on behalf of individuality against the uniformities of both nature and reason. But this revolt has had an ironic history in that romantic "individualism" so quickly became a powerful contributing force to the spirit of collectivism. The inner relation between autonomous individualism and collectivism is a highly instructive relation and one that has been explored by many contemporary thinkers. Niebuhr writes:

> From the standpoint of the vicissitudes of the idea of individuality in modern culture the significance of romanticism is that it exalts the individual more unqualifiedly, but also loses him more quickly and completely than any form of rationalism. The process of this romantic destruction of individuality can be briefly summarized as follows: Individuality is directly related to the eternal source of meaning and given unqualified significance, while idealism ascribes significance to the individual only as he is related to a rational universal value of history. Sooner or later the romantic thinker must, however, recoil from the pretension of this purely individual self-deification; and all but Nietzsche do recoil. They seek to increase the plausibility and reduce the pretension of this self-glorification by looking for the "larger individual"; which they find in the unique

nation. This collective individual then supplants the single individual as the centre of existence and the source of meaning.[29]

That which is obscured, and ultimately destroyed, in both rationalism and romanticism is the dialogical character of man's life.
This is, as we have seen, no small matter. Failure to discern the
nature of man in his relatedness is to undercut the meaning of selfhood, the radical freedom of the self, and the radical corruption of
that freedom; it is to miss both the grandeur and the misery of man.
To understand man in terms of the coherences of either nature or
reason on the one hand, or the titanic assertion of the autonomous
self in individual or collective forms on the other, is in the end to
read the life of man in monological terms. This is to lose hold of the
uniqueness of the self.

## 3.  THE RADICAL FREEDOM OF
## THE SELF

The datum with which Niebuhr always begins his discussion of
the uniqueness of man is the human capacity for self-transcendence.
As we have seen, this means the capacity of the self to transcend
not only natural processes but also its own reason, and "to stand,
as it were, above the structures and coherences of the world."[30]
Herein lies the radical freedom of the self. This does not at all
mean that the limitations of creaturely particularity are obscured;
it means rather that the self is not bound to the norms of reason.
It is further to be emphasized that this freedom is the real source
of the dignity of man. This radical freedom is the source of man's
uniqueness. His dignity lies here rather than in any of the functions
in which the self is provisionally defined or enclosed. But to place
the dignity of man in his radical freedom, rather than in any dis-
cernible structure that may be labeled virtuous, is to assert also
that man's misery has the same root as his dignity. This radical
freedom is the basis of man's creative powers; it is also the basis of
human destructiveness. Thus any attempt to identify virtue with

reason or spirit, and evil with bodily passion or vitality, is to miss entirely the fundamental fact of the self—the freedom of the self wherein the creative and the destructive powers of human life have their common root. "Man stands perpetually outside and beyond every social, natural, communal, and rational cohesion. He is not bound by any of them which makes for his creativity; he is tempted to make use of all of them for his own ends. That is the basis of his destructiveness." [31]

The radical freedom of the self is the first datum of our consideration of the nature of the self and we must take the full measure of this fact. There is no doubt that this concern has increasingly become the forward thrust of Niebuhr's thought. The immediate and significant consequence of his serious measuring of this fact is that the self cannot find its norm in either nature or reason. This is of such crucial significance both for our concern to delineate the relationship between the norm of *agape* and the constitution of the self, and the character of the debates in which Niebuhr is presently engaged, that we ought to hear him put it himself in a clear and forceful passage.

> The Christian answer to the human predicament, a divine mercy toward man, revealed in Christ, which is at once a power enabling the self to realize itself truly beyond itself in love, and the forgiveness of God toward the self which even at its best remains in partial contradiction to the divine will, is an answer which grows out of, and which in turn helps to create, the radical Christian concept of human freedom. In the Christian faith the self in its final freedom does not find its norm in the structures either of nature or of reason. Nor is either able to bind the self's freedom or guarantee its virtue, as the proponents of "natural law" would have it. The principle of rationality, the force of logic, does not secure the virtue of the self, as in the thought of Kant. For the self can make use of logic for its ends. The partial and particular self is not merely a provisional particularity which is overcome in the universal self which develops with increasing rationality. Nor is the evil in the self the provisional confusion and cross-purposes of natural passion before ordered by mind as in Aristotle. There is, in other words, no form, structure, or logos, in nature to which the self ought to return from its freedom and no such form within its reason which would guarantee that the

self will express itself harmoniously with the total structure of existence above the level of natural necessity. The self is free to defy God. The self does defy God. The Christian conception of the dignity of man and of the misery of man is all of one piece, as Pascal rightly apprehended. All Renaissance and modern emphases upon the dignity of man to the exclusion of the Christian conception of the sin of man are lame efforts to reconstruct the Christian doctrine of selfhood without understanding the full implications of the Christian conception of the self's freedom.[32]

The radical freedom of the self precludes any co-ordination of man to the coherences of either nature or reason. When we take the full measure of man's freedom, we see the necessity for understanding man in terms of his "dramatic-historical environment." Elaboration of the dialogic life alone can delineate the "nature" of a creature possessed of such a freedom over the functions to which it is organically related. Being impressed with the utter centrality of this, Niebuhr has increasingly found himself in recent years in opposition to scientism.

## 4. SCIENTISM

We began our discussion of the self in this chapter by noting that Niebuhr found himself opposing a habit of thought that had issued in a remarkable understanding of nature but which, through an illegitimate extension of its assumptions and methods, had resulted in a deplorable misunderstanding of human nature. The result has been that we have deprived ourselves of the needed insight to cope with the profound personal and political issues of our day. In short, Niebuhr has constantly sought to undercut the scientism that pervades so much of our approach to life.

He is motivated by no defensive concern. The methods of the natural sciences have produced our phenomenal technical achievements, but they have been he says, "singularly deficient in generating *wisdom* in human affairs."[33] We must pause here and make something perfectly clear. Niebuhr is not opposed to science, as some of his critics have suggested. His opposition is to scientism, the assumption that the methods of the natural sciences are the avenue to the undertanding and the solution of all human problems. Nor does Niebuhr deny or underestimate the scientific elements in all the more specifically human disciplines. His concern is to undercut the prevailing scientific imperialism, and to show the serious limitations of the scientific method in illuminating the issues of the self and history. "There are innumerable scientific elements in history. What is insufferable is that elaborate claims should be made for the resources of 'science' in the clarification of our perplexities, when it is obvious that a most rigorous application of the methods of science means a denial of everything which is characteristically human."[34]

Science is not confined to nature. Man is a creature involved in natural process and there is a very significant portion of his life accessible to scientific inquiry. However, only the natural scientist is able to fulfill the strict requirements of science. He alone stands outside the process he observes. The psychologist and the historian stand inside as well as outside the process of their study. Objectivity in these disciplines is a necessary condition. But it is as much a moral as an intellectual achievement, and at best only a relative objectivity can be claimed. Moreover, he who deals with the self and human history cannot fulfill one of the tests of a strict science: predictability of the future on the basis of analysis of the past. Who in 1945 was able clearly to foresee the power alignments of today? The network of historical causation is far too complex, and moves on too many different levels, to allow for the exactitude required by any strict science.

The serious limitation of any scientific method in dealing with the specifically human will have the result that the most significant facts about man and history are missed. This has led to the ironic outcome that an illegitimate extension of the scientific method has meant that "the climax of an empirical culture" is its "blindness to some obvious 'facts.'" Moreover because these "facts" are either obscured or improperly measured, the hidden dogmas of modern

scientism become powerfully operative to add still further confusion. What does Niebuhr believe to be the "facts" obscured, and
the "hidden dogmas" embraced by modern scientism?

They are the "facts" or "realities" with which man *qua* man,
rather than man as scientist, must daily deal and live. They are
"the self's freedom," "the self-corruption of that freedom in self-
concern," and the "self's 'historical' character." [35]

It is, however, in the field of social and political analysis where
the uncritical adoption of the scientific method has resulted in the
spread of the worst confusion and sentimentality. The assumption
that the dynamic stuff of history may be tamed, directed, and
managed by the same methods used to control nature stems from
the disastrous failure to make the sharp distinction between nature and history required by the uniqueness and freedom of the
self. Niebuhr goes so far as to say that "Almost all the misinterpreta-
tions of human selfhood and the drama of history in the modern
day are derived from the effort to reduce human existence to the
coherence of nature." [36] An example of the banality into which
this approach can descend was given us by George Brock Chisholm, the Director General of the World Health Organization.
Chisholm wrote an article to show how science could help to
develop human nature so that it would be capable of, and prepared
for, world citizenship. [37] We need to learn, as children, that our
natural urges are good; consequently we need to get rid of all the
nonsense about original sin which prompts children to "hate themselves." A still further root of evil is our insecurity, which manifests
itself in various forms of self-expression and aggressiveness. What
is needed to eliminate this insecurity is to teach mothers how to
love their children with an uncritical love so that the security that
comes with a sense of belonging might naturally arise and then
be extended into the wider communities of life. In a scathing attack
on this, Niebuhr comments: "It need hardly be stated that this
prescription for the world's ills is the most pathetic nonsense which
has ever been preached in the name of science. It would be
insignificant if it were unique. It is unfortunately typical." [38] We

may wish to argue whether the apostles of "nursery salvation" are as typical as Niebuhr suggests, but there is no gainsaying the fact that they bring clearly to the fore the hidden dogmas of those whose approach to the problems of the self is determined by the assumption that man is to be understood as a piece of nature. It is to be noted that the dogmas are the natural corollaries of this assumption and procedure. "The religious presuppositions which form the framework for most modern scientific examinations of the human scene contain two very dubious articles, which must be held responsible for most of the errors and illusions in these examinations: (A) The idea of the perfectability of man and (B) the idea of progress."[39] We shall have more to say about this at various points in our study; here it is sufficient to emphasize that the distinctively human characteristics, the radical freedom of the self, the radical corruption of that freedom, and the historical nature of selfhood are obscured both by the assumptions and the inherent limitations of the method of inquiry.

It is scientism, not science, against which Niebuhr is inveighing, and his protest is made for the positive purpose of clearing the ground to the end that we may realistically and savingly approach the problems of human togetherness and the ultimate questions of what it is to be man.

> The relation between "I and Thou" is not a scientific but an existential procedure. The turning of the self from itself as the centre of its life to God and the neighbor is also not scientific. The correlation of historic facts requires imagination, wisdom, and humility which are not properly defined as "scientific." These attitudes require existential commitments, denials of self-interest, and recognition of the finiteness of all human knowledge in which the self rather than the mind is involved. If we really analyze these characteristically human elements in history we will not only cease to worship so uncritically at the altar of science. We will be less apologetic for the essence of a religion of history and revelation.[40]

## 5. ONTOLOGY

The uniqueness of man is the radical freedom of the self which is rooted in the capacity of the self to transcend in its unity the structures in which it is provisionally expressed. Until this is seen, neither can the radical character of man's self-corruption be measured, nor will the historical character of man be clearly apprehended. "Man is primarily a historical creature."[41] This is to say that he must be understood in terms of the freedom, decision, and responsibility that characterize relationships. In a word, man is to be understood in the dramatic-historical elaborations of his dialogic life. Anything that obscures this dimension, the personal-historical character of man's life, must be resisted. For this reason Niebuhr insists that we must resist the attempts to co-ordinate man to the coherence of reason as well as nature. Theologies that emphasize ontological categories display the Hellenic tendency to obscure the indeterminate freedom of the self by reducing it to some essence of reason or nature. "The encounter between God and man, as the encounters between men in history, must be by faith and love and not by the discovery of some common essence of reason or nature underlying individuals and particulars."[42]

To speak of personality, the radical freedom of the self over its own structures, and history as the dramatic elaboration of the dialogic life of the self, as the clues to the understanding of man, is to throw into the center terms that are ontologically ambiguous. To show this is, for Niebuhr, the primary task of Christian apologetics. "We must make it clear," he says, "that the concepts of both personality and history are ontologically ambiguous. Personality, whether God's or man's, is defined only in dramatic and historic encounter. Though these dramatic and historical media of personality are not inherently 'irrational,' they are not subject to the ordinary 'scientific' tests of rational intelligibility. Nothing in history follows as it does in nature or reason, 'in a necessary manner.' The personality is bound by historical destiny rather than by natural or ontological necessity."[43]

It is this concern and perspective which has led Niebuhr to diverge from the viewpoint of his great friend and former colleague, Paul Tillich. The contrast between the biblical-historical and Greek-ontological ways of thinking is the center of the issues between them. To be sure, Tillich fully appreciates Niebuhr's concern to illuminate the full meaning of the self, and believes that his own ontology of polar opposites does justice to the dynamic aspects of being, to freedom as well as structure. But Niebuhr, along with many others, is not so persuaded. He has pinpointed the issue between them right at this question.

> Professor Tillich suggests that what he regards as my errors are derived from my preoccupation with the nature of the self. That is indeed the cause of the difference between our respective viewpoints. I do not believe that ontological categories can do justice to the freedom either of the divine or of the human person, or to the unity of the person in his involvement in and transcendence over the temporal flux or that the sin of man and the forgiveness by God of man's sin or the dramatic variety of man's history can be comprehended in ontological categories.[44]

To be sure, every thinker who uses terms like self, dynamics, and history as Niebuhr constantly does, has an implicit ontology, as Tillich states.[45] Niebuhr is fully aware of this but he is determined to keep his ontology implicit rather than explicit, because the nature of the reality with which he is dealing cannot, he believes, be truly comprehended in any ontological system.

> "It is quite true," he says in reply to Tillich, "that whenever we speak of 'being' we speak ontologically. But since ontology is the 'science of being,' it has its limitations in describing any being or being *per se* which contains mysteries and meanings which are not within the limits of reason. Among these are both the human self in its mystery of freedom within and beyond the rational structure of mind, and the divine mystery which certainly implies the 'power of being'; but the mystery of God's creative power is certainly beyond the limits of a rational ontology."[46]

And again,

> My point is simply that when we deal with aspects of reality which
> exhibit a freedom above and beyond structures, we must resort to
> the Hebraic dramatic and historical way of apprehending reality.[47]

Throughout our discussion we have been concerned to underline
the fact that for Niebuhr, the freedom of the self is such that no
coherence of reason or nature can provide the norm for his life.
That norm can be discerned only by faith received in the dialogue
of the self with God, as that encounter is shaped by the actions of
God in history which cannot be anticipated by any philosophy.

What is discerned by such faith? The Christian answers, "a suffering divine love is the final coherence of life."[48] From our standpoint, incoherence between the most righteous human will and
the divine will remains to the end. The Christian message is that
"The final answer to this incoherence between the human and the
divine will is the divine suffering mercy; and for this no reason
can be given."[49] This is the light "that shineth in darkness." As
Christians we affirm that by this light we see meaning where before
there was only a meaningless passing of time. But the meaning
has a penumbra of mystery. We see, but we see through a glass
darkly. And the meaning and the mystery penetrate each other.
When apprehended by the *agape* of the Cross we learn, as did
Charles Wesley, that when we cry " 'Tis mercy all," we must go
on at once to say, " 'Tis mystery all."

Only so radical a love as the *agape* of the Cross, and no rationally conceived law, can be the norm for a creature possessed of
such a radical freedom as man; only the mystery of a love so
spontaneous and self-giving can meet the need of a freedom so
radically self-corrupted. We can know this only when in repentance
and trust, we receive this gift of grace.

## 6. THE RADICAL CORRUPTION OF MAN'S RADICAL FREEDOM

Niebuhr's rich and profound analysis of man's sin is quite generally regarded as his most valuable contribution to contemporary theology. We have already urged that it is misleading to conceive this as his central concern. On the contrary, his analysis of man's sin was developed out of the context in which his own great concern to make relevant the insights of the Christian faith to the decisions and structures of our social life came into conflict with a shallow moralism that assumed the direct and immediate relevance of *agape* as a simple historical possibility. To say that his delineation of the sin of man is subordinated to his major concern is not, however, to minimize the immense significance it has for Niebuhr's thought or the value of the contribution he has made to theology at this point. It is simply to set the analysis of human sinfulness in its proper place in Niebuhr's total life work.

We do not propose to undertake here a full exposition of Niebuhr's understanding of sin for a number of reasons. It is the best-known aspect of his work and has been done with such power and perception in the Gifford Lectures, that it is quite impossible to compress it into a short space. Moreover, this aspect of Niebuhr's work has already received wide, indeed a disproportionate, amount of discussion. Finally, man's sinfulness must appear in all aspects of our study of the relation between love and justice and therefore does not require a full separate exposition. Our concern here will be to show that man's ultimate problem does not lie in this or that limitation or defect, but in a profound self-contradiction. The uniqueness of man lies in his radical freedom, his capacity for self-transcendence. The root of his problem, therefore, must be sought there and likewise the answer to his condition must be a life-giving relationship within the terms of his freedom.

The position of man is highly ambiguous. He is finite yet he is free. Despite the fact that he is tied to nature and his place in the historical process, he is free to survey the past and project the future. He does not want to be simply American man, Chinese man, or modern man—he wants to be man. Although he is a frail, limited creature, subject to every natural and historical contingency, he is free to reject the position of relatedness with God in and for which he was created.

In this highly ambiguous situation, man senses his insecurity; he does not possess *within himself* the basis of his own life. And it is precisely this failure to see that the "phenomenon of self-seeking may be related, not to specific forms of insecurity but to the insecurity of life itself,"[50] that Niebuhr believes to be one of the most serious limitations of much of even the most sophisticated psychological theory. Life itself is perilously insecure. Man has his life at the juncture of necessity and freedom, of involvement in nature and transcendence over it. This ambiguous position is the occasion, but not the cause, of his sin. Aware of the insecurity of his position, man seeks to overcome it. But to seek to overcome his position, to gain the basis for security within himself, he must trample on other life and thereby destroy the harmony of creation, the nature of his relatedness with both God and his fellows. "Therefore all human life is involved in the sin of seeking security at the expense of other life."[51] Any view of man's sinfulness must probe far deeper than the transgression of known laws, or the failure to live up to principles because of insufficient resolution. The insecurity of man's life goes to the roots of his being, to his position in creation.

> In short, man, being both free and bound, both limited and limitless, is anxious. Anxiety is the inevitable concomitant of the paradox of freedom and finiteness in which man is involved. Anxiety is the internal precondition of sin. It is the inevitable spiritual state of man, standing in the paradoxical situation of freedom and finiteness.[52]

Anxiety then is the precondition of sin, but it is not itself sin. It is the precondition rather than the actuality, and furthermore it is the basis of all creativity as well as sin. In a word, anxiety is descriptive of man's radical freedom, the source of both man's creativity and destructiveness, the locus of both his dignity and his misery. "It is the condition of the sailor, climbing the mast (to use a simile), with the abyss of the waves beneath him and the 'crow's nest' above him. He is anxious about both the end toward which he strives and the abyss of nothingness into which he may fall."[53] Man is free and he is anxious to realize the indeterminate possibilities of his freedom; man is a creature subject to every contingency of creaturely existence and he is anxious to overcome, or at least to hide, these contingencies.

Our awareness of the depths of man's sin is part of our awareness of the radical nature of man's freedom. Therefore we must speak, with an older and profounder tradition, of the mystery of sin. Sin is ultimately a mystery because it takes place in the depths of man's freedom. The mystery is deepened when we realize that sin is more than a sheer, deliberate act of perversity or rebellion, though it is certainly also that. The significance of biblical satanology is that it points to both these dimensions. Niebuhr puts it this way:

> The importance of Biblical satanology lies in the two facts that: (1) the devil is not thought of as having been created evil. Rather his evil arises from his effort to transgress the bounds set for his life, an effort which places him in rebellion against God. (2) The devil fell before man fell, which is to say that man's rebellion against God is not an act of sheer perversity, nor does it follow inevitably from the situation in which he stands. The situation of finiteness and freedom in which man stands becomes a source of temptation only when it is falsely interpreted. This false interpretation is not purely the product of human imagination. It is suggested to man by a force of evil which precedes his own sin. Perhaps the best description or definition of this mystery is the statement that sin posits itself, that there is no situation in which it is possible to say that sin is either an inevitable consequence of the situation nor yet that it is an act of sheer and perverse individual defiance of God.[54]

Here then is the mystery of "original sin." No matter how far back sin is traced we find an element of sin in the temptation that leads to sin. And yet the "anxiety of freedom leads to sin only if the prior sin of unbelief is assumed. This is the meaning of Kierkegaard's assertion that sin posits itself." [55] Sin is inevitable, we cannot will ourselves out of being sinners; but sin is not necessary, it does not follow necessarily from our nature or from our ambiguous position of being both finite and free. It is to be understood only as a profound self-contradiction in the depths of man's freedom.

Man seeks to overcome the anxiety of his ambiguous position, "the dizziness" of his freedom, either by seeking the basis of his security in himself, or through releasing the tension of his position by abandoning himself to the vitalities of nature. "When anxiety has conceived it brings forth both pride and sensuality. Man falls into pride, when he seeks to raise his contingent existence to unconditioned significance; he falls into sensuality, when he seeks to escape from his unlimited possibilities of freedom, from the perils and responsibilities of self-determination, by immersing himself into a 'mutable good,' by losing himself in some natural vitality." [56] The relations between pride and sensuality are extremely intimate and complex and it is not the least of Niebuhr's contributions that ne has delineated these relations with such sensitivity and perception.

Enough has been said to bring the sin of man into organic relation with the radical freedom of man. "The essence of man is his freedom. Sin is committed in that freedom. Sin can therefore not be attributed to a defect in his essence. It can only be understood as a self-contradiction, made possible by the fact of his freedom but not following necessarily from it." [57] Man is therefore responsible and Christianity is in this sense "the religious expression of an uneasy conscience." [58] But the damage is profound. Man's egotism does not proceed from his essential nature but that does not mean that it can be readily overcome. Christianity "believes that men are egotists in contradiction to their essential nature. That is the doctrine of original sin, stripped of literalistic illusions." [59] The will is bound. It is not bound by fate or by creation. It is bound to the interests of the self which, in contradiction to its essential nature, seeks the things of the self for the sake of the self and thus deepens the alienation of the self from its true self. Nor can the will so bound, unwill its condition by willing. The condition must be restored. That the condition is restored through the person, work, and promise of Jesus Christ is the message of the Christian faith.

To be sure, Niebuhr's whole analysis has presupposed the vantage point of revelation. Man can truly understand himself as he is understood from beyond himself, for he has his life as a being-in-relation, the ultimate dimension of which is his relationship with God. Therefore the ultimate reaches of selfhood can be discerned only through faith in the revelations given to us wherein the nature of the relationship between God and man is disclosed. It is of course just this vantage point which modern man finds most difficult to accept, and yet this perspective alone illumines the really distinctively human. In a word it is in the life, death, and resurrection of Christ that we see most clearly both the radical character of man's freedom and the radical self-corruption of that freedom.

The Cross reveals the divine mercy which overcomes the contradiction between the human and the divine will. God in Christ in the fullness of mercy takes the evil of our self-contradiction upon Himself and conquers it in His own "heart." But Christ is also Very Man. He is what we ought to be but cannot be. The *agape* of the Cross is the norm for the self, and thus provides a frame of meaning in which the self in its freedom can find fulfillment. Love, which is itself first a gift, is the law for man in his freedom. In this relationship of love and freedom we see the true dignity of man. But the love of Christ is the love of the crucified Christ. *Agape* enters history to be crucified. The dimension of the law of self-love is thus illuminated in all its profound and radical nature. The depth of the contradiction of man in his "fallen freedom" is revealed afresh. And in the relationship between the love of the crucified Christ and man's self-corrupted freedom the depth of the misery of man is clarified.

The Cross of Christ is, for the Christian, a victorious Cross. It is the central symbol of Christian faith because it is indivisibly linked with the Resurrection. The crucified Christ is the risen Lord. And on the basis of this resurrection faith, Christians rest their final confidence, and in its power they live the life of hope. Moreover, it is right here in the concept of resurrection that Niebuhr sees the final illumination of the nature of selfhood provided by the Christian faith.

In a quite remarkable sermon entitled "The Fulfillment of Life" in *Beyond Tragedy,* Niebuhr begins by recalling the embarrassment and distaste with which he, at the time of his ordination along with most of his generation, regarded the phrase in the creed "the resurrection of the body." He then goes on to contrast this view with his present approach, which is that no part of the creed "expresses the whole genius of the Christian faith more neatly than just this despised phrase: 'I believe in the resurrection of the body.'"[60]

We may distinguish five fundamental and clearly related facts about the nature of the self which Niebuhr stresses as being illumined by the biblical message concerning resurrection. They are precisely those which we have been discussing, so our only task here is to show how they are illuminated by, and correlated with, the Christian hope of resurrection.

First, the resurrection faith places our hope in our ultimate destiny in the only place where it can with confidence rest—in the power, mercy, and purpose of God. He alone can complete what remains with us incomplete and redeem what is distorted by sin. The ultimate destiny of man is not something which man can control—a desire which appears to be the motivation of most arguments for the "immortality of the soul"—but must come to man as a gift from the Giver of life. Our hope is in God. Placed anywhere else it will have the marks of nervous hopelessness which distinguish every idolatry.

Secondly, this faith affirms the unity of the self and guards against any and all attempts to dissect a man into "mortal" and "immortal" parts. It is the *whole* man—body, soul, and spirit—who is destined for fulfillment. Thus the ultimate hope of St. Paul is expressed in the vision of a transfigured "spiritual body." All heresies about the good spirit and the evil body are undercut completely by the affirmation "I believe in the resurrection of the body."

The Christian understanding of individuality as a fruit of both nature and spirit is asserted and illuminated by the idea of resurrection. Our creaturely particularity is not annulled, but at the same time the resurrection affirms that the "self in its final freedom transcends the conditions of nature-time and can not be fulfilled within them." [61] Or as Niebuhr has it elsewhere, "To believe that the *body* is resurrected is to say, therefore, that eternity is not a cancellation of time and history but that history is fulfilled in eternity. But to insist that the body must be *resurrected* is to understand that time and history have meaning only as they are borne by an eternity which transcends them." [62]

In the fourth place, the freedom of man is a dignity that is affirmed only in clear relationship with the misery of the corruption of that freedom. The affirmation of the hope in "the resurrection of the body" is immediately preceded by the confession of belief in "the forgiveness of sins." "The Gospel, in short, both guards the dignity of the self which transcends death and recognizes the misery of the self, which faces the problem of sin, as well as the fact of death. The tendency to disregard this part of the Gospel invariably reduces the Christian faith to the affirmation of the 'spiritual' character of man against the threat of death."[63]

Finally the resurrection hope asserts not only the individuality of the self, but also the social dimension of man's life. "The fulfillment will be a fulfillment for the *whole* man and for *all* men who have lived through the years and have entered into history and its making." [64] This is the meaning of the symbol of the "general resurrection." Thus the drama of God's mighty deeds and promises to man is brought to its climax, and from the vantage point of faith and hope the believer affirms, with quiet penitence and trust, the misery and the grandeur of man.

## 7. THE COMMITMENT OF THE SELF AND THE FREEDOM OF THE MIND

The relationship between religion and education remains a burning social issue for Americans. It is an exceedingly complex question and the issues interlock at many different levels. Of fundamental importance is the manner in which we conceive the relation between the commitment of the self and the freedom of the mind.

There is simply no use trying to water down the total and absolute claims of the Christian Gospel. To do so is to falsify everything about it. Moreover, our analysis of selfhood has shown that man is that kind of being who must be committed if he is to be whole. This is so because the center of his life as a creature in relationship with God is beyond himself. He comes unto his true self only in a relationship of commitment. To seek the center of life within himself is to seek to realize the self too narrowly and thus to destroy the self. But the presupposition of any worthwhile education must be freedom of inquiry into the most "sacred" of traditions. This seeming contradiction has often led, particularly in America, to a radical separation of these two aspects, to the mutual impoverishment of religion and education. Niebuhr has dealt with this issue in an important address bearing the title "The Commitment of the Self and the Freedom of the Mind," given on the occasion of the bicentennial celebrations of the founding of Columbia University.[65]

To trace his argument here would involve us in undue repetition. He discusses the questions of how we can prevent the religious commitment from being unduly restrictive and how we may establish community with those of different religious loyalties. He then discusses the assumptions and surveys the attempts of a "secular culture" to free the mind, and of the manner in which extremely important truths have ridden into history on the back of error. His conclusion is such a packed summary, not only of this address but also of his wider thought, that our best procedure will be simply to quote it, despite its length.

If we are sure enough of the truth which we hold as religious people, we will not be too anxious that what is false in these disciplines, will ever permanently obscure the truth about man and God which we have seen. This is the more true in our own day in which the rationalistic and naturalistic illusions are being dispelled; and the truth is again coming into view. The path of truth has been a tortuous and circuitous one. But it has come through the journey of the past centuries enriched by this encounter with its "enemies," and also purged of many aberrations which were the consequence of human folly seeking its last hiding place in the sanctuary of God. Therefore we have no reason to despair of either commitments of faith or of the freedom of the mind, which are logically incompatible, but both of which are necessary for a wholesome life.

The reason for this relationship between religion and a free mind can be briefly summarized: (a) The self is not identical with its mind. (b) The mind may enrich the self, but it cannot free the self from its interests. (c) The self is emancipated from itself by its faith and trust beyond itself, but these commitments bind the mind as surely as the self's interest bind it. (d) The worship of idols in modern political religions are more binding to the self and to the mind than mild forms of egocentricity, and the fact that these religions should have arisen in a period of "enlightenment" is proof that the relation between the self and its mind is more complicated than a culture with rationalistic illusions could realize. (e) Even the worship of the true God who convicts all historic interests of their parochialism is no guarantee against restrictions upon the mind, for these partial and parochial interests participate in the ultimate religious commitment by becoming identified with the divine. (f) This tendency to corruption and pretension in religion makes freedom of religion necessary in order that no religious community may have a monopoly of power and remain unchallenged by other faiths. Such freedom is necessary in order to preserve tolerable community under conditions of religious heterogeneity; but it is even more necessary to purify the various faiths. (g) The freedom of the mind in a society has its own justification, because of the enrichment of life through the disciplines of culture which freedom makes possible. It has its special justification in relation to religion because the free mind, while less potent in delivering the self from its self-concern, is nevertheless able, not only to enrich the self, but provisionally to free the self from too narrow concerns and divert its interests to the larger world. Furthermore the rational analysis of all the coherences and sequences of life and history is an antidote against the cultural obscurantism into which the disciplines of faith periodically fall because they avail themselves of poetic, rather than scientific, ways of knowing. This freedom is necessary even though it is apparent that the disciplines which avail themselves of it usually propagate either one of two heresies: (1) that the self and the mind are identical and that God is identical with the rational order of the world, and (2) that the self is not significantly different from the brutes of nature and that it does not have the freedom which is the basis of all its religious striving. These heresies must be tolerated for the modicum of truth which emerges from the labors of these disciplines of culture.[66]

## 8   THE SELF AS CREATOR AND CREATURE OF HISTORY

Just as Niebuhr has emphasized that individuality is the fruit of both nature and spirit, of creaturely particularity and the freedom to transcend natural necessity, so here man is to be understood both as creature and creator of history. This is, in one sense, a rather obvious observation, but the history of modern political thought and movements quickly persuades us how easily one of these facts can be obscured, or the relation between them misunderstood. The question contains political issues of immense importance, but it is really a facet of the problem of the self as creature and creator, and thus requires some discussion at this point. The issue is to what degree we conceive human communities as organisms and as artifacts.

Communities are artifacts "insofar as the form of cohesion and the integration of the community have been consciously contrived."[67] They are primarily the creations of the human will and reason. The most outstanding modern symbol of this approach is the social contract theory propounded by thinkers as diverse as

Locke, Hobbes, and Rousseau. It gave expression to the sense of mastery over historical destiny and the liberal idea of the autonomous individual that distinguished the rising bourgeois class, the dynamics of which have touched every phase of modern life. As such the social contract theory is much more than a theory about the nature and origin of government. "It assumes that communities, and not merely governments, are created by a fiat of the human will." [68] In short, the self is regarded primarily as the creator of history. The assumption that world government is a simple possibility if only we could awaken and organize "public opinion" and persuade the "bad guys" (the Russians and the Chinese) of the folly of their ways, is what Niebuhr has termed the "final and most absurd form of the 'social contract' conception of government." [69] Such exaggerated notions of man's capacity as a creator of history must be regarded as belonging to the class of not-so-harmless illusions. To overlook so completely the primordial nature of communities will involve us in disastrous errors of political judgment and strategy. "The fact is that even the wisest statecraft cannot create social tissue. It can cut, sew and redesign social fabric to a limited degree. But the social fabric upon which it works must be 'given.' " [70]

The temptation to overestimate the capacity of man as a creator and master of history is particularly strong for Americans. There are many good historical reasons for this, especially the fact that America emerged in so short a period from the security of continental mastery to the position of the world's greatest power. Moreover, all this occurred when it was assumed that the ideas of the French Enlightenment embodied the final political wisdom of man. We shall have a good deal to say about this when we discuss Niebuhr's political philosophy. Our only concern here is to emphasize the immense political and social significance of the views we hold of the nature of the self and particularly the significance of the coincidence of the rise of America to a position of unprecedented power with a heritage that overestimates the capacity of man as a creator of history, and a master of historical destiny.

The great social movements and philosophies of the modern period with their strange combinations of determinism and excessive voluntarism are highly instructive about the view of man as a creator of history. We may take *laissez-faire* theories and communism as examples. The foundation of *laissez-faire* ideas is the physiocratic philosophy in which there is no essential difference between nature and history. The "laws of nature" govern both, and men ought not to interfere with their working. But this determinism was joined with an excessive voluntarism. Nature not only has its laws which direct its course, nature can also be mastered by those who know its laws. When history is viewed as nature it can be controlled by those who combine the requisite knowledge and vision, e.g. the scientific humanism of Comte.

This combination of determinism and voluntarism is much more dangerous in Communism. "It has a self-appointed elite, the Communist Party, who, by reason of being the only ones who are privy to the logic, which supposedly determines historical events, are able to intervene at the crucial moments to further the logic and finally to take the heroic step which will insure not only the victory of the 'proletariat,' but change the whole human situation by making man the unambiguous master of historical destiny rather than merely both creature and creator." [71] Man now "not only proposes but disposes."

What is the root of this affinity between these violently warring creeds? It can be variously described—their common tendency to view history as nature which at one and the same time assures them that history possesses its own "logic" and that man has the capacity, if he rightly apprehends the logic, to manage the stuff of history and so on. But the root of the affinity is the degree to which they are both informed by rationalistic, utopian conceptions of man. Both possess the idea of man as an essentially tame and harmless creature. Neither apprehends either the radical freedom of man or the radical self-corruption of that freedom. The liberal bourgeois finds the evil of the self in the ignorance of the individual mind; the communist, in a defective social organization, specifically in the institution of property. Neither sees the self in either its grandeur or its misery. Thus both, from an initial determinism, are able to exaggerate the freedom of the self as a creator of history, because both regard history in terms of nature, and the evil of man as rooted elsewhere than in the center of the self. The philosophies of both are, in their different ways, "based upon erroneous estimates of the disinterestedness and the wisdom of the mind which is called upon to manage the stuff of community and history, and of the malleability of the stuff which is to be managed."[72]

Communities possess a primordial character that places serious limitations upon our capacity to build by conscious contrivance. Every decision or plan is limited by prior actualities. Failure to acknowledge this will result in a wanton destruction of those organic processes and achievements of the past necessary for the growth and maintenance of all communal values. Man is a creature as well as a creator of the historical process. But if man as a creature of history is so emphasized that recognition of the organic aspects of community obscures the degree to which every community is an artifact, the basis has been laid for an endemic conservatism, an undue reverence for existing structures of authority. Man has the capacity to transcend, in measure, the historical process of which he is a part. He has, therefore, both the right and the duty to criticize inherited traditions and to seek for the establishment of new structures which will more adequately provide for justice.

Man is both a creature and a creator of history. Neither dimension of his life can be obscured without ill consequence. This ambiguous position is rooted in the very nature of the self and can be ignored only at the peril of developing a social structure which denies the essential meaning of selfhood.

Throughout this chapter we have emphasized that there are three great "realities" which describe the uniqueness of human selfhood—the freedom of the self over all its functions with which it remains in organic relation; the radical self-corruption of this freedom which infects all the relations and structures in which the self has its existence; and the historical character of the life of the self. This view of the self is intimately correlated with all that we have said about the relation between love and justice. We need only restate the framework of this relation. *Agape*, as the final coherence of life, alone provides an adequate framework of meaning for man in his freedom. God's condescending, suffering love alone is able to forgive and to heal man in his condition of profound self-contradiction, entailed through the self-corruption of his freedom. Love actualizing itself in the structures of society as justice is alone an adequate norm and task for the self which, conscious both of the law of love and the law of self-love, seeks to act responsibly in the concrete situation.

*Four*

# LOVE, JUSTICE, AND HISTORY

Many factors have conspired to place the question of history in the center of contemporary concern. The events of our time, the rise of demonic political absolutist creeds upon the soil of relativism, the collapse of trust in historicism, and the powerful thrust of existentialism have all contributed to this end. In a word, history has become the central question of our time because of a crisis of ultimate meaning in the context of a profound and perilous social dislocation. Simply to put the matter this way is to see once again, how a central question of the day is met by the heart of Niebuhr's concern and encompassed by the structure of his thought.

By way of getting inside Niebuhr's thought on the question of history, we may begin by asking three questions. What does he conceive to be the "nature" of history? How does he view the problem of historical knowledge? How does he approach the question of "the meaning of history"? We can then proceed to a more detailed discussion of Niebuhr's presentation of the dialogue between the Christian faith and the human story.

## 1. HISTORY AND THE POSSIBILITY OF HISTORICAL KNOWLEDGE

We have already discussed Niebuhr's insistence upon understanding the self as a historical creature. We can expect, therefore, that his understanding of history will be intimately correlated with his understanding of selfhood. Just as the entrance to the understanding of the self is the recognition of the freedom of the self over the coherences through which it is expressed, that the self is both creator and creature, so history is a bewildering mixture of freedom and necessity. History is rooted in the natural process, inasmuch as man is involved in the natural flux. Man is never freed completely from natural necessity. But man's capacity to transcend the necessities of nature enables him both to reorder and to transmute the causal sequences of nature, and thereby both to make and to know history. Or to put it in a word: "History is the fruit and the proof of man's freedom."[1] Since the character of man's freedom is elaborated through the dialogues of man's life, history is comprised of the dramas which result when these dialogues precipitate action. "These actions," Niebuhr continues, "are formed into dramatic patterns which constitute a web of destiny for the individual, determining subsequent actions and dialogues. These dramatic patterns may extend to various communities, family, local or national. The dramatic patterns are historic realities in which freedom and necessity are variously compounded."[2]

Two consequences follow immediately from this approach. First, in order to comprehend the distinctively human, we must understand its history. Man is that being who has a history. If we are to understand the human, in either its personal or collective dimensions, we must know its history. Not only is man in history, history is in him. Therefore history is never simply something "back there," it is the depth dimension of our present. The study of history is thus never merely an inquiry into far off and forgotten things, it is a venture in self-understanding. But since history is the realm, not of necessity alone, but is a compound of freedom and necessity, then to apprehend any historical event properly we must understand it *in its uniqueness*. The second consequence now presents itself: history must be sharply distinguished from nature. The patterns of historical reality are much more complex than the structures of nature, not only because historical patterns are compounds of freedom and necessity, but also because of the manner in which they are superimposed upon, and interwoven into, each other. The

complex of events which constitutes history is thus such a bewildering confusion of freedom and destiny, that the historical cannot
be made to conform to the patterns of either logical or natural
coherence. This leads us directly to a consideration of our second
question—the possibility of historical knowledge.

It is important to note where Niebuhr finds the basis for historical
knowledge. If the historical is such that it possesses a uniqueness
that cannot be comprehended either by logic or by the coherences
of nature, then some other facet of man's freedom must more truly
correspond to the nature of the historical. This is memory. "Memory is thus that aspect of human freedom which is most determina-
tive in the construction of historical reality. It gives meaning to
historical events without reducing them to natural necessity and
recurrence; and it thereby gives the agent of action a dimension of
freedom in the present moment which proves history to be a realm
of freedom as well as of destiny."[3] Memory is that aspect of man's
freedom which is able to grasp the historical event in its uniqueness; and the uniqueness of the historical event lies precisely in
the manner in which freedom encounters destiny. For this reason,
Niebuhr is perfectly right when he says that, "Memory is, in short,
the fulcrum of freedom for man in history."[4] He is also right when
he expands this by pointing out that that "is why the study of history is an emancipating force in human life. The less disclosed the
past and the human contrivance which entered into present realities, the more do present facts appear in the guise of irrevocable
facts of nature."[5]

Niebuhr is, of course, careful to note that memory is not the
only way by which the past lives in the present. History is the realm
of destiny as well as freedom. Decisions of the past have their own
way of developing social configurations that cannot simply be
revoked by human freedom.

> Actually the past is present to us not only in our memory of its
> events but in the immediacy of the accomplished events which it
> places upon our door steps. We do not merely remember the acci-
> dent we had in our childhood but we have a scar upon our forehead

as a "reminder." We do not merely remember that our fathers brought slaves to this country from Africa. We are reminded of their action by our colored fellow-citizens. The problems which arise from the actions of our fathers remind us that past actions are not simply revocable. . . . No statesman in modern Europe can undo the complex of facts which resulted from Hitler's political adventures, however much he may have freedom to choose between new alternatives which arise from the irrevocable facts thus created.[6]

Memory reaches another serious limitation the moment it confronts the question of ultimate meaning. Memory certainly can create a framework of meaning for the tribe and the nation as well as for the individual. Herein is the root of the idolatrous strength of all "religions of memory" or culture faiths. But like all polytheisms, ethnic they are and ethnic they remain. Memory is incapable, by itself, of giving unity to the total history of mankind, or of providing a framework of meaning able to comprehend that history in its unity.

Man is a creature as well as a creator of history. Enough has already been said about that, but full recognition of man's ambiguous position is sufficient to bring the problem of historical relativism clearly before us. How can a person or a culture involved in all the mutabilities of finiteness achieve either the perspective or the disinterestedness necessary to view the human story, without using a framework of meaning which is conditioned by the limitations of his own historical perspective? Just to raise this question is to place a serious doubt before the very possibility of historical knowledge.

The problem posed by historical relativism manifests itself on two main levels—the complexity of historical causation, and the ambiguous position of the observer of history.

The study of history is the study of human situations, and the human subject is incomparably variable. Every historical event stands in such a complex of causation that it becomes impossible for the historian to approach the exactitude of the natural sciences. Indeed, failure to recognize this, will lead him to a distortion of the very characteristics of the historical. "There are, of course," as Niebuhr says, "valid social or historical sciences. They are most legitimate when the scientists know themselves to be historians rather than natural scientists; and therefore recognize that their generalizations are hazardous and speculative. The real historians have an instinct for the peculiar quality of history and know the hazards of predictions of the future."[7] The complexity of historical causation is such that we must begin by acknowledging the thoroughly relative nature of our knowledge of history.

The position of the observer of the historical scene is, moreover, such that he cannot claim the same measure of objectivity that a natural scientist can. The observer is involved in the temporal flux and must view it from a particular locus. Extravagant biases can be refuted, the honest historian can be distinguished from the obvious propagandist, but there is no neat line by which this distinction can be drawn. History is in the observer; every historian has his own framework of meaning which cannot help but condition his construction and interpretation of events. Thus it is impossible to get an interpretation of the French Revolution, the American Civil War, or the destruction of the medieval synthesis which will refute all conflicting interpretations.[8] The limitations imposed by the particular historical perspective, together with the "ideological" taint to which all men are subject, significantly qualify the "objectivity" of even the most disinterested historian.

Ludwig Freund, in an important and appreciative review of *The Self and the Dramas of History*,[9] has criticized Niebuhr for failing to make sufficient distinctions "between the learned and the naïve attempts at reconstructing historic realities" and for failing to give sufficient weight to the fact that "care for the real scientific prerequisites to historical analysis" does very significantly mitigate the "ideological" character of historical writing. Freund uses Niebuhr himself as an illustration of the achievements of one who has fulfilled these conditions. "His *methodological* analysis is therefore incomplete. A redeeming feature is, that in the *systematic* portions of this as well as all his other works he unfailingly applies the scientific tools of research, observation, introspection, analogy, description and exemplification to illumine his points. One may add, that what emerges is not an iron-clad proof, but partly artful inspiration, partly scientific result, precisely as it should be, and as it must."[10] This criticism is more appropriate to *The Self and the Dramas of History* than to the rest of Niebuhr's work. The polemical context of this book, the concern to show that the approach of the natural scientist is ill-fitted for the task of understanding man and his history, has been the occasion for his underplaying the significance of the achievement of a disciplined, though admittedly still relative, objectivity on the part of the observer of the human scene.

Niebuhr's point, however, that "there is . . . no complete rational solution for the problem of historical relativism,"[11] ought surely to be everywhere granted. The only "solution" is the combination of discriminating, careful, and honest historical inquiry in a society that has the wisdom to prefer its historians to report from their different perspectives rather than to seek a "scientific" solution to a perennial and distinctively human problem.

The interpretation of history cannot be completely divorced from the ultimate framework of meaning, whether explicitly or only implicitly held. To consider the nature of human life, is we have contended, to consider the nature of history. But the "nature" of history cannot be profoundly discussed without raising the question of its meaning. Thus the question of the meaning of history is the question of the meaning of life itself. To ask the question of the meaning of history is to ask the question of the "end" of history. To this question of the meaning of history, Christians and skeptics unite against all utopians and most "philosophers of history" in saying that there is, and can be, no immanent solution to the question of meaning. Either the question of meaning must be completely disavowed as with the thoroughgoing skeptic, or it must find its resolution in faith. History does not yield its own meaning. "History in its totality and unity is given a meaning by some kind of religious faith in the sense that the concept of meaning is derived from ultimate presuppositions about the character of time and eternity, which are not the fruit of detailed analyses of historical events." [12] For this reason Niebuhr can speak of a "theology of history." This is not an arbitrary construction, it is simply reflection upon the Christ-event as a basis for understanding history, and for answering the questions so poignantly asked by the moral ambiguity of history.

Since the framework of the meaning of history is derived, not from an examination of history itself, but from religious faith, a fundamental distinction must be made between "historical" and "non-historical" religions and cultures. This distinction, Niebuhr says, "may thus be succinctly defined as the difference between those which expect and those which do not expect a Christ. A Christ is expected wherever history is regarded as potentially meaningful but as still awaiting the full disclosure and fulfillment of its meaning. A Christ is not expected wherever the meaning of life is explained from the standpoint of either nature or supernature in such a way that a transcendent revelation of history's meaning is not regarded as either possible or necessary." [13]

This is a highly suggestive way in which to draw the distinction between "historical" and "non-historical" interpretations of history. However, the following classification comes to grips more with the specific motifs of the interpretations which have entered so richly into our heritage.

> Western culture embodies three approaches toward the vexing problem of the nature of human history: (1) The approach of Greek classicism which equated history with the world of nature and sought emancipation of man's changeless reason from this world of change; (2) the Biblical-Christian approach which found man's historic existence both meaningful and mysterious and which regarded the freedom of man, which distinguished history from nature, as the source of evil as well as of good; (3) and the modern approach which regarded the historical development of man's power and freedom as the solution for every human perplexity and as the way of emancipation from every human evil. [14]

Here we have the outlines of Western man's dialogue concerning the nature and meaning of history.

Niebuhr believes that to disclose the inadequacies of rival positions is an important aspect of the apologetic task. He considers this a necessary procedure in order to clear the ground so that the Christian message may be apprehended in its full power and relevance. In this respect his approach is not inaccurately described as "the technique of demolition." It is of even more importance to see that for Niebuhr this "commerce with the wisdom of the world" is entered into in such a way that the truth embodied in rival views may be appropriated in such a manner as to save the Christian understanding from the distortions it suffers at the hands of its own apologists. Our procedure will be to indicate, briefly, the character of Niebuhr's criticism of the classical and modern views of history and then proceed to outline the structure of his own presentation of the Christian understanding.

## 2. NIEBUHR'S CRITIQUE OF THE CLASSICAL VIEW OF HISTORY

Oriental thought and Western classical thought as elaborated by Plato, Aristotle and the Stoics are distinguished by their ahistorical spirituality. The differences between Oriental mysticism and Greek rationalism are, of course, obvious, but the thrust of their spirituality is fundamentally the same. "The common characteristic in all of these approaches is that a rigorous effort is made to disassociate what is regarded as a timeless and divine element in human nature from the world of change and temporal flux."[15] History, like nature, belongs to the world of change, the world of "coming to be" and "passing away." Life must either be reduced to the meaninglessness of the changing natural order or secure its meaning and fulfillment in being emancipated from it.

Niebuhr thus begins his discussion of the classical view of history by estimating the significance of its "profound metaphysical impulse to resolve life's mysteries into rational intelligibility," [16] and to proceed to its understanding of time and the significance of this for its view of history. "In brief summary the situation is this: classical culture regarded neither time nor history as self-explanatory. Time was made intelligible in terms of its relation to a world of changeless forms; and history was made intelligible by its unqualified identification with natural time." [17] The dominant conception is thus the cyclical view of time through which the world of change participates in the changeless world. This conception of time, as a cycle of recurrence, determines the classical view of history, since history, being part of the world of "coming to be" and "passing away," has been equated with nature. The ambiguity of history is thus overcome by making it intelligible in the same way as nature is made intelligible, through its participation in the endless cycle of birth and death.

Life can be fulfilled because of the presence of the divine in man. But to be fulfilled it must be emancipated from the body which belongs to the world of change and decay. Fulfillment thus involves the negation of the conditions of history. Niebuhr sums up his critique of the classical approach to history in a remarkably compressed passage as follows:

> The various versions of the classical idea of the meaning of life and history are sufficiently similar to justify the idea of a common classical approach to life and to history. In this approach history is equated with nature, its intelligibility is proved by its subjection to natural recurrence; and the distinctive interrelation of freedom and destiny, of human decisions and a pattern of meaning transcending human decisions, is obscured. The meaning of life is equated with a higher form of rationality which can be realized by the emancipation of the unique freedom and reason of man from the ambiguities of human history. Thus there is intelligibility on two levels; but life is not meaningful in its wholeness; and history is meaningful only in its recurrences but not in the novelties which human freedom introduces into the temporal process. Two parts of human existence are correlated to two realms of intelligibility; but the life and the history of man in the unity and the ambiguity of their freedom and finiteness are not meaningful. [18]

## 3. NIEBUHR'S CRITIQUE OF THE MODERN VIEW OF HISTORY

Niebuhr sees modern culture, despite its great diversity and warring creeds, as possessing unity through a common faith in the redemptive power of history. "A single article of faith," he says, "has given diverse forms of modern culture the unity of a shared belief. Modern men of all shades of opinion agreed in the belief that historical development is a redemptive process."[19] Development rather than order has been the dominant motif, and in this sense the modern faith has been primarily faith in history rather than faith in reason. This is merely a form of modernity's faith in man since history has been everywhere regarded as "the story of man's increasing power and freedom."[20] A *nisus* toward progress was regarded as the inner dynamic of the historical process. The development of this dogma has been the subject of too many inquiries to warrant any discussion of it here. A paragraph from the January 4, 1851, issue of the British *Economist* will suffice to indicate the mood.

> When we refer to a few only of the extraordinary improvements of the half century just elapsed—such as the 35 years' peace, so far as morals are concerned; such as the philanthropic and just conviction that the welfare of the multitude, not of one or two classes, is the proper object of social solicitude; . . . the advances in religious toleration, and in forbearing one with another . . . the extended application of machinery to all the arts of life . . . :—when we refer to a few events of this kind, we become convinced that the half century just elapsed is more full of wonders than any other on record. . . . All who have read, and can think, must now have full confidence that the 'endless progression' ever increasing in rapidity, of which the poet sung, is the destined lot of the human race.[21]

It is not necessary to argue that the idea of progress has been rudely refuted by the tragic events of the twentieth century. The spiritual crisis of our time consists precisely in our awareness that our faith in the upward movement of history by virtue of a force immanent in history has been shaken, but we have not yet secured another faith by which to interpret and approach history and its problems. We need therefore to see the ingredients of the dogma of progress in more detail.

This calls, first of all, for a re-examination of the Renaissance view of man and history. We cannot here discuss such a complex subject, but we can indicate the character of Niebuhr's approach. Whatever else we have to say about the Renaissance, it was a combination of the recovery of classical thought and disciplines with an altogether fresh enthusiasm for the creative powers of man. The classical confidence in man was united with the biblical sense of the meaningfulness of history. However, history was conceived in much simpler terms than it is in the Bible. The Renaissance luxuriated in history as the realm of endless possibilities, but instead of conceiving this as endless possibilities for both good and evil, its confidence in the power and goodness of man's freedom were such as to make the dogma of progress inevitable in its view of the historical progress. Thus although it shares the Biblical-Christian view of the dynamic nature of history, the Renaissance truncates and secularizes this view. History possesses its own immanent *logos*. It carries within itself its own meaning and power of fulfillment. To be sure, the Renaissance did not regard history as a steady upward line. The frailty and evil of man was such that history's progress would frequently be interrupted by periods of retrogression. But faith in the dynamic nature of history would not permit of a simple return to the cyclical view of history. The consequence was that historical cycles became spirals of advance. The spiral concept has come down right to our own day in one form or another and has been one of the favorite images of the apologists of the Renaissance—modern view of history.[22] But whatever changes the images have experienced the basic concept remains the same, history possesses the capacity for its own redemption and fulfillment. It is this which gives unity to the period from the Renaissance to the present day. Niebuhr summarizes his approach in the following paragraph.

The Renaissance as a spiritual movement is best understood as a tremendous affirmation of the limitless possibilities of human existence, and as a rediscovery of the sense of a meaningful history. This affirmation takes many forms, not all of which are equally consistent with the fundamental impulse of the movement. But there is enough consistency in the movement as a whole to justify the historian in placing in one historical category such diverse philosophical, religious and social movements as the early Italian Renaissance, Cartesian rationalism and the French enlightenment; as the liberal idea of progress and Marxist catastrophism; as sectarian perfectionism and secular utopianism. In all of these multifarious expressions there is a unifying principle. It is the impulse towards the fulfillment of life in history. The idea that life can be fulfilled without those reservations and qualifications which Biblical and Reformation thought make is derived from two different sources; from the classical confidence in human capacities and from the Biblical-Christian impulse towards sanctification and the fulfillment of life, more particularly the Biblical-eschatological hope of the fulfillment of history itself. [23]

There is a very real strength in the modern view of history. Its dynamic conception of history enables it to do justice to the novelties of history, to acknowledge its indeterminate possibilities and to recognize the positive meaning of the historical process. But its errors have been filled with grievous consequence. Those errors in brief are (1) an exaggerated estimate of the growth of man's freedom and power over history which issues in an obscuration of his ambiguous position as both creator and creature of history; and (2) a too easy identification of freedom and virtue which fails to do justice to the tragic antinomies of history which are a consequence of that freedom, and this has issued in serious political misjudgments. [24]

The question of the meaning of history involves the question of the end of history. When history is conceived as its own redeemer, growth is the meaning of life and some form of utopia is its end. This dimension of the modern view of history needs some more discussion before the Christian understanding can be apprehended in its full relevance.

Utopianism is not a small matter to be dismissed as a harmless illusion. It is an expression of the sinful aspiration of man to master and control his destiny, and is therefore in some form or another deeply imbedded in every man. But serious perils inhere in it when it is embraced as a conscious social aim. The perils stem from the fact that it wrongly locates the source of evil outside of man in the inertia of either our social institutions or our "brute inheritance." This gives rise to the crusading approach to social and political evils which is productive of both political blindness and the fury of self-righteousness. It further "interferes with an interest in proximate, rather than ultimate, goals, and that is the point which distinguishes a sane political movement from one that is corrupted by false religious visions." [25] The ultimate evil of utopianism is the fanaticism it both breeds and sustains. Anything is legitimate if it can be construed as contributing to the realization of the ultimate goal.

Niebuhr has, at this point, made a useful distinction between what he terms "soft" and "hard" utopianism. "Hard utopianism," he writes, "might be defined as the creed of those who claim to embody the perfect community and who therefore feel themselves morally justified in using every instrument of guile or force against those who oppose their assumed perfection. Soft utopianism is the creed of those who do not claim to embody perfection, but expect perfection to emerge out of the ongoing process of history." [26] There is a common root in the view that the fulfillment of history will come in history through a power resident in history. Perhaps the greatest peril results when a "hard" utopianism is met by the pacifistic notions and the political confusion that usually mark a "soft" utopianism.

The ultimate perils of utopianism have become most clearly apparent in the "hard" utopianism of Marxism. The dictatorship of the proletariat is not the utopia of Marxist dreams; it is rather the classless society in which each gives according to his ability and receives according to his needs. The dictatorship of the "transition" period is, however, justified by this ultimate vision. The utopianism of the Marxist creed thus sanctifies a thoroughly ruthless, though supposedly provisional, tyranny.

The Marxist insight into the ideological taint that corrupts our reason and our ideals ought to have mitigated the fierceness of its own utopianism. But Marxism failed to carry this insight through with any consistency for two principal reasons. First, because it made this insight into a weapon of conflict by attributing the ideological taint to every group but its own. The second reason in turn supports the first: it attributed ideology to economic class interest alone. Since the institution of private property is the root of all evil, the proletariat was thus free from the ideological corruption that affected every other group. Thus the Marxist theory of ideology instead of mitigating the fury of communist utopianism serves only further to strengthen, justify, and sanctify it.

Marx was altogether right when he said that "The beginning of all criticism is the criticism of religion." This is true, as Niebuhr remarks, "because the claim of ultimate and absolute validity is always involved in religion . . ." [27] What needs to be recognized is that communism is a religion and that "religion *qua* religion is idolatrous." Communism is a total interpretation of life; it seeks ultimate ends and its political maneuvers are justified in the light of its total understanding of man and history. Its appeal has been almost entirely religious. It grants the believer a purpose in harmony with the "movement of history," it provides a world view which defines and sustains his values, it challenges him with a sacrificial purpose, and it assures him of ultimate victory. One need not argue that it has been one of the most powerful religions of our time even though for many it has proved to be "the God that failed."

When the religious nature of communism is recognized we realize how inept and beside the point are the usual charges against its "atheism" and "materialism." It is not this that makes communism so vicious but its idolatry which stems from its utopianism. It puts its trust in something less than God. Idolatry is always the worship of a god in which the claims of the self are maintained and sanctioned. In communism, this god is the unqualified ally of one group in society and the implacable foe of all the others. It is this idolatry that is the source and sustaining power of the fanaticism and the ruthless tyranny of communism. Only the voice of faith which knows the ineradicable tendency of the human heart to turn even a religion of contrition into an expression of pride and complacency, can speak to the roots of the issue.

Niebuhr has remarked that "the ultimate similarity between Marxist and bourgeois optimism, despite the provisional catastrophism of the former, is, in fact, the most telling proof of the unity of modern culture."[28] There is no doubt, as Niebuhr goes on to say, that conflict between these two warring creeds has contributed to the refutation of the hope they held in common. But the refutation of a fallacious hope by such a circumstance in no way means that we have achieved a sufficiently positive and structured perspective to take its place. That, in turn, but indicates the importance of the apologetic task and achievement of Niebuhr.

## 4. NIEBUHR'S CRITIQUE OF HISTORIC CHRISTIAN VIEWS

The inadequacy of the modern view of history in comprehending the tragic antinomies of man's historical life has cleared the way for the Christian understanding to be spoken and heard with a fresh relevance. But before this can be done there must be a contrite recognition of the various errors that have distorted the Christian understanding in its major historic traditions. Just as truth frequently rides into history on the back of error, so "the profoundest truth may become the source or bearer of grievous error."[29] The contemporary apologetic task thus requires both a detecting of the errors which have been compounded with Christian truth and an appropriation of the truth in the modern view of history, the more significantly to present the Christian understanding. It is an exceedingly complex and difficult question. The distinctions between good and evil constitute the moral substance of history; the possibilities for actualizing the good in history define the social obligation of the Christian. But such distinctions as we make, and must make, and such actualizations of good that are achieved must be constantly submitted to the judgment of the Gospel where the relative nature of both our distinctions and our achievements will be clearly revealed. Such an approach to social decisions and strategies involves us at once in a re-examination of the whole structure of our theology.

For this reason, the whole of Niebuhr's apologetic has involved him in a running debate with various Christian traditions. Properly to assess his criticism would take us too far afield. Our procedure will simply be to lift up briefly the point at which he sees the most serious weakness, or most dangerous tendency, of those traditions to which he has addressed himself, to the end that this will enable Niebuhr's own thought to be thrown into clearer relief.

Niebuhr's constant criticism of Roman Catholicism is the perennial Protestant protest—that Rome too readily identifies the Church with the Kingdom of God. In the Church it finds the place in history where sin is transcended, the ambiguities of history overcome. The Church as a "supernatural order" is the place where evil is overcome, at least in principle. Immense social consequences always arise from this position. Both political power and self-righteous pretension are distilled from this principle of sanctity. The Church cannot repent. Niebuhr recognizes, of course, that Catholicism is different in different places and he is one of the few Protestant theologians in America who seems to be able to enter into a living conversation with Catholic theologians. Nevertheless, Niebuhr's criticism of Catholicism at the point of the pretension of the Church runs throughout his work and is the subject of many a scathing article. The Spanish hierarchy has been the object of his severest strictures, but the following excerpt from his article commenting on the Pope's message initiating the holy year, is typical of his central criticism.

We often define the difference between us in terms of our varying attitudes toward freedom. We persuade ourselves that we Protestants would rather run the risks of anarchy for the sake of spiritual freedom than gain the boon of unity and order at the price of spiritual tyranny. But that was only one issue in the Reformation. A more important issue was derived from the Reformation conviction that Catholicism was involved in idolatry because it allowed the Church to usurp the majesty of God. It pretended that the Church would mediate the divine mercy and judgment without itself standing under that judgment or requiring that mercy. It was, in short, involved in an intolerable pretension. [30]

To be sure, such criticism would lack all point, if it were not accompanied by, and supported with, a criticism of the entire structure of Roman Catholic theology—which is a consistent whole. Niebuhr has not failed to do this. It will be sufficient for our purposes just to point to the character of his criticism of the Catholic understanding of sin, grace, and the Church.

The Catholic doctrine usually views sin as a privation of original perfection rather than a positive corruption. Thus the tragic dimension of history is not sufficiently comprehended and is too easily overcome. The world is not so much incomplete and finding its completeness in the Incarnation extended in history in the Church; ours is a tragic world troubled by "false absolutes" which express themselves most powerfully in the highest reaches of spirituality. Thus the Roman doctrine of sin fails to deal profoundly enough with the human situation, which in turn opens the door for the pretension of the sinlessness of the Church.

This weakness corresponds to a similar failure in the Catholic doctrine of grace. We need not concern ourselves with anything but the center of Niebuhr's criticism. That may be succinctly stated: Catholic thought obscures the complex relation between grace as pardon and grace as power with the consequence that justification is subordinated to sanctification. "This subordination of justification to sanctification," writes Niebuhr, "becomes definitive for the whole Catholic conception of life and history. It contains the roots of a new self-righteousness and a new pretension that man is able to complete life and history. The difference between it and Hellen-istic conceptions is that it expresses man's consciousness of his inability to realize the good by his own power; but it assumes that it can be accomplished by the aid of divine power." [31]

These two "errors" of overestimating the sinlessness of the re-deemed and of failing to comprehend the really tragic nature of history culminate in the doctrine of the Church. The Church has become the sole dispenser of grace and this mission means that the Church herself has escaped the ambiguities of history. This is in-dicated by the significant shift of conceiving the Church as the "extension of the Incarnation" instead of the Pauline "body of Christ." What or who can stand in judgment upon the extension of the Incarnation? By definition, the church *qua* church can neither be judged nor repent. But, as Niebuhr points out, this can hardly be what is meant by the phrase "body of Christ." "For when con-ceived as the body it is clear that it remains subject to the laws of historical reality. Its ideal and norm is, that all its members should be perfectly coordinated to one another by being subordinated to the 'head' which is Christ. But the actual realities always betray some of the contradictions which characterize historical existence. In history there is always 'another law in my members, warring against the law of my mind.' This war is certainly as apparent in the collective, as in the individual, life of the redeemed." [32]

The Roman Catholic doctrines of sin and grace culminating in the doctrine of the Church, obscure the tragic character of history, overestimate the sinlessness of the redeemed; Catholicism is thus forever tempted to introduce "false eternals" into history, with endless political and social consequences.

Niebuhr thinks that the Calvinist Reformation also obscured the contradiction between the historical and the divine. It gave the Christian an unjustified confidence in the transcendent perfection of moral standards derived from Scripture, obscuring both the relativities of judgment involved in the application of a Scriptural standard and the historical relativities embedded in the Scriptural standards themselves.[33] This in turn prompted the Calvinist to appeal "prematurely to Biblical authority for answers to every conceivable moral and social problem."[34] From this basis, the theocratic impulse of Calvin issued in the various attempts to build "holy commonwealths," which "have all proved how dangerous it is for the Christian faith to equate any form of historic virtue or power with the sanctity of Christ."[35] Insofar as historic Calvinism has failed to make the proper reservations about the "rule of the saints," Niebuhr's criticism is well founded. It is my opinion, however, which I cannot argue here, that Niebuhr has not always sufficiently estimated the contribution to democratic thought that inheres in the whole thrust of Calvin's thought. Niebuhr fully acknowledges the significant contribution of later Calvinists, and it would of course be nonsense to try to make Calvin out to be a democrat, but my contention is simply that the structure and thrust of Calvin's total thought have contributed more significantly to democracy than is generally acknowledged. Calvin's successors at least did not have a heritage to overcome. Be this as it may, Niebuhr in pointing to the assumption, undergirded by biblicism, that the Church in Calvinism constituted a new social order, has put his finger on a tendency to self-righteous pretension that has more than once marred the Calvinist tradition.

Niebuhr sees Lutheranism as having been guilty of the opposite error. Luther has exercised an immense influence on Niebuhr. Indeed, John Bennett is probably right in saying that it was the influence of Luther and the Reformation heritage generally, which has made Niebuhr's message so difficult for American liberal Protestants.[36] But that tells us more about the condition of American Protestantism than it does about the thought of Niebuhr. Despite his great indebtedness to Luther there is one criticism that Niebuhr has repeatedly throughout all the years of his writing leveled at both Luther and Lutheranism. That criticism in summary is this: that although the ultimate religious relationship is illumined in the Lutheran Reformation as nowhere else, it failed dismally to throw light on the problem of securing justice, of the relation between *agape* and justice, of the relation between the ultimate dependence of man upon the mercy of God and the task of making discriminate judgments for the achievement of proximate, but very important, social ends. He even goes so far as to say that "The Lutheran Reformation is . . . that particular locus in the history of Christendom where the problem of justice is most nearly disavowed." [37]

The burden of all his criticisms are centered in this one weakness. Luther's conception of the relation of grace to law relaxes tension at all intermediate points so that it does not deal seriously with the task of extending justice.[38] The "final experience of grace" is severed from "all the proximate possibilities of liberty and justice." [39] The attitude to government is thus "at once too negative and too sacrosanct." [40] Luther thus develops a "private" and a "public" ethic, which despairs of the possibility of redemption in man's social life.[41] The relationship between *agape* and the task of securing justice is not conceived in sufficiently dialectical fashion, with the result that the relevance of the Kingdom of God to every historical decision and structure is obscured.

Wilhelm Pauck has vigorously taken Niebuhr to task for this presentation of Luther's position.[42] Niebuhr's thinking "appears to be conditioned by a strange animosity against Luther which is all the more surprising in view of the fact that he is more closely related to Luther's faith than any other." [43] The burden of Pauck's criticism is that Niebuhr failed to make the necessary distinction between Luther and Lutheranism, and that he misreads Luther when he thinks that Luther subordinated sanctification to justification.

This is an exceedingly complex historical debate, which will serve no purpose for us to enter. Two things might be said. It is, I think, true that Niebuhr has not made the distinctions between Luther and German Lutheranism and between German and Scandinavian Lutheranism, that ought to be made,[44] and that his description of a private and public morality in Luther is open to a

good deal of discussion. With these reservations, I think his judgment that the Lutheran Reformation failed to see the real relevance
of *agape* to the struggle for justice is well taken. Luther did not
think in sufficiently structured political terms for the nature of
the relationship to acquire proper delineation. That this had some
real evil social consequences cannot, I think, be gainsaid, nor
does it dim the glory of Luther to admit it.

Sectarian Protestantism has always been tempted by the perfectionist heresy. This is conceived very differently from Roman
Catholicism inasmuch as sectarianism shares with the Renaissance
the impulse toward completing life within history. Significant distinctions must be made *within* sectarianism, between the pietistic
and eschatological sects, but still the common impulse remains and
the basic relationship with the Renaissance views of history is
maintained. Niebuhr has succinctly analyzed this relationship as
follows:

> The root of the error of sectarian perfectionism is to be found in a
> conception logically and historically related to those held by secular
> perfectionists. The "hidden seed" and the "inner light" is an im-
> manent Christ, which corresponds to the immanent *logos* of the
> main stream of Renaissance thought. The immanent Christ may be
> conceived more dynamically than the immanent *logos*; and con-
> version and redemption may therefore involve the total personality
> to a larger degree than the various secular *logos* doctrines do. But
> the idea of an immanent Christ in man, just as a completely im-
> manent *logos* in history, obscures the real dialectic between the
> historical and the eternal. It fails to recognize that the freedom of
> man in history, whether conceived in rational or mystical terms
> contains possibilities of both good and evil. [45]

When we consider the failures of both Christian and secular
approaches to history, the ways in which both the tragic dimension
of history and the relevance of *agape* to history can be obscured,
we see both the predicament of modern man and the complexities
involved in securing a perspective that discloses both the genius of
Christian faith and the realities of historical existence. But it is
just this task that has engaged the full energy of Reinhold Niebuhr

over the past three decades. Our attempt now will be to indicate
the structure of his understanding of the Christian view of history.

## 5. THE STRUCTURE OF NIEBUHR'S UNDERSTANDING

### a. THE SOVEREIGNTY OF GOD AND THE UNITY OF HISTORY

The biblical idea of the sovereignty of the Creator God over
historical destiny is not in itself unique. But the biblical concept
does possess a unique quality. Israel does not choose God. God,
out of sheer grace, chooses Israel. God is not conceived as a pro-
jection of the nation's desires or values, nor as an extension of the
nation's power. On the contrary, God is the limit of the nation's
power and the judge and enemy of all her pretensions. Out of this
conception of the relation of God to historical destiny, two basic
ideas of the Hebraic-Christian interpretation arise—the idea of a
universal history and the complexity of that history.

The God who chooses is not the possession of Israel or the
cosmic guarantor of her values. He is the ruler of all nations, and
his choice of Israel but lays upon her the great responsibility of
testifying to that grand fact. There is no special security in thus
being the object of God's choice. Israel is always tempted to make
herself the center of universal history, but this temptation only
serves to show that her election exposes her to a special peril. "You
only have I known of all the families of the earth; therefore I will
punish you for all your iniquities." (Amos 3:2) And from the standpoint of the revelation in Christ, all nationalistic corruptions of
Messianism are negated. All history, including the events in which
God's self-disclosure is effected, stands under God's sovereign rule.
In this manner the "scandal of particularity" becomes the source
of the conception of the unity of history. Again it is to be noted
that it is the unique quality of this relationship that enables such
a concrete and particular revelation to be the basis for the idea of
a universal history. Or as Niebuhr has put it, "The scandal that

the idea of universal history should be the fruit of a particular revelation of the divine, to a particular people, and finally in a particular drama and person, ceases to be scandalous when it is recognized that the divine Majesty, apprehended in these particular revelations, is less bound to the pride of civilizations and the hopes and ambitions of nations, than the supposedly more universal concepts of life and history by which cultures seek to extricate themselves from the historical contingencies and to establish universally valid 'values.' "[46]

The first word, then, to be said about the Christian view of history is that history is conceived as a unity because all historical destiny is under the sovereignty of the one God. The unity of history is discerned by faith. It is not the result of empirical investigation. And once again, believers and skeptics (historians) unite against the attempts of the philosophers of history to reduce the variety and complexity of historical phenomena to intelligible patterns.

The second basic idea of the biblical understanding, derived from the distinctive quality of the relation of God to Israel, is the complexity of history. The people of God's choice are not immune from idolatry. On the contrary, they who have encountered the Sovereign of all history, alone know the real meaning of idolatry. History is thus not only the realm over which God exercises dominion, it is the arena in which He is engaged with Man's universal tendency to deny that dominion in the effort to make himself or some value the center of existence. In a word, the relation of God to Israel discloses the depth and universality of evil as well as God's sovereignty. This evil springs from the same source as man's creative power, from his freedom. Its root is in man rather than nature, and it is in all men not just some men. The historical drama is therefore "not so much a contest between good and evil forces in history as a contest between all men and God."[47] History is the realm of both the providence of God and the confusion of man.

The complexity of history is thus rooted in its moral ambiguity. Individuals and nations are destroyed not just because they are vain and proud, but also because they are powerless. And when it is discerned that the judgment of God is being meted out, the executors of the divine judgment are frequently anything but exemplars of the divine righteousness. The moral ambiguity of history is such that we are tempted either "to the despairing conclusion that there is no meaning in the total historical enterprise and that history is merely a bewildering confusion of 'death for the right cause, death for the wrong cause, paeans of victory and groans of defeat,' or that it is under a sovereignty too mysterious to conform fully to the patterns of meaning which human beings are able to construct. Yet this sovereignty is not pure mystery, since the experiences of life, in which egotism and self-worship are punished, are in rough and inexact relation to an ultimate judgment upon the self, perceived by the self in the experience of repentance and faith." [48]

Faith in the sovereignty of God over historical destiny illumines both the unity and the complexity of man's history. Here is the root of the distinction between the biblical interpretation of history and both the classical and the modern views. "In contrast to ahistorical cultures, Biblical faith affirms the potential meaning of life in history. It is in history, and not in a flight from history, that the divine power which bears and completes history is revealed. In contrast to idolatrous historical cultures the revelation of the divine, which manifests itself in history, casts down everything which exalteth itself against the knowledge of God." [49] One further comment must be made. Meaning is set in the context of mystery. This relationship between meaning and mystery is crucial in all Niebuhr's work. "Mystery," he says, "does not annul meaning but enriches it." [50] There is meaning in history, there is a relationship between purpose and value. This is not annulled but enriched by being interpenetrated with mystery. "It prevents the realm of meaning from being reduced too simply to rational intelligibility and thereby being given a false center of meaning in a relative or contingent historical force or end." [51] The freedom of man, the complexity and ambiguity of his history introduced by the self-corruption of that freedom, the depths of a divine love which is both able to illuminate and overcome the contradictions of that history—in these relationships man finds the meaning of his historical existence, but it is a meaning that cannot be simply discerned but which is apprehended in repentant faith. Meaning is set in a Mystery which does not becloud, but enriches, the meaning experienced by the free self. Our days are set in the "interim" between the disclosure of that meaning and the "day" when we shall know even as we are known. The concept of History as Interim is of such significance to Niebuhr, that we must consider it in more detail.

### b. HISTORY AS INTERIM

Niebuhr's interpretation of history is simply the result of continuous reflection on the meaning of the Christ-event for the interpretation of the whole range of human experience. The Cross is the central vantage point. But the Cross itself must be related to the heritage of prophetic Messianism if both its relation to history and its uniqueness are to be clarified.

The messianic age was never conceived simply as the culmination of the historical process; it was always looked upon as the result of divine intervention. It is this which distinguishes it from all utopianism, however much Hebraic futurism lies at the basis of the modern view of history. Prophetic Messianism in its highest form was, moreover, profoundly aware that all peoples are involved in rebellion against God. Thus the ultimate "problem of the meaning of history according to prophetism is how history can be any more than judgment, which is to say, whether the promise of history can be fulfilled at all." [52] It is this problem which becomes "the unsolved question of prophetic Messianism." [53] The problem is whether God possesses mercy great enough to redeem as well as to judge men, and if so what the relationship between His mercy and His justice is.

Christianity enters the world with the stupendous tidings that in Jesus, Messiah has come. That in Him God overcomes the contradictions of history not by destroying the "wicked" and vindicating the "righteous" but by Himself bearing the evil of all men, both the "wicked" and the "righteous"; and that the depth of His mercy thus revealed does not annul but deepens, while at the same time transcends, His judgment upon evil.

In exploring the meaning of this for the Christian interpretation we must first estimate the significance of the assertion that history is an "interim." In Christ the hidden sovereignty of God is disclosed, the Kingdom of God has come, the "eschaton" is realized, the meaning of life and history is revealed. "But we see not all things put under his feet." Sin still abounds, life remains morally ambiguous, history awaits its culmination, the Kingdom is coming. History is an interim between the disclosure of the meaning of life and history, and the fulfillment of that meaning.

The concept "interim" being conceived in these terms, it has, says Niebuhr, the capacity to illumine all the facts of human existence. "History, after Christ's first coming, has the quality of partly knowing its true meaning. Insofar as man can never be completely in contradiction to his own true nature, history also reveals significant realizations of that meaning. Nevertheless history continues to stand in real contradiction to its true meaning, so that pure love in history must always be suffering love. But the contradictions of history cannot become man's norms, if history is viewed from the perspective of Christ."[54] The Christian revelation does not promise that the fragmentary and contradictory aspects of life will be overcome, history remains ambiguous to the end. The Christ is crucified in history. But here, suffering innocence which, from our standpoint reveals the problem of history's moral ambiguity, becomes the answer to the problem. The suffering love of Christ is the love of God who bears the sins of the world and overcomes its contradictions, by taking them upon Himself. This is the ultimate dimension in the sovereignty of Him who rules. Because this power may be laid hold of in the relationship of faith, history has the possibility of indeterminate renewals; but this love is the love of the Cross, the contradictions of history remain to the end. Our days are set in the interim between the disclosure of the meaning of history and the fulfillment of that meaning. In the light of this grand fact we are called to live a life of responsible action, "to show forth the Lord's death till He come." This is of such immense importance in Niebuhr's thought, that we must consider further how he views history in the light of the coming of Christ and the hope of the "second coming," the relationship between the Cross and eschatology.

### c. History in the Light of the Cross

We have spoken frequently of the centrality of the Cross in Niebuhr's thought. Now we must consider this specifically in terms of the doctrine of the Atonement, for here as we have already seen, Niebuhr's thought on the meaning of the Christ event is centered. "The doctrine of the Atonement and justification is the 'stone which the builders rejected' and which must be made 'the head of the corner.' It is an absolutely essential presupposition for the understanding of human nature and human history." [55]

The reasons why the atoning work of Christ is viewed as "the head of the corner" have been touched on numerous times and we need only summarize. It is at the Cross that we learn the exceeding sinfulness of human sin, that the best as well as the worst in history is involved in rebellion against God, that "every majesty or virtue, which is tenable in history, is involved in the crucifixion of a 'prince of glory.' " [56] But He who dies upon the Cross is essential man, and we learn that sin is not a necessary part of our nature. "Life is thus not at war with itself." [57] Here also is the revelation of the suffering love of God who takes the frustrations and contradictions of man's self-corrupted freedom upon, and into, Himself and overcomes them. We further learn that this love, which judges us to the roots of our beings, has the power to uphold and reconcile, "and man is no longer afraid, even though he knows himself to be involved in the crucifixion." [58] We can be saved by faith and hope; the chain of evil that binds all men is not a natural fate. At the Cross we see the great realities which constitute our inner and outer environment—the might of evil and the even greater power of redeeming grace. Therefore we are called to be neither complacent nor hysterical, but watchful and sober. The meaning of history is not completed within itself. History is completed beyond history by a power above history. The name of that power is *agape* revealed in history at the Cross as sin-bearing love.[59]

The Atonement is the content of the Incarnation, the revelation is accomplished through the act of reconciliation. Christian theologies which subordinate Atonement to Incarnation (as Catholic and Anglican theologies are inclined to do) obscure the fact that the problem of man is sin not finitude. The question is not primarily how the eternal is to invade time, but how the justice and mercy of God are related in the overcoming of the truly tragic antinomies of history. The Atonement is the "head of the corner." It is both the wisdom and the power of God.

### d. THE CROSS AS THE WISDOM OF GOD

St. Paul recognized that the claim that the Cross was the final revelation of God and the relation of God and man, was to the Greeks neither human nor divine "wisdom," but "foolishness." It was foolishness to them "because history belonged to nature and made such a revelation impossible; and human reason belonged to eternity and made it unnecessary."[60] But to the "called," the Cross is both the "wisdom" and the "power" of God.

To assert that the Cross is the wisdom of God is to say that "the final mystery of the divine power which bears history is clarified; and, with that clarification, life and history are given their true meaning."[61] What is that final mystery? We have been asserting throughout that it is the relation between the mercy and the justice of God. Does the mercy of God exist *alongside* His justice? Does the one finally abrogate the other? Niebuhr's way of putting the Christian answer is this: "The *wisdom* apprehended in Christ finally clarifies the character of God. He has a resource of mercy beyond His law and judgment but He can make it effective only as

He takes the consequences of His wrath and judgment upon and into Himself."[62]

The mercy of God does not abrogate the justice of God, but it represents the freedom of God over his own law. The love which is the law for man has a dimension which is able to overcome and forgive the violation of the law. Thus the justice and forgiveness of God are the same, but forgiveness is the deeper dimension.

It is of the utmost importance for our study, that we note that the dialectical relation between love and justice finds its ultimate basis in the "wisdom" of God, in the relation between the mercy and the justice of God. The justice of God is the love of God acting against the corruptions of His order. To seek to have love without justice is to sentimentalize the whole Gospel. But the justice of God does not exist apart from His love; its ultimate dimension is the unfathomable depth of a love which takes into itself our violations of that same law of love. Such is the theological rootage of Niebuhr's ethics.

The truth of Christ apprehended in faith becomes also the source of a new wisdom for the understanding of human experience. This is so because history possesses a meaning which points beyond itself. The wisdom discerned by faith is never in complete contradiction to human experience. Therefore the truth of the gospel, although it cannot be derived from experience, can be validated and confirmed in experience. "Revelation does not remain in contradiction to human culture and human knowledge. By completing the incompleteness, clarifying the obscurities and correcting the falsifications of human knowledge it becomes true wisdom to 'them that are called.' "[63]

It must be emphasized that the Cross is wisdom "to them that are called." That is to say, the meaning of life as dependence upon the judging-redeeming love of God is not some truth that can be simply added to our store of worldly knowledge. It must be constantly apprehended inwardly by faith. The Cross is neither wisdom nor power to those who accept it gracelessly. The "wisdom" of God is not appropriated apart from the "power" of God. There is an intimate relation between the content and the mode of knowing. The wisdom of the Cross is known only to him who appropriates it in contrition and trust. To him who thus apprehends the truth of Christ, the wisdom of God is also the power of God; the disclosure of the meaning of life carries with it resources for the fulfillment of that meaning. This leads us to a consideration of the meaning of grace.

### e. Grace as Power in, and as Mercy towards, Man

The Cross is not only the "wisdom" of God but also the "power" of God, the power of God in us and the power of God over us. The manner in which these two facets of the grace of God are emphasized and related comprehends a good deal of the history of Christianity.

The grace of God is effective. The pride of the self is broken, life can be recentered, there is "newness" of life. The self becomes freed from the constrictions of self-concern and thus is made free for responsible action. The Cross is power as well as wisdom, the power of God *in* us. There is growth in grace. But we must be careful here. For growth in grace is growth in faith and hope and love. It is not a possession of our own to which we can lay claim. The grace of God is new every morning only to those who have both the humility and the boldness to receive it as a gift every morning. "What hast thou that thou hast not received?" Christ remains the one continuing ground of Christian experience. Still the power of God is effectual in leading men to repentance and new life and the name of its working is grace.

But all Christian history testifies to the fact that the other facet of grace must be equally emphasized. Even in the "new life" the contradictions between human self-will and the divine purpose remain. Indeed human pride and arrogance manifest themselves most demonically under the guise of sanctity. Thus without minimizing the reality of the power of God in us, we must rely ultimately on the power of God *over* us, in the power of his forgiveness to overcome the corruption we introduce into even the gifts we have received. Thus the final peace is not the "moral" peace of achievement but the "religious" peace that springs from the certainty that there are divine resources of mercy to overcome the continued contradiction between our self-love and the divine purpose.

Niebuhr fully recognizes the difficulty involved in doing justice to both of these facets of the meaning of grace. His own formulation, "Sin is overcome in principle but not in fact," fails to do justice, as Niebuhr himself acknowledges,[64] to the real measure of sanctification that results when the self is turned from itself to God. Both facets must be held together. Saints remain sinners, but recognition of that must not obscure the indeterminate possibilities for the realization of good, individually and collectively. The Gospel is mighty unto the bringing of new life, but that must not obscure the reality of sin which appears on every new level of virtue.

The significance of Niebuhr's thought on this question is the clarity with which he sees that "the two sides of the experience of grace are so related that they do not contradict, but support each other"[65] and the immense importance of this in providing motivation and humility for the exercise of social responsibility. "To understand that the Christ in us is not a possession but a hope, that perfection is not a reality but an intention; that such peace as we know in this life is never purely the peace of achievement but the serenity of being 'completely known and all forgiven'; all this does not destroy moral ardour or responsibility. On the contrary it is the only way of preventing premature completions of life, or arresting the new and more terrible pride which may find its roots in the soil of humility, and of saving the Christian life from the intolerable pretension of saints who have forgotten that they are sinners."[66]

History is a meaningful process but it can neither yield nor fulfill its own meaning. The distinctions between good and evil in history are of the utmost importance, indeed of ultimate significance. Yet every realization of good is tainted with evil, every structure of justice is incomplete, and all our finest achievements stand in need of the divine mercy to complete their incompleteness and to destroy their sinful distortions. For this reason the doctrine of the Atonement is the "final key" to the Christian interpretation of history.

> The Christian doctrine of the Atonement is therefore not some incomprehensible remnant of superstition, nor yet a completely incomprehensible article of faith. It is, indeed, on the other side of human wisdom, in the sense that it is not comprehensible to a wisdom which looks at the world with confident eyes, certain that all its mysteries can be fathomed by the human mind. Yet it is the beginning of wisdom in the sense that it contains symbolically all that the Christian faith maintains about what man ought to do and what he cannot do, about his obligations and final incapacity to fulfill them, about the importance of decisions and achievements in history and about their final insignificance. [67]

### f. THE END OF HISTORY

The question of the meaning of history is always a question of the completion of history. We have already discussed the significance of the Christian understanding of history as interim, between the disclosure of the meaning of history and the fulfillment of that meaning. The finite mind can not comprehend that which will fulfill history, nor really conceive the nature of fulfillment. Therefore the biblical symbols of the "end" of history cannot be taken literally. But they must be taken seriously because "they express the self-transcendent character of historical existence and point to its eternal ground." [68] Four basic symbols require consideration, the Antichrist, the return of Christ, the last judgment, and the resurrection.

The Antichrist belongs to those events that herald the "end" of history. To take this symbol seriously would be to undercut all utopian illusions at once. History does not solve the problem of the ambiguity of history, the future cannot guarantee increasing virtue or security. The Antichrist symbolizes that the "most explicit denial of the norm of history must be expected in the most ultimate development of history. Closely related to this idea of the final evil at the end of history, is the general anticipation of evils in the course of history, which believers will understand but by which the world will be taken unawares."[69] This is entirely consistent with the whole New Testament view of history. Evil is commingled with the good; evil does not have a separate history, an independent existence. Evil is demonically powerful, but it is not independent of good. It is *Anti*-Christ.

> The final evil is thus dependent upon the final good. Either it consciously and explicitly defies the Christ, in which case it requires Christ as a foil; or it is a lesser good, claiming to be the ultimate one, in which case it requires Christ as a cloak. The one form is the Antichrist of the sinners and the other the Antichrist of the righteous. But in either case the force of the Antichrist, though parasitic and negative in origin, is so positive in effect, and so stubborn in purpose that no force, immanent in history, is capable of encompassing its defeat. The Antichrist who appears at the end of history can be defeated only by the Christ who ends history.[70]

The symbol of the "second coming of Christ," despite the fact that it has been so fantastically abused in Christian circles, involves, as Niebuhr once remarked, "all the profoundest characteristics of the Christian religion."[71] It distinguishes the Christian hope from all rationalistic and mystical otherworldliness; the parousia is at the "end" of history not above it. The fulfillment of history is thus relevant to historical forms. But the "second coming" is at the "end" of history; it is not a point *in* history and thus the Christian expectation is distinguished from all utopianism.

Niebuhr distinguishes three important facets for the Christian understanding of history contained in the symbol of the last judgment. (1) It is Christ who will be the judge of history. The importance of this is that the historical is judged by its own possibility, by Christ who is Very Man. The norm by which we are judged is given with the very constitution of selfhood. "The judgment is upon sin and not finiteness."[72] (2) This symbol emphasizes the distinction between good and evil. To be sure "all have sinned and come short of the glory of God," all are dependent upon the divine mercy. But this symbol emphasizes that "the ultimate mercy does not efface the distinctions between good and evil."[73] (3) The last judgment is a "last" judgment. This emphasizes, what we have already stressed, that history is not its own redeemer. No achievement is so freed from sin as to mean that it escapes the last judgment. (4) We have already discussed at length in Chapter Three, the significance of the symbol of the resurrection. One quotation will therefore suffice to show how Niebuhr sees the relevance of this symbol to the problem of history. "The hope of the resurrection," he writes, ". . . embodies the very genius of the Christian idea of the historical. On the one hand it implies that eternity will fulfill and not annul the richness and variety which the temporal process has elaborated. On the other it implies that the condition of finiteness and freedom, which lies at the basis of historical existence, is a problem for which there is no solution by any human power."[74]

We have endeavored in the foregoing to outline the structure of Niebuhr's presentation of the Christian understanding of history. At numerous points we have emphasized that the whole approach is rooted in faith. This must be underlined. The Christian walks by faith and not by sight. The meaning of history as he affirms it is discerned by the "eyes of faith." It is not derived from experience; no empirical analysis of historical structures and patterns can yield the Christian perspective, peculiar understanding, and ultimate hope. Nor can it be proved to be true by rational analysis and demonstration. Nevertheless, Niebuhr's entire apologetic task is directed to the end of establishing the relevance of the Christian understanding so that it may be an available resource of discriminate insight and healing. It is Niebuhr's contention, therefore, that although the Christian revelation is given to experience and not derived from it, nevertheless its truth can be validated or confirmed in experience. The truth of the Gospel is not subject to rational proof, "but a limited rational validation of the truth of the Gospel is possible."[75] The validation of the truth of the Gospel involves us in a task possessing both negative and positive aspects.

### g. THE QUESTION OF VALIDATION

The negative aspect of the task is that "of exploring the limits of human knowledge and the fragmentary character of all forms of human virtue."[76] According to St. Paul the defect of the "wisdom of the world" lies in the fact "that it knew not God" (I Corinthians 1:21). The consequence is that it either identifies God too simply with some historic truth or value and falls into idolatry issuing in complacency, or it is so impressed with the fragmentary character of human knowledge and virtue that it finds no meaning in life and falls into atheism and despair.[77] No amount of rational analysis of the limitations of "worldly wisdom" will, of itself, persuade one of the truth of the Gospel. The acceptance of the Gospel is always a gift of grace, a mystery "which is not subject to manipulation."[78] However, if one is "to make room for the Gospel" in the world it is important to puncture the idolatrous pretensions of a culture, awaken it from its complacency, and interpret the significance of its despair. When both forms of worldly wisdom are shown to provide an inadequate interpretation of the total human situation, the Christian understanding secures a fresh relevance and a limited negative validation. This engagement of the "wisdom of the Cross," of a faith which "is perplexed but not in despair," with the "wisdom of the world" is of special significance to a generation which has moved so rapidly from optimism to pessimism, from complacency to despair. This neither proves the "truth" of the Gospel nor makes it acceptable, but if the engagement is real and vital the Christian faith can be shown to be "the apprehension of a wisdom which makes sense out of life on a different level than the worldly wisdom which either makes sense out of life too simply or which can find no sense in life at all."[79] This is what Niebuhr means by the negative task of validating the truth of the Gospel.

The positive apologetic task is not a different task, it is simply a different thrust of the one and the same task. "It consists in correlating the truth, apprehended by faith and repentance, to truths about life and history, gained generally in experience."[80] Insofar as this shows the Christian faith to be a more adequate "source and center" for interpreting life than alternative interpretations, such a correlation can be said to validate the truth of the faith. Having said this, it is perhaps indicative of Niebuhr's caution in this affirmation that he proceeds at once to list three major temptations to which such a procedure is peculiarly prone. The temptations he sees are: (1) To regard "the truth of faith as capable of simple correlation with any system of rational coherence and as validated by such a correlation."[81] This will issue in the capitulation of the faith to a given culture's scheme of meaning, e.g. liberalism. (2) The second temptation is that of obscurantism, the guarding of Christian truth by insisting on its validation by "miraculous historical fact" and divorcing the faith from all commerce with the wisdom of the world, e.g. Protestant literalism. (3) "The third error, to which Catholic rationalism is particularly prone, is to validate the truth of faith but to explicate it rationally in such a way that mystery is too simply resolved into ostensible rational intelligibility."[82]

The truth of the Gospel can be apprehended only in repentant faith and its truth stands at the limits of all systems of meaning. Only in that spirit and from that vantage point can the wisdom of the world be either challenged or appropriated.

Karl Löwith and Niebuhr are akin in much of their understanding of the Christian faith but it is at this point of the relationship between the "truth of the Gospel" and "the wisdom of the world" that their differences have become sharp and clear. In the conclusion to his valuable book *Meaning in History*, Löwith writes, "The importance of secular history decreases in direct proportion to the intensity of man's concern with God and himself. While we are overflooded with secular history but dried up religiously, the *Confessions* of Augustine do not contain the slightest hint at a serious interest in secular events as such."[83] One is tempted to ask just what can be meant by the phrase "secular events as such." In any case, this way of putting the matter smells very distinctly like a religious cloak for social irresponsibility. This suspicion seems to be confirmed, when in his essay on Niebuhr in the *Library of Living Theology* volume, Löwith says: "And since the story of salvation does not refer to historical empires, nations, and civilizations but to each human soul, one cannot dismiss the thought that Christianity, that is, faith in Christ, is essentially indifferent over against world-historical differences, even over against the difference between civilization and barbarism."[84] *Agape* apparently has no relationship to the task of securing justice. Niebuhr's reply to Löwith grasps the difference between them with such firmness, and the issue is of such pertinence to our inquiry, that the reply ought to be quoted at length.

> The difference is essentially that Professor Löwith finds no tangents of meaning in the historical drama which are clarified by Christian revelation. He seems to me to be saying that the drama is "full of sound and fury, signifying nothing," and that only revelation and salvation rescue life from meaninglessness. I know how easily any "Christian" interpretation of history can give it false meanings, analogous to the false meanings elaborated by Hegel or other philosophers. I know that Christ is the "light that shineth in darkness." The question between us is how absolute the darkness is. If it is as dark as he assumes, there cannot be any relevance between faith and our life as historical creatures. Professor Löwith says that responsibility is a moral and not a religious category. Is this distinction absolute? Is there no wisdom in the Christian faith which might prevent a powerful nation and a secure culture from plunging into catastrophe by its pride? Or which would prevent individual Christians from fleeing into complete irresponsibility about the fate of their civilization?
>
> We ought to be quite clear what is at stake in this issue. If we declare "history" to be totally meaningless, we also absolve the individual of responsibility for the health of the various collective enterprises, cultures, and civilizations which make up the stuff of history. The Christian faith is reduced to a purely individual transcendence over a very inscrutable collective life. I cannot see this as the meaning of New Testament faith, even though "world history" is not specifically mentioned in the Bible. Incidentally, it is worth remembering that the Bible contains both Old and New Testaments.

In the Old Testament the prophets are certainly concerned with the sovereignty of God over the history of all the nations, and over the problem of whether the historical drama has any meaning. They assert that it has meaning which will be clarified in the Messianic age.[85]

This difference between Löwith and Niebuhr serves to underline what has been a contention of our whole discussion, that the relationship between love and justice in Niebuhr is thoroughly integrated with, and rooted in, his view of the Christian faith and history. It must be asserted in the strongest terms that this relationship is integral and not a case of similar thought structures running parallel to each other. Niebuhr is writing theological ethics, and it is nonsense to speak of him as an "ethicist" if by that it is meant that he is not a theologian, or if by that it is implied that Christian theology and Christian ethics can exist in separation.

The Kingdom of God is relevant to the kingdoms of this world. It hovers over every moment of history both in judgment and in revelation of the indeterminate possibilities of history. In a word, "The kingdom which is not of this world is always in this world in man's uneasy conscience."[86] "In every moment of existence those 'who are of the truth' hear the Christ's voice, warning, admonishing and guiding them in their actions. The real truth condemns their lies; pure justice indicts their injustice; the law of love reveals their selfishness; and the vision of God reveals their true centre and source of existence. They may continue to be disobedient to the heavenly vision; but they can never be as they have been."[87]

But the kingdom of God is not a simple historical possibility. It lies at the end of history, which is not a point in history. The Kingdom of God does enter this world but it enters it through the crucifixion of "the prince of glory." The contradictions of our history are such as not to allow a complete union between power and pure love. Power and love are united only in God. The Kingdom enters the world through the King who is crucified in history. The Cross is not a strategy of historical success, the kingdom of God is not a simple historical possibility. The tragic antinomies of history cannot be overcome by more persuasive sermons on the kingdom of love.[88] Their life destroying power is mitigated by structures of justice which are demanded, negated, and completed by love.

The dialectical relation between love and justice is not just an aspect of Niebuhr's thought but the point at which the whole dialectical relation of the Gospel and the world finds its focus. Conversely, if the full richness of the relation between love and justice is to be apprehended it must be seen in the context of his total theological reflection, in which it has its base, and of which it is his most characteristic expression.

*Five*

# THE RESOURCES OF LOVE
# FOR A RESPONSIBLE SOCIETY

In the previous chapters we have endeavored to delineate the structure of Niebuhr's theological ethics especially as it is focused in the dialectical relation of love and justice. It is our conviction that Niebuhr's understanding and presentation of the Christian revelation not only provide illumination for the nature and dimensions of the social task but also clearly hold before us those resources of spirit that are at once the fruit of faith and the prerequisite for a responsible approach to concrete social issues. It must, however, be acknowledged that there is a widespread impression abroad, especially in religious circles, that it is at this point that Niebuhr is most defective. It is quite generally held that although Niebuhr has been effective in the destruction of illusions, he fails to provide adequate positive direction; that his thought has been more significant for the casting down of idols than for the illuminating and focusing of the resources of faith for the fulfillment of social responsibility.

The widespread impression that Niebuhr's understanding fails on the side of giving positive direction and motivation has been given focus in an article by Professor Mack B. Stokes entitled "Passivity in the Thought of Reinhold Niebuhr." [1] This article is of some importance for our inquiry because it illustrates so clearly the difficulties of so much of American religious thinking to get inside

Niebuhr's thought, and therefore its failure to appreciate and appropriate the positive dimensions of his teaching. For this reason it will be instructive for us to analyze this article.

The thesis of the article is that Niebuhr has contributed to the idea and nurtured "the tradition of passivity within the Protestant mind."[2] The "unmistakable theme of passivity" runs throughout his thought.[3] Stokes sees this theme in the first place in Niebuhr's theory of Christian ethics, specifically in his view of the relation between love and the structures and decisions of history. It must be said bluntly that Stokes's treatment in this brief section is notorious for its misrepresentation. He makes no attempt whatever to deal with the dialectical relation between love and justice in Niebuhr. The burden of his complaint is that Niebuhr places "the life-subserving purpose of Christian love in jeopardy" by disconnecting it from its mighty purpose of influencing and transforming the social order. This protest is bolstered by three quotations and by a criticism of Niebuhr's understanding of vicarious love. The quotations are all taken from *An Interpretation of Christian Ethics.* The first quotation[4] is given without any reference to its context. The context is a discussion in which Niebuhr is distinguishing the "ethic of Jesus" from both "natural self-regarding impulses" and prudentialism. The context of the second quotation (page reference is not given but it may be found in the same book on page 51), in which Niebuhr expresses a measure of agreement with Karl Barth, is simply that no detailed social ethic is to be derived from *agape.* For the third quotation the reader is sent off to the wrong book to do his checking.[5] Having persuaded himself that Niebuhr's thought nurtures the tradition of passivity, Stokes proceeds to an even more grievous misrepresentation while discussing vicarious love. Stokes quotes Niebuhr's remark that vicarious love may have "its triumph in the knowledge that it is ultimately right and true" (*The Nature and Destiny of Man,* volume 2. p. 45). Here Professor Stokes appears to think that Niebuhr has been presenting his own views instead of discussing the tragic conception of history. The very next sentence would have saved Stokes from this mistake. "Such a tragic conception still leaves the problem of the evil in history unresolved."[6]

Stokes next contends that Niebuhr's view of the ambiguity of all historical action contributes to passivity. In particular he pounces on Niebuhr's view that it is only in prayer that we are lifted to that vantage point where we gain a perspective upon the self-love that insinuates itself into even our best actions. This Stokes thinks "would seem to be a call to prayer and contemplation *as over against* active participation . . ."[7] The fact that the whole of Niebuhr's thought is directed against these as the only alternatives is in no way discussed. The vantage point provided by faith above the battle is precisely what motivates us to engage in the battle, and to temper the spirit in which we do our battling. Moreover, it is exactly this joining of humility and resoluteness that is the distinguishing mark of Niebuhr's thought which Stokes tears asunder, and then, seemingly, deplores its absence in Niebuhr. Mr. Stokes is also certain that Niebuhr's conviction that God can still make the wrath of men to praise him has the effect of "blurring our moral distinctions and therefore of weakening the sense that we are really doing the right thing whenever and wherever we fight the forces of tyranny in the name of Christ."[8] This goes right to the heart of the problem of much historic Christianity on the one hand, and serves, on the other, to throw into clear relief, not the passivity of Niebuhr's thought, but its urgent relevance. Mr. Stokes apparently cannot conceive that we have sufficient motivation for resolute action unless we persuade ourselves that God is the simple ally of our cause. He does not apparently see that God's purposes transcend, as well as include and negate, our causes. Surely if God is not able to make the wrath of men to praise him then we are all betrayed either into despair or complacency; into despair because we are all "men of wrath" who stand before him with no claims to our own righteousness, or into complacency because we have allowed the greater evil of our opponents to persuade us of our own innocence. The political implications of such a philosophy of history, with its neat division between good and evil men, are most frightening to contemplate. Mr. Stokes clearly reveals that, despite his glowing tributes to Niebuhr, the moralism of his own thought has not really been breached. Be that as it may, the importance of his little article lies in the fact that it reveals both the urgent need for American religious thought to appropriate Niebuhr's illumination of the *positive resources of faith for the social task,* and the difficulties that stand in the way of that appropriation.

In our discussion of the resources of faith for the securing of a responsible society our procedure will be to draw attention to those concepts and motifs which run through all Niebuhr's works, and which clearly disclose his understanding of the distinctive resources of spirit inhering in biblical faith. To a discussion of these we now turn.

## 1. HUMILITY

No theme courses through the whole of Niebuhr's writing with greater strength or constancy than the theme of the social relevance of the humility born of faith's encounter. We need to read his articles as well as his books fully to realize how large this theme looms in his total work, and how significantly it informs his whole approach. One frequently hears the remark that although the reader of Niebuhr may not always understand Niebuhr, he cannot read Niebuhr without coming to a better understanding of himself. Perhaps the basis of this capacity lies right here in the meaning of humility and the place it has in Niebuhr's whole thought structure. He has himself faced—and he makes us face—the condition of the self before God. We cannot wriggle out because he does not point us to himself, but always to the Cross. To be sure, this is what happens whenever we encounter any authentic religious soul; what is distinctive about Niebuhr in this respect is the power and insight with which humility is set in a wider social context. He not only knows, as does every sensitive spirit, how pride insinuates itself into our very desires to be humble; he also sees so clearly the immense significance of this for social relations.

It is perhaps best to begin by saying what humility is not. It is not spinelessness, it is not the lack of firm resolution and decisiveness. It is not an inaccurate estimate of our own capacities. Indeed humility is not a virtue among other virtues at all. It is that relationship before God and our fellows which is the source and spring of all other virtues. Humility is the pervasive quality of that relationship with God in which we stand before Him in the unity of our being, know and accept His judgment upon us, know and appropriate His forgiveness and seek to live in the light of that grand fact. Humility is not something we can wring from ourselves, that we possess within ourselves, or that we can control. It is ever a gift of grace, appropriated in faith and renewed in love and obedience. Therefore when we speak of humility as one of the resources of faith for the social task, we speak not of some virtue or other but rather the social significance of the whole tonal quality of the life of faith. It has been Niebuhr's peculiar strength to illuminate, as perhaps no other, the points of contact of such humility with the concrete social issues of daily life.

The first fruit of humility is self-knowledge. "The truly religious man does know himself as no one else does."[9] This is not spoken of religion in general. Religion as such is neither a cure for human pretension nor a source of self-knowledge. "It is," rather, "the final battleground between pride and humility."[10] This is another way of acknowledging the inveterate tendency of the human heart to invest its own values and causes with divine sanction and thus turn even a religion of contrition into an instrument of pride, a repentant faith into a new security for the self in its sin. Nor is it claimed that real contrition eliminates all the selfishness of the human heart. What is acknowledged is this: that when we measure ourselves by ourselves, although we may and do experience conviction and shame, we are always ultimately righteous. "Thus we never know anything against ourselves ultimately. The self is always righteous in its self-analysis and secure in its self-esteem until it feels itself under a more ultimate judgment than its own."[11] But when that happens, when before the *agape* of the Cross, we are convicted in the center of our beings and see ourselves as we really are, such self-knowledge emerges as a component of that humility which arises in the relationship which knows the divine judgment upon every human pretension. We are moved to recognize and acknowledge that our wisdom is fragmentary, our power limited, and our virtue tainted with guilt. And that we are bound to our fellows in this common guilt and limitation, for this is the universal human condition.

Humility thus rooted in repentance expresses itself in the spirit of forgiveness which is at once the crowning fruit of biblical faith and the perennial need of all personal and social relations. The evil in the other is to be "borne without vindictiveness because the evil in the self is known."[12] "Mercy to the foe is possible only to those who know themselves to be sinners."[13] Herein the sensitive compassion of the profoundly religious spirit is joined with the resolute action of the political realist and the discriminating judgments of the morally serious person. The foe remains a real foe; he must be resolutely opposed. But the temper of the struggle will be mitigated by the knowledge that the righteousness of our cause, though real, is not absolute. Thus are we enjoined to be "angry and sin not." "The avoidance of sin in anger is not achieved by a position of detachment but by a recognition of the partisan and partial character of our actions and of the majesty of the divine judgment above all our judgments."[14]

This is no "nurturing of the tradition of passivity"; the contrite recognition of our own sinful involvement issues in neither the blunting of our moral discrimination nor the paralyzing of decision to resist social evil. On the contrary: the very divine majesty which reveals to us our own sin compels us resolutely to resist the greater evil, but leaving vengeance to God alone. Years before the outbreak of the war, Niebuhr had forcefully answered the moralists who opposed both his emphasis upon religious contrition and his political realism, and who stood aghast at his joining of the two.

Emphasis upon political and religious realism and Christian contrition does not mean that there should be or that there would be less moral idealism and a less genuine effort to understand the interest of the other person and to meet it by voluntary action. All justice established by pressure is in need of being elaborated by love; and there is no reason to suppose that people who know themselves to be selfish will be less anxious to try to approximate unselfishness than those who imagine that unselfishness is an easy attainment. In a final conflict only those who have learned the grace of humility can be loving, for in a conflict love requires forgiveness and forgiveness is possible only to those who know themselves to be sinners. Moral idealists never forgive their foes. They are too secure in their own virtue to do that. Men forgive their foes only when they feel themselves to be standing under God with them and feel that under divine scrutiny all "our righteousness is as filthy rags."[15]

We hear a great deal these days about the relationship between Christianity and democracy but the deep-rooted heritage of idealistic moralism in American Christianity means that we usually hear the wrong thing. A healthy democracy requires not only a sustained devotion to moral ideals, it also requires the spirit of religious humility. This, Niebuhr urges, is the real point of contact between democracy and profound faith. "Democratic life requires a spirit of tolerant co-operation between individuals and groups which can be achieved by neither moral cynics, who know no law beyond their own interest, nor by moral idealists, who acknowledge such a law but are unconscious of the corruption which insinuates itself into the statement of it by even the most disinterested idealists."[16] The real point of contact is the humility which combines a fervent devotion to values with a clear recognition that these values are fragmentary in character and tainted by our prejudice. But again let it be emphasized that Niebuhr never allows humility to be construed in such a way as to obscure the moral seriousness involved in all our political decisions and social strategies.[17] For not only does humility mean the recognition of the perversions in even our best achievements, it also impels us to more complete realizations of social values.

At no point has Niebuhr proclaimed the message of Christian humility with greater prophetic power and insight than in the post-war years of American power and leadership. As victory loomed into sight in 1943, we find him wrestling with the question of the distinctive resources of faith that would serve the Anglo-American nations to fulfill their highest responsibility of providing leadership for the restoration of a shattered world. There was no question, in his mind, of the comparative virtue of the Anglo-American nations. But the temptation of a virtuous nation is always "to claim eminence by the right of its virtue" and thus to obscure those factors, other than virtue, that are responsible for its eminent position. As with Israel of old, the special mission laid upon the victors carries with it neither special security nor advantages but places them in "a precarious moral and historical position." Nothing is more relevant for the responsible discharge of such a solemn mission than the humility born of faith.

> There is no cure for the pride of a virtuous nation but pure religion. The pride of a powerful nation may be humbled by the impotence which defeat brings. The pride of a virtuous nation cannot be humbled by moral and political criticisms because in comparative terms it may actually be virtuous. The democratic traditions of the Anglo-Saxon world are actually the potential basis of a just world order. But the historical achievements of this world are full of violations and contradictions of these principles. "In God's sight" they are not just; and they know it if they place themselves under the divine scrutiny, that is, if they regard their own history prayerfully rather than comparatively and measure themselves by what is demanded of them rather than by comparing their success with the failure of others.
>
> Thus a contrite recognition of our own sins destroys the illusion of eminence through virtue and lays the foundation for the apprehension of "grace" in our national life. We know that we have the position which we hold in the world today, partly by reason of factors and forces in the complex pattern of history which we did not create and from which we do not deserve to benefit. If we apprehend this religiously, the sense of destiny ceases to be a vehicle of pride and becomes the occasion for a new sense of responsibility.[18]

It became increasingly clear in the years following the war that the greatest peril threatening the responsible discharge of her high mission, was the complacency that settled over the American community. The temptation complacently to make a simple correlation between American power and American virtue was reinforced by the fact that its new foe embodied all the evils of a demonic religion.[19] The task of the Church in this situation seemed clear.

> The Christian church must therefore regard it as one of its important missions to disturb the mood of national self-congratulation into which our nation is sinking. If the Church is to perform this task it must know however that the "prophetic" mission does not come easily or automatically to the Church. Religion qua religion is naturally idolatrous, accentuating, rather than diminishing, the self-worship of men and nations, by assuring them of an ultimate sanction for their dearest desires. Insofar as our congregations are merely religious communities in which an uncritical piety is nourished, they also do no more than to mix patriotic self-congratulation with the worship of God. It requires both courage and astuteness to penetrate the armor of the nation's self-righteousness. But above all it requires knowledge of and devotion to the one true God who declares to even the most righteous of nations: "You only have I chosen; therefore will I visit you with your iniquities." [20]

The message of humility thus became for Niebuhr not only a major point at which he sought to bring the resources of faith to bear upon the national task but also a call for a total renewal of the life and thought of the Church. There is no question that America has recently experienced a resurgent interest in religion. Much, though not all, of this revival has been distinguished by a cult of "faith in faith" with the result that it has been too shallow and sentimental to speak a significant word of either judgment or redemption to the national life. Niebuhr has had a good deal to say about the contemporary religiosity of American life but one quotation will suffice to reveal his evaluation of it.

> One must come to the conclusion that religion *per se* and faith *per se* are not virtuous, or a cause of virtue. The question is always what the object of worship is, and whether the worship tends to break

the pride of the self so that a truer self may arise, either individually
or collectively. If worship and faith do not serve this rebirth of men
and of nations they are the source of confusion. We can therefore
take no satisfaction in the prevailing religiosity of our nation. Much
of it is a perversion of the Christian gospel. It aggravates, rather
than mitigates, the problems of a very successful people.[21]

Our world teeters on the brink of disaster because of the conflict
of different forms of idealism busily engaged in establishing their
own righteousness. The task of the Church is not that of making
constant exhortations to obey the moral law in which the competing
forces alike believe, but interpret differently, or that of turning
religion into an instrument for the securing of some other value;
its task is above all to face anew the majesty of Her Lord who
reveals the pharisaism of every human heart and who wounds in
order to heal.

In this sense the first task of the Church, in opening the hearts
of men to the resources of grace, is to issue a call to serious prayer.
One hesitates to use that phrase, because none has become cheaper
than the phrase "call to prayer." But prayer is not easy, for prayer
is work, a wrestling with God. So conceived, prayer becomes a
first "means of grace," an experience wherein the grace of humility
is most frequently vouchsafed. Since Niebuhr's writings are as far
removed as can be imagined from "the devotional writings of the
conventionally pious," it sometimes comes as a surprise to realize
the place he accords prayer whenever he discusses the resources of
faith for responsible social witness. But it ought not, when we
measure the meaning that humility holds in all his writing.

Prayer is that expression of the life of grace in which the whole
of life is held before the purposes of God. Thus confronted with
the Holy God, we become conscious in a new way of the taint of
sin in the cause of our devotion and the need for grace which
unites us with our foes.[22] More than that: it is in the experience
and context of prayer that the life of the spirit is extended so that
we are enabled to sense the breadth and dimensions of our relations and obligations. Niebuhr spoke most eloquently on this in an

article written during the war. "The breadth of our responsibilities, compared to the narrowness of our imagination in the present world situation, accentuates a very old spiritual problem of man. We are constantly called upon to extend the limits of our insights so that they will correspond more nearly to the boundaries of our mutual relations and obligations. This must be done in many ways; but one of the most effective means of such extension is intercessory prayer."[23] If the spirit of humility and forgiveness is the content of seeing life in its total dimension and of achieving a measure of transcendence over its conflicts, then prayer is the vehicle. As such nothing can take the place of real prayer in resisting the temptations either to complacency or despair. "Our imagination is so limited in comprehending, from the perspective of security and comfort, all the sorrow and anguish of the world. If we do not, in prayer, transcend those limits, how can we be saved from the intolerable complacency of the secure in a tragic time? One might almost claim that only intercessory prayer is adequate for the spiritual peril of America, which (with the exception of its fighting men) becomes involved only peripherally in the convulsions of modern history."[24]

In prayer we are stabbed awake, our spirits are sensitized, our imaginations are extended, and we learn anew the real meaning of Christian peace. When the security we possess within is anchored in the divine mercy alone, the acrimony of the struggles in which we are, and must, be involved become mitigated.

This is not passivity. On the contrary: it is a resolute call to responsible action in which decisiveness is joined with a sensitive awareness of the ideological taint that accompanies all our actions. The Christian revelation unmasks all ideological corruption—both the corruption of the "ideology of interest" and the "ideology of conscience." This distinction Niebuhr defines succinctly: "The one is meant to hide particular sins of particular groups. The other is meant to hide the moral precariousness of all human striving."[25] It is particularly the latter which the Christian revelation illuminates. But the recognition of the ambiguity inhering in all human virtue, far from dissipating the motivation to social action, is instead the precondition of action that is in conformity with the realities of existence as illuminated by the Christian Gospel.

## 2. TOLERANCE

The question of tolerance has its own way of going to the roots of religious faith, of what is claimed by it and how the truth of faith is understood and apprehended. The meaning of tolerance is, however, so intimately correlated with humility, that our discussion can be brief and pointed.

The manner in which we view the issue of tolerance will depend upon how firmly and vitally we grasp the altogether fundamental paradox of grace as this is applied to the question of truth. Niebuhr expressed it in this fashion: "The truth, as it is contained in the Christian revelation, includes the recognition that it is neither possible for man to know the truth fully nor to avoid the error of pretending that he does. It is recognized that 'grace' always remains in partial contradiction to 'nature,' and is not merely its fulfillment." [26] The acceptance of the "truth of faith" is the acceptance of a truth *over* us and not just *in* us. And we will the more certainly possess it when we acknowledge that it cannot be possessed. The very nature of the truth affirmed by the Christian believer forbids its being simply identified with our apprehension or expression of it. The paradox of grace related to truth is this: we can affirm this truth properly only when we do not claim it as *our* possession.

The test as to how well this paradox has been comprehended is found in the issue of toleration. It is a twofold test including "both the ability to hold vital convictions which lead to action; and also the capacity to preserve the spirit of forgiveness towards those who offend us by holding to convictions which seem untrue to us." [27] Here lies the root of the Protestant criticism of Roman Catholicism. The latter destroys the paradox of grace by pretend-

ing "to have as a simple possession, what cannot be so possessed." [28]
The Christ becomes identified with "my Christ." The Reformation
understanding of "justification by faith" pierced through this, but
the Reformation itself failed to apply this understanding to the
realm of truth. This failure necessitated the revolt of sectarian and
secular movements in their recognition of the fragmentary character of our apprehensions of truth and their appreciation of the
futility of attempting to maintain truth by coercion. Modern culture thus was enabled to meet one test of toleration—the capacity
to entertain diverse views without rancor. However the individualism and subjectivism informing so much of this achievement un-
dermined the capacity of the "Renaissance heritage" to meet the
other test, the capacity to affirm and act upon its deepest convictions, with comparable success. This resulted in the enervation of
modern culture which has issued in its contemporary oscillation
between skepticism and the embracing of new fanaticisms.

Thus the problem is nicely posed. "Loyalty to the truth requires
confidence in the possibility of its attainment; toleration of others
requires broken confidence in the finality of our own truth. But if
there is no answer for a problem to which we do not have the answer, our shattered confidence generates either defeat (which
in the field of culture would be scepticism); or an even greater
measure of pretension, meant to hide our perplexities behind our
certainties (which in the field of culture is fanaticism)." [29]

It is to be stressed that the problem for the Christian is not completely set by saying that it is a problem of how to combine deep
conviction with toleration of opposing views. The reason for this
lies in the nature of the truth he affirms. The truth he affirms is
not just a truth for him which will die with him. It is true for him
because it is true for all men. The Lordship of Christ remains
whether I witness to it or not. In that respect it is an objective truth.
The Christian affirmation is an affirmation about the nature of
things and it is an exclusive affirmation. It is that Jesus Christ is
Lord and that no one comes to the Father but by Him. But this is
not an objectively verifiable truth. Our certainty of the truth of

the Lordship of Christ issues only from an existential appropriation of this truth.

The objective and exclusive nature of the Christian affirmation poses the problem of toleration. The Christian must not allow the truth to which he testifies to be obscured in the name of love. At the same time the nature of the truth affirmed and the mode of its apprehension give rise to a profound toleration. How is this so? Because the Lordship of Christ is the Lordship of the crucified and our affirmation is an affirmation of faith which is itself a gift of grace. Here is the basis of Christian tolerance. The Christ we affirm as Lord is the same Christ who died *for* those who rejected Him; we who confess His Name must learn to bear and suffer, in His Name, for those who deny His Name, and thus speak the truth in love. Moreover the very faith by which we make our affirmation is itself a gift of grace. Such faith is not at our disposal, it is not a simple possession of our own. Our task is not to do what we cannot do—coerce faith, give faith, or seek to have others create faith—but to do what we can, and must do, and that is by thought, word and deed point to the Giver of all grace.

The tension between truth and love must ever remain in the life and witness of the Christian. The truth to which he testifies concerns the salvation and destiny of man; it must not be obscured. But the truth he proclaims is the truth of divine love, of Him who died for the untruthful. Thus does the "truth remain subject to the paradox of grace."[30] It is most surely ours when we do not claim it as our own, when we recognize the broken character of our apprehension of it, and know that it can be truth *in* us just insofar as we acknowledge it to be truth *over* us. "In any profound Christianity the spirit of tolerance must be derived from the knowledge that, however necessary it may be to judge one another and even to fight one another . . . we are all sinners who stand under God's ultimate judgment."[31] The motivation to contend vigorously for the truth and the spirit of toleration as we so contend, have ultimately the same root. From such faith we might derive the resource to overcome the two besetting temptations of our day: to become sentimental in the name of tolerance and to become fanatical in the name of faith.

## 3. IRONY

Continuous reflection on the manner in which the Christian revelation illumines the historical scene, unmasks the ideologies of both interest and conscience, and throws into clear light the ambiguity of all virtue has led Niebuhr to the increasing clarification and use of the category of irony for the interpretation of social experience. The concept of irony is, for Niebuhr, intimately intertwined with all that has been said about the meaning of humility. Indeed just as the spirit of tolerance is one of the cultural expressions of the humility engendered by the encounter of faith, so irony is its principal interpretative expression. As such, one of the distinctive resources that the Christian faith brings to the social enterprise is its understanding of the ironic aspects of historical existence.

Niebuhr clarifies his understanding of the ironic by distinguishing it from both the tragic and the pathetic. The tragic arises from the fact that good and evil are so intertwined that it becomes necessary to do evil in order to accomplish good. Destruction is a necessary consequence of human creativity. The tragic hero must break the moral law in order to assert his own integrity. Thus a tragic choice is purest when it is deliberate.[32] The ironic arises not from the evil inherent in the gift of freedom but from the corruption of that gift, with the result that ironic situations are not usually the consequence of deliberate choice. Irony must also be distinguished from the pathetic. Pathos, Niebuhr understands to be constituted "of essentially meaningless cross-purposes in life, of capricious confusions of fortune and painful frustrations."[33] The characters of Thomas Hardy generally fit this category. The distinctions which Niebuhr makes between these three elements may now be summarily stated: "An ironic situation is distinguished from a pathetic one by the fact that a person involved in it bears some responsibility for it. It is distinguished from a tragic one by the fact that the responsibility is not due to a conscious choice but to an unconscious weakness."[34] Irony then, "consists of apparently fortuitous incongruities in life which are discovered upon closer examination, to be not merely fortuitous. . . . If virtue becomes vice through some hidden defect in the virtue; if strength becomes weakness because of the vanity to which strength may prompt the mighty man or nation; if security is transmuted into insecurity because too much reliance is placed upon it; if wisdom becomes folly because it does not know its own limits—in all such cases the situation is ironic."[35]

Such a definition makes clear the degree to which this has been the operative concept in so much of Niebuhr's analysis and interpretation of contemporary history. It will be sufficient here to indicate briefly the pertinence of the concept for the understanding of the American scene and as an instrument for self-criticism.

Contemporary history offers many ironic refutations of American hopes and illusions and the situation is made doubly ironic by the fact that "the experience which furnishes the refutations is occasioned by conflict with a foe who has transmuted ideals and hopes, which we most deeply cherish, into cruel realities which we most fervently abhor."[36]

Communist Russia is, by definition, an innocent nation. It has abolished the root of evil, the institution of private property. But next to Russia, America according to its traditional theory, is "the most innocent nation on earth." "Whether our nation interprets its spiritual heritage through Massachusetts or Virginia, we came into existence with the sense of being a 'separated' nation, which God was using to make a new beginning for mankind."[37] America had turned its back on the vices, corruption, and kingcraft of Europe and made a fresh beginning. This concept was nurtured through the opulence of the American continent and the years of isolation. The ironic climax is that America now is the custodian of weapons of ultimate destruction which she must not disavow using because of the evils derived from the pretensions to innocency in her foe. Thus the "innocent" and comparatively righteous America is placed in a position of historical responsibility from which there is no escape from guilt, and the heritage of innocence ill equips her for dealing with the realities of power involved in such a position. Nevertheless, a full awareness of the ironic character of the total situation will assist America to "slough off many illusions which were derived both from the experiences and the ideologies of its childhood. Otherwise either we will seek escape from responsibilities which involve unavoidable guilt, or we will be plunged into avoidable guilt by too great confidence in our virtue."[38]

The Communist elite makes the pretension that it has made "the leap from the realm of necessity to the realm of freedom" and thus imagines itself the master of historical destiny. Once again the irony of the situation exists in the fact that America, which must lead the opposition to the tyrannical results of such pretensions, represents the culmination of a liberal culture which shared (happily in only a vague sort of way) in the same illusions about the managing of history. The relation between power and the mastery of history has further ironic elements. America now possesses power far greater than she ever dreamed or even sought. The ironical element in this "lies in the fact that a strong America is less completely master of its own destiny than was a comparatively weak America, rocking in the cradle of its continental security and serene in its infant innocence."[39]

America is a relatively "virtuous" nation, but she is not so virtuous as she thinks, and her tendency to make a simple correlation between her virtue and her power makes her insufferable to her allies and hinders her from dealing as creatively with political situations as she might. America is a very powerful nation but a complacent security in her power leads her to overlook the limitations inherent in all power in the managing of history, and thus further compounds the weakness that attends great power. Thus virtue turns ironically into vice, and power into weakness, when pretension stretches them beyond their limits. "Israel is un-

doubtedly a 'good' nation as compared with the great nations sur-
rounding it. But the pretensions of virtue are as offensive to God
as the pretensions of power. One has the uneasy feeling that
America as both a powerful nation and as a 'virtuous' one is involved in ironic perils which compound the experiences of Baby-
lon and Israel."[40]

America has, however, been wiser in her practice than she has
been in her creed. But this too has been due to "the ironic triumph
of the wisdom of common sense over the foolishness of its wise
men."[41] The modern world has witnessed a continuous debate
between bourgeois and Marxist ideologies. The "wisdom of democracy itself" has prevented either strategy from being carried
through to its logical conclusion. The ironic feature in American
history "consists of the fact that we have achieved a tolerable
synthesis between two conflicting ideologies in practice while we
allowed the one to dominate our theory."[42]

The important point for us to note is the manner in which the
insight of an ironic interpretation calls for a complete reorientation
of the spiritual context and criticism of our political thought. The
manner in which this is integral to the entire structure of his thought
will be immediately apparent in the following passage.

> Our moral perils are not those of conscious malice or the explicit
> lust for power. They are the perils which can be understood only if
> we realize the ironic tendency of virtues to turn into vices when too
> complacently relied upon; and of power to become vexatious if the
> wisdom which directs it is trusted too confidently. The ironic ele-
> ments in American history can be overcome, in short, only if Ameri-
> can idealism comes to terms with the limits of all human striving,
> the fragmentariness of all human wisdom, the precariousness of all
> historic configurations of power, and the mixture of good and evil
> in all human virtue.[43]

If it be granted that this describes the need of America, it must
further be acknowledged that the whole focus of Niebuhr's thought
and apologetic has been to make available the resources of Christian faith which are peculiarly fitted to meet this need. "Con-

sciousness of an ironic situation tends to dissolve it." [44] But the source of such awareness of our own pretensions to wisdom, virtue, and power which help to fashion the ironic incongruity, can be no other than the sense of an ultimate judgment upon such pretension. That judgment can be mediated only by a profound faith in the God before whom "the nations are as a drop in the bucket and are counted as small dust in the balances." Thus the spirit of humility not only mitigates the fury of the struggle in which we must engage, it also provides the context for the perception of the ironic incongruities which hinder the most fruitful prosecution of the struggle.

It is, to be sure, an extremely difficult achievement for an active participant in a momentous struggle to gain that measure of detachment and transcendence over the conflict to yield the spirit here described. And yet the greatest model of this spirit was just such a participant—Abraham Lincoln. It is interesting to note that in the first issue of *Christianity and Crisis,* as he sought to give articulation to his position which transcended the alternatives of irresolution and fanaticism, Niebuhr turned to Lincoln. In Lincoln resolute action against evil was joined with that awareness of the purposes of God which contradicted the pretensions within the "righteous" cause. Lincoln's sense of the over-arching providence of God in no way diminished the resolute nature of his action, but it tempered the spirit in which he engaged in the struggle, and was the source of his charity throughout its course, and at its end.

## 4. THE ETHICS OF JUSTIFICATION BY GRACE: THE NONCHALANCE OF FAITH

We have been emphasizing that Niebuhr's theology and ethics are thoroughly integral and that the whole task of his apologetic has been to elaborate the insights of Reformation understanding, more dialectically than the Reformation succeeded in doing. It is clear that both in terms of concepts and the dynamics of motivation, his ethic is an ethic of Justification by Grace through Faith. The whole range of his social thought is focused in this cardinal doctrine of the Reformation. He has stated the social meaning of this doctrine precisely: "Justification by faith in the realm of justice means that we will not regard the pressures and counter pressures, the tensions, the overt and the covert conflicts by which justice is achieved and maintained, as normative in the absolute sense; but neither will we ease our conscience by seeking to escape from involvement in them. We will know that we cannot purge ourselves of the sin and guilt in which we are involved by the moral ambiguities of politics without also disavowing responsibility for the creative possibilities of justice."[45]

From here is derived the spirit with which the man of biblical faith engages in the social task, and which Niebuhr has frequently, in recent years, described as the "nonchalance of faith." One may question whether the word nonchalance is rich enough to bear his meaning, but be that as it may, it indicates that "measure of serenity" and "spiritual relaxation without which all moral striving generates a stinking sweat of self-righteousness and an alternation of fanatic illusions and fretful disillusionments."[46] Again let it be said, this is no easy or cynical passivity. It is no escape from history. On the contrary it "gives us a fulcrum from which we can operate in history. It gives us a faith by which we can seek to fulfill our tasks without illusions and without despair."[47] Such a spirit is derived from the ultimate dimension of the Cross, the divine forgiveness which takes upon itself the evil in our good. It is also derived from confidence in the gracious providence of God. Rightly interpreted, faith in divine providence does not mean any escape from our responsibilities. Quite the contrary: "It represents the only possibility of performing our duty without the alternate distractions of illusion and despair. We cannot, from the standpoint of our faith, either promise a bright tomorrow or threaten mankind with the possibility of ultimate disaster. History is today, as it has always been, filled with hours of decision in which we can relate ourselves to its promises or contribute to its disasters. It is therefore more important to seek to do our duty in watchfulness and soberness than to speculate overmuch about the perils which lie before us."[48]

Frequently an index into the focal points of an apologist's thought can be gained from observing his favorite biblical texts. Those receiving most prominent use by Niebuhr during the period of the cold war all illustrate the theme of the nonchalance of faith. The following are used repeatedly: "Whether we live, we live unto the Lord; whether we die, we die unto the Lord; whether we live therefore, or die, we are the Lord's" (Romans; 14:8). "If in this life only we have hope in Christ we are of all men most miserable" (I Cor. 15:19). And perhaps above all the Pauline injunction, "Therefore let us not sleep, as do others; but let us watch and be sober. For they that sleep, sleep in the night; and they that be drunken are drunken in the night" (I Thess. 5:6–7). Only the resources of a faith which does not have its final ground in the historical can provide a spirit capable of dealing with the perilous issues of contemporary history. "Sleep is a symbol of complacency and drunkenness is a symbol of hysteria. If we avoid both complacency and hysteria and seek, as a nation, to cultivate the habits of watchfulness and soberness, we still have an excellent chance of averting world conflict and of laying the foundations of a stable world community."[49] This troubled world is still God's world. Therefore we must labor for freedom, justice, and peace, but the fruit of our efforts is in His hands. Our work is done in the knowledge that God reigns. Thus freed from both idolatrous expectations and despair we can do our work, even in hopeless situations, as men whose hope is indestructible. This is the "nonchalance of faith."

## 5. THE CHURCH

Consideration of the resources of faith for witness in the social order necessarily involves a discussion of the nature and mission

of the Church. What is the significance of the Church as a redeemed and redeeming community for the collective life? It must
be acknowledged that discerning and sympathetic critics seem to
agree that the most obvious and serious defect in Niebuhr's apologetic lies right at this point, in an inadequate understanding of the
Church or, what is intimately related, in his defective doctrine of
the Holy Spirit.

Since this criticism is so pertinent to our present discussion, it
will be instructive for us to sample it. W.J. Wolf remarks that the
Church is the "undeveloped area" in his thought which constitutes
"a critical omission in Niebuhr's social picture of redemption."[50]
Paul Scherer also regrets that the doctrines of the Holy Spirit and
the Church receive "little attention" in Niebuhr's sermons.[51] The
doctrine of the Holy Spirit still awaits "the full creative attention of
the Church," Paul Lehmann remarks; and although, as he continues, Niebuhr's Christology "has already drawn suggestive boundaries and broken fertile ground," nevertheless he feels that the
doctrine of the Spirit is the major defect in Niebuhr's Christology.[52]
The same complaint is voiced by Hans Hofmann who goes on to
add, "Also does not much more need to be said and said more
definitively about the church? Certainly a much fuller criticism of
the church is needed."[53] The only serious criticism registered by
Davies is at this point of the Church. He feels that Niebuhr's apparent lack of concern for the issues of ecclesiology "has resulted
in the neglect of a fundamentally significant field of theology."[54]

All of these critics have been immensely influenced by Niebuhr,
and all of them are profoundly grateful to him for all that he has
meant to them for thought and life. The unanimity with which
they voice this criticism is in itself compelling. Before attempting
to weigh their judgment, however, we ought to hear what Niebuhr
himself has had to say concerning the Church, for although the
Church may be an "undeveloped area" of his thinking, it has not
been completely omitted.

The Church for Niebuhr is first of all people—the people of God.
The concept of the Church as a community of grace dominates all

considerations of structure, form, and order. The Church is that community of believers which lives in the light of the fact that our history is set in that "interim" between the disclosure of the meaning of history and the fulfillment of that meaning. It is that community which lives its life by the meaning and the power of God's redemptive act in Jesus Christ and, thus rooted and grounded, looks with confident hope to the mercy and power of God to fulfill the gift by which she lives. The Church is a community of believers, and as such, it is an eschatological community. The eschatological dimension is emphasized in all Niebuhr's descriptions of the Church. Without this dimension it is in danger of becoming Anti-Christ by resting on something which it possesses in itself, and thus bringing the meaning of life to another premature conclusion. The Church is a community that lives by faith and hope.

> The Christian church is a community of hopeful believers, who are not afraid of life or death, of present or future history, being persuaded that the whole of life and all historical vicissitudes stand under the sovereignty of a holy, yet merciful, God whose will was supremely revealed in Christ. It is a community which does not fear the final judgment, not because it is composed of sinless saints but because it is a community of forgiven sinners, who know that judgment is merciful if it is not evaded.[55]

The doctrine of justification by grace through faith has as much meaning and relevance for the life of the Church as it has for the individual believer. Herein the Church finds its true and only security. The security of the Church does not lie in any of its own historical configurations in which the grace of God is always mixed with the pretensions of man. "The secure church," he writes, "is precisely that community of saints, known and unknown, among whom life is constantly transformed because it is always under the divine word."[56] As such the Church is the place where the Kingdom of God is always impinging upon man's history. The Church is not that kingdom but it lives from, and for, that kingdom. Because of this it can never be "at home" in any culture or nation. Its task is ever anew to find the right way to be "in" but not "of" this world. The Church is an eschatological community and the more surely it knows that "God gave the church its gospel and the Holy Spirit keeps faith alive in it," [57] the more relevant will be its message and life to the world in which it is set.

As Christ is the foundation of the Church, and the content of her hope, so a living relationship with Him, in which the gifts of grace are appropriated, is the sole source of her renewal. It is this concern for the renewal of the total life and witness of the Church that determines most of Niebuhr's writing on the Church. His plea, in a word, is for reality—reality in her preaching, worship, and common life. The Church is called to make manifest by word, deed, and common life the reality of God's reconciling grace which brought her into being and through the power of which she has her life. But to respond to such a call, demands a total reformation of the Church in theology, liturgy, preaching, and social practice. Only such a profound and comprehensive renewal can enable us to overcome "the appalling corruption of sentimentality and banality in our American Protestantism which expresses itself in such varied ways as worship services in which the minister engages in chatty intercourse with the Almighty, in sermons which spin ideal possibilities of a warless world without ever coming to grips with the sins of the human heart, in social meetings which never rise above the spirit of Rotarianism and in church conferences which hold the candle light of the obvious to the daylight of common experience." [58] That is a strong indictment but it is not true that Niebuhr only deplores the sentimental morass into which contemporary American Protestantism has been sinking. The positive character and direction of his call to renewal of the common life of the Church may be indicated by calling attention to something of what he has said concerning worship.

A profound cleavage runs through the liturgical heritage of American Protestantism, producing a most disturbing situation over which, unfortunately, few American theologians appear to be giving much concern. American Protestantism has stemmed very largely from the sectarian heritage which protested against all established forms of the Church, liturgical and governmental. This anti-historical bias was powerfully reinforced by the frontier history of American Christianity in which the cultural concepts of "new beginnings" blended with sectarian notions of repristination of the forms and life of the New Testament Church. The religious spontaneity marking this heritage, which spurns "devotion's every grace except the heart," had its depth, and even its meaningful form, in the lonely farmhouse. But confronted with the dynamics of our contemporary culture this "religious spontaneity without adequate forms degenerates into something even more graceless than a graceless formalism. It degenerates into a void which is filled by the potent symbols of a cinema secularism." [59] The problem is only worse confounded when, as has been so frequently the case in recent years, the situation is not seen as a profound theological issue and attempts to solve it take the form of "prettying up" the service by rearranging the furniture and introducing a full quota of choral responses.

The liturgical churches which know full well that the religious community can be nurtured only through fully developed forms of prayer and praise are of little help to the other churches in overcoming the emptiness and banality of their liturgical chaos. The reason for this is, as Niebuhr says, that the former "are usually touched by idolatrous conceptions of both the church and its order, regarding them not as means of grace but as necessities of salvation." [60]

We must begin by asking ourselves some fundamental questions, directly and simply. What is it that we are doing when we meet as a Church for divine worship? Why do we do what we do when and where and how we do it? Simply to put the question that way forces us again to wrestle with the meaning of the revelation of God in Christ and the nature of the community founded upon that revelation. That means liturgical concern and reform.

It cannot be said that Niebuhr has made any particular contribution to this task. What he has done has been to throw us hard upon the basic questions by his "symptomatic" criticisms of American

Protestant worship. In one particular article he enumerates and discusses eight major deficiencies of the worship of "non-liturgical" churches. (1) "The pastoral prayer is too long and too formless." (2) "Without the discipline of traditional and historic prayers there is a tendency to neglect some of the necessary and perennial themes of prayer." (3) "The language of the prayers . . . is either too common, too sentimental or too extravagant." What is lacking is "chastity." (4) A closer relation to biblical truth is needed both to purify the expression and correct the thought of the prayers. (5) The worship service "centers too frequently in the personality of the leader of worship." (6) The reading of the Scripture leaves much to be desired both in the manner in which it is usually read and the lack of any systematic selection. (7) "The participation of the congregation . . . is too minimal." (8) "Choir music in the non-liturgical churches and in some liturgical ones is still affected by the sentimentality which began to corrupt religious music in the latter part of the last century." [61]

This is, to be sure, anything but an exhaustive list, and itself proceeds from no evident systematic approach. But it does serve to make us face the basic questions and to open us to the wealth of our liturgical heritage on which we have, to our impoverishment, turned our backs. If the Church is to experience the renewal we so desperately need and desire, it is necessary that the entire liturgy of the Church "become thoroughly informed by the whole Biblical faith and by the spirit and form of the traditional disciplines." [62] It is only as we seek renewal of the churches, in this as in other respects, in the depths of the faith wherein the "traditions of men" can be separated from the "truth of the gospel" that we will find the basis of both Christian unity and a redemptive witness of the Gospel to a despairing world. [63]

As a prophet concerned with the prophetic and apologetic task of the Church, we would expect that preaching would assume a central place in Niebuhr's view of the Church. This is true but it need not detain us here because our whole inquiry has to do with the message the Church exists to proclaim, and also because

Niebuhr's own preaching has received such a splendid analysis from Paul Scherer.[64] It will be sufficient to remind ourselves of the spirit in which the Church's message of God's work of judgment, forgiveness, and reconciliation must be proclaimed. The Church is a *koinonia*, participating in the gifts of the Gospel, because it has faced the judgment of God and heard through and beyond His judgment the deeper word of mercy. The Church is that place in history where the full depth of sin is known because it is seen in the light of the Cross where the divine mercy which is stronger than our sin and our death is known, appropriated, and again betrayed. This is what determines the spirit in which the message is proclaimed.

> If we preach repentance, it must be repentance for those who accept the Lord as well as for those who pretend to deny Him. If we preach the judgment of God upon a sinful world, it must be judgment upon us as well as upon those who do not acknowledge His judgments. If we preach the mercy of God, it must be with a humble recognition that we are in need of it as much as those who do not know God's mercy in Christ. If we preach the obligation of the love commandment, the preacher must know that he violates that commandment as well as those who do not consciously accept its obligation.[65]

Only in such knowledge and spirit can the Gospel of redemption be savingly proclaimed.

At no point is American Protestantism more confused or in need of renewal than in its understanding of the sacraments. Niebuhr has not written a great deal on this subject, and yet at no point does his view of the Church as the eschatological community within and subject to the limitations and corruptions of history become more clearly articulated. "A community of grace, which lives by faith and hope, must be sacramental. It must have sacraments to symbolize the having and not having of the final virtue and truth. It must have sacraments to express its participation in the *Agape* of Christ and yet not pretend that it has achieved that

love."[66] The sacrament perfectly expresses the fundamental paradox of grace, the historical and eschatological dimensions of faith.
God is active in and through His Church. He is present in judgment, forgiveness, and redemption. He is able to enter our history,
no matter how tragic, in order to redeem its meaning. But nothing
historical can capture or contain Him. He is a free and sovereign
Lord. We possess the grace of Christ only insofar as we do not
make it a simple possession, but rather with gratitude and expectation await His new command. He who in the past has met us in
mercy is always He who comes. Indeed it is just insofar as we open
ourselves to Him who meets us out of the future that our past is a
true history instead of a dead fate. Failure to give the eschatological dimension of grace its due place exposes the Church to the
idolatrous pretension of claiming to possess what cannot be simply
possessed. Thus Niebuhr remarks the "identification of Christ
with the 'Sacred Host' on the altar is the perfect fruit of the
Catholic error."[67] The symbol, to use Tillich's words, does not
enclose but participates in the reality to which it points. Moreover,
the sacrament of the Lord's Supper, which is the point at which
the divisions of Christendom become most painfully visible, can
become the symbol of unity only if the eschatological dimension of
this sacrament is seriously considered. Niebuhr is most explicit
about this:

> It may be observed that this sacrament can never become the
> effective symbol of the unity of the church if its original eschatologi-
> cal motif does not receive new emphasis. ("For as often as we eat
> this bread and drink this cup, ye do show forth the Lord's death,
> *till he come.*" (I Cor.11:26.) This eschatological emphasis in the
> sacrament is a true expression of the eschatological character of the
> church. It does not have the unity in fact which it desires in prin-
> ciple. The divisions of history and the chasms of nature and sin
> leave their mark upon it. It cannot overcome them completely in
> fact; but it would overcome them more completely than it does if
> it would recognize its inability to overcome them more contritely.
> It would thus live in memory ("This do in remembrance of me")
> and in hope ("till he come"). Such memory and such hope would
> not leave the present unaffected. The church could have the more

of grace, if it admitted that the truth was subject to the paradox of having and not having.[68]

One comment here is perhaps in order: Niebuhr's view of the sacrament is thoroughly integrated with his understanding of the nature and mission of the Church and indeed the total structure of his thought. His thinking here has not gained the elaboration which we desire, or even perhaps feel to be necessary, but it cannot be said that the nature of the Church, her proclamation of the Word, her sacraments, and her liturgy have been beyond the horizon of his concerns.

Nor has the difficult pastoral and ecclesiastical problem of Church discipline escaped his attention. But in characteristic fashion, Niebuhr discusses this question in a wider social context than is customarily the case. The question may be posed this way: What is the significance for the individual churchman of a consensus on social issues and philosophy arrived at in the churches through their responsible organs? It cannot of course be rigidly binding. But that is not the problem facing contemporary Protestantism. The problem is one of taking such a consensus with any seriousness at all. The occasion which prompted Niebuhr to raise this issue was the wide publicity given to a chapter of John T. Flynn's *The Road Ahead* with its undiscriminating attack upon the Federal Council of Churches and many of its leaders. The social position attacked was one in which a real consensus appeared to have been reached not only in the Federal Council but also in the World Council of Churches and many Catholic encyclicals since *Rerum Novarum*. Niebuhr puts the issue before us this way:

> On the whole, Christian laymen and pastors have a proper regard for the moral and spiritual authority of the church, though the church cannot bind the conscience of individuals in economic and political decisions. But the Flynn book has revealed one of the great weaknesses of Protestantism. There are members of Protestant churches, both lay and clerical, who treat the consensus in the church with complete disrespect upon the prompting of a second-rate and hysterical critic. They seem to have no understanding that

when the church regards all social and political institutions as standing under divine judgment this conviction is no vagary, but a consequence of having its mind renewed by the mind of Christ.[69]

The point here does not at all concern the question of the machinery of ecclesiastical discipline. The whole concern is with the inner renewal of the life and witness of the Church. A great amount of penetrating study has been done in recent years by commissions of the churches. If we are to experience an effective renewal in our social understanding, witness, and practice, this work must be appropriated and extended in a manner not yet envisaged by many of our churches. This will in turn demand from us a renewal of our churchmanship, and the concern and critical respect for the consensus of the Church that is the mark of responsible churchmanship. This concern goes right to the heart of the question of the resources of faith for a responsible society.

We began this section of our discussion by noting the amount of criticism directed at Niebuhr for his defective view of the Church. How are we to evaluate this criticism? The charge that he has no doctrine of the Church, or that the Church receives no attention in his consideration of the reality of God's redemptive activity, may be simply dismissed. It must be said, however, that his analysis would be strengthened by an elaboration of his own view of the nature and mission of the Church. His understanding of the Church is integral with the totality of his thought, but it needs to be bodied out and more explicitly related to his Christology. The doctrine of the Church is rightly securing much more attention in our own day. But a peril attends this right and necessary task. The peril is that undue concentration upon the doctrine of the Church may tempt us to obscure the ambiguity of the Church's life. Perhaps behind Niebuhr's reticence to say more than he has in this connection is a recognition of this. This is the burden of his reply to W. J. Wolf.

> The Church is the one place in history where life is kept open for the final word of God's judgment to break the pride of men and for the word of God's mercy to lift up the brokenhearted. Inasmuch as

this has been only a growing recognition, Professor Wolf's criticism is justified. But when I see how much new evil comes into life through the pretension of the religious community, through its conventional and graceless legalism and through religious fanaticism, I am concerned that my growing appreciation of the Church should not betray me into this complacency.[70]

Our concern in this chapter has been to lift up the resources of biblical faith for the achieving of a responsible society as they appear in Niebuhr's thinking. It is our conviction that this is one of the most fruitful, but also one of the most frequently neglected, dimensions of Niebuhr's thought. He knows and rejoices in the reality of God's redemption and his whole concern is to show wherein this has relevance for the structures of our collective life. But his delineations of the actuality of redemption through such concepts as humility, awareness of the ironic, tolerance, and the nonchalance of faith are so free from the perfectionist illusions that characterize our conventional ideas of the redeemed life that we often fail to discern how firmly he has grasped and interpreted the *operative* wisdom and power of the Cross. Paul Lehmann has remarked that "Niebuhr's ethics had, so to say, correctly pinpointed the ethical target, but it had not satisfactorily explained how to live constructively in the gap between the will of God, theologically understood, and the concrete human situation, pragmatically understood."[71] Lehmann feels that this gap can be filled by taking full measure of the fact that Christian ethics is *koinonia* ethics. "In the *koinonia* one learns to understand and to talk about the will of God as one sees it in action. A *koinonia* ethic, therefore, defines the will of God as forgiveness and justice and reconciliation, rather than as love. This does not mean that the will of God is something else than love. It means, on the contrary, that the concrete reality of love in the *koinonia* in the world, is forgiveness and justice and reconciliation."[72] It is difficult to see wherein this adds anything in the way of operative wisdom and power to Niebuhr, for this is precisely what Niebuhr means by *agape* in action in the world.[73]

The Christian lives under the grace as well as the demand of *agape*. In his struggle to secure justice, which Lehmann, along with Niebuhr, rightly says "belongs with forgiveness and reconciliation," the Christian can draw not only on the wisdom concerning the self and human history contained in the revelation of the Cross, but also, when this wisdom is livingly appropriated, upon a power and a resource of faith and hope and love which guide, sustain, and temper his endeavors. Nowhere has Niebuhr expressed this more memorably than in the following paragraph:

> Nothing that is worth doing can be achieved in our lifetime; therefore we must be saved by hope. Nothing which is true or beautiful or good makes complete sense in any immediate context of history; therefore we must be saved by faith. Nothing we do, however virtuous, can be accomplished alone; therefore we are saved by love. No virtuous act is quite as virtuous from the standpoint of our friend or foe as it is from our standpoint. Therefore we must be saved by the final form of love which is forgiveness.[74]

PART TWO

# Six

# POLITICS

If the resources of insight and spirit of the Christian faith are to be brought to bear upon the issues of our time, then there must also be a wise and perceptive engagement with the actual political realities of our world. Politics has thus been the very center of Niebuhr's thought and work, his daily meat and drink. His unique authority is derived from the penetrating insight into the modern situation given him by the Christian understanding of man in history, and the pragmatic flexibility of one who knows and daily engages the intricacies of concrete political situations. The increasing, and already quite remarkable, extent of his influence can be seen by a reading of leading political thinkers.

Our attempt in this Second Part will be to present and discuss Niebuhr's thought and judgments on a number of major political and social issues and events of our time. The nature of the issues and the character of his thought are such that our total discussion could with some propriety be brought under the heading of Politics. However, in order to facilitate a broader and more detailed inquiry it seems advisable to break the discussion into four major areas—Politics, War and Peace, Economics, and Race. In this way we can with some detail and thoroughness show just what Niebuhr's judgments and positions have been on a variety of occasions and issues, and thus more completely delineate the character of his thought and the structure of his theological ethic.

The scope and character of Niebuhr's political philosophy can be clearly discerned by seeing his views upon four major areas—democracy, communism, political realism, and American foreign policy. To a discussion of these we now turn.

## 1. DEMOCRACY

Niebuhr has written an immense amount about the presuppositions, philosophy, aims, and functioning of an open or democratic society. The bulk of it has been directed at three levels of democracy—its necessity, its task, and its structure. For these three levels or dimensions of democratic life, Niebuhr has also given us three memorable epigrams. Both the possibility of and the necessity for democracy are rooted in the nature of man: "Man's capacity for justice makes democracy possible; but man's inclination to injustice makes democracy necessary."[1] Its task is never ending: "For democracy is a method of finding proximate solutions for insoluble problems."[2] Both the necessity and the task shape the structure: "It is the highest achievement of democratic societies that they embody the principle of resistance to government within the principle of government itself."[3] The burden of Niebuhr's political thought and activity has been directed to the providing of an adequate philosophy, the analyzing of the cultural preconditions, and the maintaining and perfecting of a functioning structure for an open and responsible society.

Being a Christian theologian, Niebuhr is a normative thinker. This provides him with his greatest strength and at the same time sets his most difficult problems. It is, however, from this vantage point that Niebuhr has contributed so powerfully to the recovery of political philosophy in America. By this we mean that Niebuhr has helped many to see that political understanding and inquiry cannot be divorced from a clear understanding of human nature. Or as Kenneth Thompson has remarked, Niebuhr's alternative to the scientific method is political philosophy. "The political philosopher observing the pattern of history is obliged to articulate the basis on which he interprets its meaning. At some point he must make explicit his theory of human nature."[4] Niebuhr's political thought is always held in organic and inseparable relation with his anthropology. We need not discuss that here. The discussion of Part One has dealt with that and is relevant in its entirety. It will be sufficient to remind ourselves once again that when Niebuhr discusses political questions, he has not left off being a theologian; on the contrary the real color and character of his theological thought become clearly displayed in this "worldly" dress.

Man is a creature distinguished by the radical nature of his freedom and the radical self-corruption of that freedom. The possibility of, and the necessity for, democracy are rooted in this complex reality. Man's moral and rational capacities make such a system of government possible and the corruptions of interest and passion make it necessary. The broader and more inclusive the perspectives and loyalties of a community, the better will be the functioning of its democratic life. Nevertheless it is still true that "no matter how wide the perspectives which the human mind may reach, how broad the loyalties which the human imagination may conceive, how universal the community which human statecraft may organize, or how pure the aspirations of the saintliest idealists may be, there is no level of human moral or social achievement in which there is not some corruption of inordinate self-love."[5] Democracy is thus predicated upon the fact that no man is good enough or wise enough to be entrusted with irresponsible power over his fellows. Herein lies the immense social significance of the doctrine of "original sin."

Something of the richness of Niebuhr's work in this matter may be suggested by indicating the character of his thought in three areas: (1) his criticism of the philosophy that has informed the democratic enterprise through much of its history: (2) the necessity for a realistic philosophy to deal with the perennial, but urgently modern, question of individualism and collectivism; and (3) the cultural foundations and conditions for the proper functioning of democracy.

The subject of *The Children of Light and The Children of Darkness* is, as the subtitle succinctly puts it, a vindication of democracy and a critique of its traditional defense. The thesis of this book is "that democracy has a more compelling justification and requires a more realistic vindication than is given it by the liberal culture with which it has been associated in modern history."[6] The optimistic estimates of human nature informing liberal middle-class culture are a real peril to democracy. It is thus imperative that we learn to disassociate the basis of democracy from the prejudices of bourgeois culture and history, and properly ground it in a realistic understanding of human nature. This is imperative because, although bourgeois culture is a transient phenomenon, the necessity for the diffusion of power and the keeping of power within responsible limits is a permanent necessity required by man's freedom and sinfulness.

The philosophy informing the last two centuries of democratic development is inadequate to this task. Having generally rejected the offensive doctrine of "original sin," liberal social philosophy has been largely predicated upon a fatuous view of man. It has consistently "underestimated the power of self-interest, both individual and collective. The children of light have not been as wise as the children of darkness."[7] Its conception of man has been that of "an essentially harmless individual" whose "egotism did not rise beyond the limits of nature's impulse of self-preservation."[8] This serious defect in its view of man was not too dangerous in the heyday of bourgeois youth, but it has almost brought the great democracies to complete disaster in our time. A far more realistic estimate of the depths of collective, as well as individual, egotism must inform their policies if they are to withstand the pressure and competition of a ruthless foe over an indefinite period of time.

The wisdom necessary properly to estimate the power of self-interest in the "children of darkness" will also illumine the depths of this power among ourselves. This too is an absolute necessity, not only for recognizing and dealing with major domestic issues, but also for achieving that self-knowledge prerequisite for any fruitful working with our allies in the contemporary world struggle.

We have already drawn attention to the similarities between bourgeois estimates of man and the Marxist understanding and the ironies produced by this fact.[9] "Marxism expects men to be as tame and social on the other side of the revolution as Adam Smith and Jeremy Bentham thought them to be tame and prudential on this side of the revolution."[10] Neither properly considers either the final dimension of man's spirit, his transcendent freedom over the natural and historical processes in which he is involved, or the radical corruption of that freedom. For this reason communist collectivism and bourgeois individualism have certain marked affinities of thought, however different they have been in practice.

We have already noted [11] the curious similarity between the relationship of determinism and voluntarism, man as creature and creator of history, in *laissez-faire* and communist credos. Here we shall note two other dimensions of the relationship between the individual and the community to which Niebuhr has given a good deal of thought—the difference between individual and group morality and the twofold relation of the individual to any community.

Niebuhr's first great book bore the arresting title *Moral Man and Immoral Society* and made him at once the subject of wide and controversial discussion. Its opening sentence reads: "The thesis to be elaborated in these pages is that a sharp distinction must be drawn between the moral and social behaviour of individuals and of social groups, national, racial, and economic; and that this distinction justifies and necessitates political policies which a purely individualistic ethic must always find embarrassing."[12] The latter half of the sentence points the direction of the polemical interest of the book. The rationalism of much of the American political heritage and the individualism, sentimentalism, and sectarianism of the American religious heritage combine to obscure the necessity for a view of collective man which will properly assess, and use, the realities and instruments of power.

Niebuhr did not say that man is moral and society is immoral, although a number of readers of the book seem to have thought he did. In the second sentence of the Introduction he acknowledges that the title "suggests the intended distinction too unqualifiedly." But it later became necessary, in the debate over the thesis of the book with George A. Coe, to say more explicitly: "I do not regard the individual as moral and society immoral, though I chose that title for my book for pedagogical purposes."[13]

The immense significance of the distinction observed between the behaviour of individuals and groups for Niebuhr's later thought lies in the fact that it enabled him to grasp the basic reality for the elaboration of a philosophy of political realism on the one hand, and for bringing into clearer focus the central problem of his life work, the relationship of *agape* to the task of securing justice in the realities of collective existence. It served to pose sharply the question of the very possibility of a Christian ethic, the use of power for the purposes of love. The distinction between the power, extent, and persistence of egotism in individuals and groups is not absolute but it is real.

To make this rather obvious observation is not, however, to explain it, to disclose its root. It would not be too much to say that if we are to uncover all that he sees to be involved in this distinction the whole of Niebuhr's thought must be brought to bear. The fundamental fact, though, is that the collective does not possess the same developed organs of self-transcendence that the individual does. This in turn means that although it is more long-lived than the individual, it is much more bound to nature than he. This also means that the collective is further removed from the ultimate source of meaning than the individual.[14] The collective and the individual have the same source of meaning; they both stand under the same norm, but the relationship is more indirect for the community. Thus the community never feels the same degree of judgment and contrition that an individual does. It lacks the same degree of self-transcendence, the acute awareness of the source of meaning that breaks down and renews. Again, let it be emphasized, the distinction is not absolute. The whole power and purpose of Niebuhr's work rests on the judgment that the distinction is not absolute. The Christian gospel is relevant to our collective life. But the character of his thought rests on the reality of the distinction. *Agape* becomes relevant through the securing of justice which is dependent upon both the use and the diffusion of power.

The relationship of the individual to the community is the very substance of the tension of modern history. In the modern era, the individual has been emancipated by the progress of technics from the traditional organic ties to the community; on the other hand the community has acquired, through the same technical advances, a cohesion and intensity lacking in previous civilizations. The relation of individual and community thus brings into sharp focus the major problems and perils of our age.

The community is both the fulfillment and the frustration of the individual. Man has his being in relationship. If he is to enter into true selfhood, the individual must be drawn out of himself into wider relationships. No simple limits can be placed upon the extent of community required by the individual self. The community sustains his existence and is necessary for self-fulfillment.

But the community ever remains the frustration of the individual. "It is bound to nature more inexorably than he. It knows nothing of a dimension of the eternal beyond its own existence."[15] The individual's question after ultimate meaning cannot be answered, without perilous self-abasement, by the community. That the community can command the ultimate loyalty and self-sacrificing purpose of the individual is the claim of every totalitarianism. The distinctively human resides in this capacity to transcend all the natural and historical processes upon which he is dependent. The fulfillment he seeks cannot be supplied by the morally ambiguous life of all historical communities. The community remains ever the fulfillment and the frustration of the individual.[16]

Failure to measure the full height of human self-transcendence —and the radical corruption of this freedom—is the basis for the tendency of modern civilization to oscillate between an individualism that makes the individual his own end, and a collectivism which makes the community the end of the individual's life. Individualism and collectivism are opposites indeed, but the point to see is that they are dialectical opposites. The whole history of bourgeois individualism is necessary to explain the emergence of Nazi and Communist collectivism. Both individualism and collectivism are "blind to one of the two dimensions of selfhood."[17] No one has put this more memorably than Martin Buber:

> Individualism understands only a part of man; collectivism understands man only as a part. Neither advances to the wholeness of man, to man as a whole. Individualism sees man only in relation to himself; but collectivism does not see *man* at all, it sees only "society."[18]

Two things must be said to the credo of individualism. The community is as primordial as the individual, it is not simply an instrument of the individual. The person does not have his existence apart from it. The second thing is that an individualism which prates about the "inherent dignity of man" misses the full meaning of man's self-transcendence as surely as it does the social substance of human existence. "The individual is not an end in himself and cannot live within himself. Love is the law of his existence."[19] He finds his true end only in God. Of the credo of collectivism two things must also be said. The person is not a part of something. He is a whole engaged in a *triadic* dialogue. As with the individual, so the community is not its own end. It does not possess within itself the law of life. Love is the norm of its existence also, which it seeks to actualize in structures of justice. Or as Niebuhr has put it: "The problem of the individual and the community cannot be solved at all if the height is not achieved where the sovereign source and end of both individual and communal existence are discerned, and where the limits are set against the idolatrous self-worship of both individuals and communities."[20] This means discernment of *agape* as the only norm for man in his freedom, and the establishment of the conditions of justice for man in his sin. This in turn means that use, diffusion, and control of power which it is the nature and purpose of democracy to provide.

To speak in this manner is to root the democratic enterprise in the Christian understanding of man. However, the cultural foundations and historical forces have obviously been much more complex than this. Democracy has certainly not been the simple outcome of a Christian civilization. It has emerged rather from a context of Christian presuppositions and a secular revolt against the pretensions of Christian institutions. What are the distinctive contributions that have been made by these two forces?

Christianity offers three indispensable insights to democracy. It provides the individual with a source of authority that enables him to defy the authorities of this world. It appreciates, as does no other philosophy, the unique worth of the individual and locates that dignity in the position he holds before God. It recognizes the depth of man's sin as well as his creative powers and thus justifies the checks upon man's power provided by democratic institutions. Christianity also provides, when it is true to itself, that spirit of humility and toleration without which democratic institutions are constantly imperiled.

Christians ought not to claim too much. Great portions of Christianity have contributed very little to the development of democracy. Moreover, the story of religious authoritarianism and fanaticism is such a sorry chapter in the history of Western culture that any claims for the necessity of the insights of biblical faith must begin with a contrite confession of the depths of Christian betrayal of those insights. The Christian faith has been so deeply involved in the religious sanctification of historic structures of injustice, that to a considerable degree the struggle for justice has been borne by "secular" forces.[21]

Both Christianity and secularism have contributed to the development of democratic institutions. In the American heritage one need only note the confluence of ideas stemming from New England Puritanism and Jeffersonian deism. The complexity of this story becomes visible when we estimate how frequently in our history a religiously sanctified absolutism, caught in a betrayal or obscuration of the Christian understanding of man, has been challenged by a humane secularism which just as often was informed by an erroneous estimate of human nature. But it is this mixture of ideas and forces which operated so strongly in the development of democracy, that in turn points to the necessity for the maintenance of an open society. "Sometimes new truth rides into history upon the back of an error." [22] Secular philosophy erroneously estimates human nature, it understands neither the height nor the depth of man, neither his grandeur nor his misery; and when consistently employed it reveals dangerous tendencies toward totalitarianism. But it has been the bearer of important truths, and the fact that both the errors and the truths were used so often to undermine religious absolutism, and that this attack resulted in the obscuration of Christian insight as well as the undermining of ecclesiastical pretension, serve to indicate the complexity of the cultural and intellectual foundations of modern democracy.

To change the terms, this means that Niebuhr decidedly favors a pluralistic society. Democratic institutions are both the consequence and the cause of social pluralism. Such a society is open to many serious dangers. Chaos is a perennial peril of freedom, and the temptation of every social anarchy is to solve its ills by accepting a strong absolutism. But to acknowledge the peril is simply to define the challenge to accept and cultivate the necessary discipline, because "coerced uniformity is more decadent than freedom. Mature cultures must finally face the necessity of achieving communal harmony within the conditions of freedom." [23] The internal perils besetting a society marked by ethnic, religious and economic pluralism are real and permanent. To accept the continuous tension and to learn to deal creatively with the daily problems presented by such a situation, demand our full resources of mind and spirit, but above all that combination of conviction and humility engendered by biblical faith. It is at this point where we see the deepest "point of contact" between Christianity and democracy. [24]

The foregoing discussion of the necessity for democracy and its spiritual and social preconditions clearly points up the nature and limits of the democratic task. It is, as has been said, "a method of finding proximate solutions for insoluble problems." It neither believes in, nor seeks after, the total solution. It is really predicated upon the belief that there are no total solutions to be found in history. The freedom of democracy thus "makes for a fortunate confusion in defining the goal toward which history should move; and the distribution of power in a democracy prevents any group of world savers from grasping after a monopoly of power."[25] Its problem is insoluble and its task is endless, because it seeks to "achieve justice without disturbing the order of the community."[26]

The task is to find the proper relation between order and justice. "The actual situation is," writes Niebuhr, "that the first task of a community is to subdue chaos and create order; but the second task is equally important and must be implicated in the first. That task is to prevent the power by which initial unity is achieved, from becoming tyrannical."[27] Order precedes justice, but only if the order achieved implicates justice can the order remain secure.

Justice is dependent upon the diffusion and balancing of power. This means a measure of conscious contrivance and manipulation. "There must be an organizing center within a given field of social vitalities."[28] This center, the government, is not only the seat of order, it also bears responsibility for the securing of justice. "This center must arbitrate conflicts from a more impartial perspective than is available to any party of a given conflict; it must manage and manipulate the processes of mutual support so that the tensions inherent in them will not erupt into conflict; it must coerce submission to the social process by superior power whenever the instruments of arbitrating and composing conflict do not suffice; and finally it must seek to redress the disproportions of power by conscious shifts of the balances whenever they make for injustice."[29] Order precedes justice but finally justice is of more importance. The securing of justice is a major task of government.

But all history testifies to the moral ambiguity of government. Justice is dependent on the power and will of government to balance the competing vitalities of social life. But what is to prevent government itself from developing its own imperialistic and authoritarian impulses?

Just as the task of democracy is the securing of justice within the framework of order, by a progressive equalization of power, so the check against government is achieved by embodying "the principle of resistance to government within the principle of government itself." In this way the inordinate ambitions of rulers, as well as the perennial temptation of communities to secure order at the price of liberty, is held in restraint. Justice is as dependent upon the responsible control of governmental power as it is upon the power of government to redress the disbalances of power throughout society.

There is no phrase that better sums up the genius and the nature of the democratic structure than "Her Majesty's loyal opposition." The opposition is of equal importance with the government in a democracy. It is far beyond the scope of our concern to make any comparisons between the American system of constitutional democracy and British parliamentary government. They both evidence their peculiar strengths and weaknesses. Niebuhr has frequently revealed a deep appreciation of parliamentary government amounting almost to a decided preference. The necessity for the minority, as well as the majority, to act responsibly is a valuable restraint under which Congress has not always felt itself to be placed. Moreover, the American constitutional system, which does not provide for "responsible government" in the parliamentary sense of the phrase, is dangerously dependent upon the presence of a strong President in times of crisis and war.[30] We need not pursue this further. The American constitutional system is so hallowed that nothing short of catastrophe could induce a significant structural change, and whatever may be its limitations, the constitution—much more than the Declaration of Independence—is rooted in a realistic, and indeed, a biblical estimate of man.

The power of government is derived only in part from the fact that it possesses instruments of coercion. It derives part of its

power from "the reality and the pretension of 'majesty.'"[31] The
acknowledgment of the "majesty" of government, that in some
sense it is an ordinance of God, raises acutely the question of the
Christian attitude toward government. Not a little of the story of
Church History can be subsumed under this head. We can here
neither enter a discussion of the various stands and viewpoints of
Christians in history, nor even into Niebuhr's evaluation of some
of the critical moments in this story.[32] Suffice it to say that here his
thought is, as always, thoroughly integrated with his views of the
self and history. Thus he recognizes the roles of both organism and
artifact in the creation of government, distinguishes between a
reverence for the principle of government and a critical approach
to particular governments, clearly recognizes the reality of majesty
that attends government and the idolatrous pretensions which
particular governments are usually tempted to derive from this
majesty.

> The Bible contains two approaches, which taken together and held
> in balance, do justice to the moral ambiguities of government. Ac-
> cording to the one, government is an ordinance of God and its
> authority reflects the Divine Majesty. According to the other, the
> "rulers" and "judges" of the nations are particularly subject to divine
> judgment and wrath because they oppress the poor and defy the di-
> vine majesty. These two approaches do justice to the two aspects of
> government. It is a principle of order and its power prevents
> anarchy; but its power is not identical with divine power.[33]

We have been discussing Niebuhr's political philosophy as it
is revealed in his thinking on the necessity for, the task and structure of, democracy. Democracy is not an absolute. On the contrary,
it is conceived in the light of the one absolute wherein is revealed
the height of man's freedom, and the corruption of that freedom,
which makes democracy both possible and necessary.

## 2. COMMUNISM

In getting the structure of Niebuhr's political thought before us,
it is instructive to set his understanding of democracy and critique

of its traditional defense, in sharp juxtaposition with his views on communism. This procedure is instructive because, as we shall see, at every crucial point communism stands as the negation of his interpretation of the philosophy and structure of democracy. Niebuhr has written a great deal on the subject of communism—and there have been some changes across the years—but he has gathered up most of his thought in one compact essay entitled *Why is Communism so Evil?* [34] His whole interpretation is clearly disclosed in the answers he gives to this question.

In distinguishing the sources of communist evil, Niebuhr puts down first of all the monopoly of power which it establishes. "Disproportions of power anywhere in the human community are fruitful of injustice, but a system which gives some men absolute power over other men results in evils which are worse than injustice." [35] This is no mere fortuitous corruption of the original Marxist ideal. It is the inevitable development of the concept of the "dictatorship of the proletariat." When society is divided between the powerful and the powerless, it is inevitable that the monopoly of the class becomes the monopoly of the *avant-garde* of the class which is the party, and from the party through an oligarchy to the single tyrant. A second reason for the inevitable development of this power monopoly is the erroneous Marxist theory that "economic power inheres solely in the ownership of property and obscures the power of the manager of property. It therefore wrongly concludes that the socialization of property causes economic power to evaporate when in fact it merely gives a single oligarchy a monopoly of both economic and political power." [36]

The death of Stalin, the "thaw" that many thought they saw in the Geneva summit conference, Khrushchev's amazing revelation of the crimes of the Stalin era in his special report to the Twentieth Congress of the Communist Party, led many hopeful people to think that a significant change had taken place. Niebuhr was not for a moment beguiled by these developments. For whatever may have been the changes, or the modifications of tyranny that had taken place, it was still collectivism, still a monopoly of power that denies the basic preconditions of freedom and justice. This warning was the substance of a number of articles.[37]

The second source of the evil of communism is its utopianism. We have already touched on this in Chapter Four where we noted Niebuhr's distinction between the "soft" utopianism of much of liberal culture, and the "hard" utopianism of communism. We have also noted the basic similarities between bourgeois optimism and communist utopianism in the common belief in history as its own redeemer. Such utopianism springs from the fact that it, in contrast with the premises of democracy, envisages a total solution to the problems of man. Utopia is the god who, for many, has not yet failed. It is rooted in its sentimental reading of man and its construing of the source of evil in something outside man, specifically in the institution of private property. Its evil is that "It provides a moral façade for the most unscrupulous political policy, giving the communist oligarch the moral warrant to suppress and sacrifice immediate values in the historical process for the sake of reaching so ideal a goal."[38] The evil of communism stems from its completely erroneous view of human nature. It is this utopianism which undergirds the self-righteous fury and fanaticism of communism on the one hand, and which makes it so attractive to idealists cut loose from biblical faith on the other.

Niebuhr has frequently drawn the distinction between Communism and Nazism just at this point. The distinction is important if we are properly to gauge the power of the evil against which we contend. Nazism was morally cynical while communism is morally sentimental and utopian. "That they should turn out to be so similar in practice is one of the most instructive aspects of our contemporary situation. It proves that the self-righteous fury of a consistent Marxism may be as dangerous to the establishment of community as the cynicism of a consistent fascism. This similarity in practice, despite differences in principle, can only be understood from the standpoint of a Christian interpretation of life and history; for only from that standpoint is it possible to see how quickly human virtue turns to evil when men forget the sinful corruption in every expression of human interest."[39]

Niebuhr finds the third great source of the evil of communism in the conviction that the proletarian class can, by a "revolutionary" act, change not only history but the entire human situation. Through such a "revolutionary act" man ceases to be both a creator and a creature of history, but becomes simply its creator. We have already discussed this question in considering the self in its dimensions of creature and creator of history. Here we need only stress how this assumption (based, to be sure, on Marxist-Leninist science!) that the party is endowed not only with an understanding of present events but also with the capacity to penetrate the future, reinforces the monopoly of power and intensifies the evil contained therein. "This tendency of playing God to human history is the cause for a great deal of communist malignancy".[40] It is no idle play. The entire assumptions of this creed add up to an unqualified faith in man. No one can understand the driving power of communism without seeing that it is the great substitute religion of our time. It is premised upon an uncritical faith in Man, in his omniscience (he is able to penetrate the future, he knows its "end"), and in his omnipotence (he can, through a "revolutionary act" bring redemption to pass).

The fourth source of communist evil, distinguished by Niebuhr, is the coupling of Marxist dogmatism and pretensions with scientific rationality. "The communist irrationality and dogmatism consists of a rigorous adhesion to dogma in defiance of the facts."[41] But the dogma receives strength through its pretension to being scientific. To be sure, this has not been the case in the researches of the natural scientists, but it has remained consistently true in the areas of social philosophy. Indeed, the fact that scientific and technical advance is not at all incompatible with tyranny is not the least disquieting feature of the contemporary struggle. In any event, the scientific pretension of an inflexible dogma illustrates still another facet of the character of a total faith in Man.

At every point of philosophy and structure, communism stands as the antithesis of democracy. Communism establishes a monop-

oly of power; democracy insists upon a control, a balance, and
diffusion of power. Communism believes in man, in his capacity to
restore himself to his own essential nature. Democracy is predicated upon the sin of man, on the idea that no man or group of
men is good enough to be entrusted with absolute power over his
fellows. Communism believes in a total solution to the human
problem. Democracy eschews the attempt thus to mix absolutes
with relative tasks; it assumes the task of seeking proximate solutions to perennial, communal problems. Communism, seeking a
total solution, pretends to be scientific; democracy is anything but
scientific, it is based upon the conflict of legitimate, limited interests
within the body politic.

To be sure, the democracies face a perennial danger of being
corroded from within. This danger is most acute when we mistake
its nature and task and begin to talk about the "democratic faith."
But its greatest virtue resides in the fact that it provides the kind
of structure whereby it can be recalled to its own authentic roots.
It presupposes human imperfection at every point. Democracy is
an imperfect method for imperfect men to work at the problems
of an imperfect world.

## 3. NIEBUHR'S POLITICAL REALISM

The intimate relationship between Niebuhr's theology and political philosophy is clearly evident in the foregoing. His understanding of the nature of man and history informs his entire approach
to such questions as the philosophy, task, structure, and limits of
government as we have illustrated through his interpretation of
democracy and communism. We must now inquire whether this
intimate relationship remains when we seek to describe more explicitly the character of his political orientation. Neibuhr is generally regarded as a realist in politics. But what is the character of
his political realism and how is this related to the normative
aspects of his thought?

Niebuhr has not done his work as a political philosopher with the result that his definitions of the political task do not always possess the precision that a political philosopher desires and demands. [42] He does not, for example, define and differentiate politics with such precision as does Hans Morgenthau, who speaks of politics as the "pursuit of interest defined in terms of power." The political realism of Niebuhr is, nevertheless, clearly and consistently evident, as also are the ingredients of the term. Realism, for Niebuhr, is a clear recognition of the limits of morality and reason in politics; the acceptance of the fact that political realities are power realities and that power must be countered by power; that self-interest is the primary datum in the actions of all groups and nations.

A few quotations, taken almost at random, will serve to show the rigor and consistency of this disposition to deal with the facts as they present themselves. In 1932 he complained about the unrealistic approach of all kinds of moralists to political problems: "Hardly anywhere, from either academic or ecclesiastical political moralists does one hear a word about the limits of morality in politics." [43] It ought clearly to be recognized that "No nation, or any other group for that matter, will ever sacrifice itself for another." [44] Moralists who put their trust in the persuasive power of appeals to love or reason can never come to grips with the political question because "They do not recognize that when collective power, whether in the form of imperialism or class domination, exploits weakness, it can never be dislodged unless power is raised against it." [45] These moralists, whether religious or rationalist, simply will not come to grips with the reality and the power of self-interest in all group relations. At a later date, he made substantially the same criticism of the philosophy informing UNESCO: "The difficulty with UNESCO on the ideological side is in short that its idealism is informed by a too simple universalism. Its idealists burke at the tragic realities of life: the conflicts of interests which cannot be easily composed; the perils of war which cannot be simply overcome; the power of collective egotism which is not easily sub-limated."[46]

That self-interest is, and must be, the basis of national policy is a fact that Niebuhr clearly recognized in an era when it was not fashionable to do so. "Every nation is guided by self-interest and does not support values which transcend its life, if the defense of these values imperils its existence. A statesman who sought to follow such a course would be accused of treason. On the other hand nations do become the bearers of values which transcend their national interests."[47] And again: "No nation is good enough to do what is right, unless its sense of duty is compounded with its sense of survival."[48] To look for solutions of international problems by avoiding, or minimizing, the reality of national self-interest is either to indulge in irrelevant fantasies or to court disaster by jeopardizing that measure of order which is achieved by the competition of nations.

Such a realistic approach to political realities involved Niebuhr not only in a vigorous rejection of moralistic idealism, but also in an equally vigorous assault upon the so-called "scientific" approach to politics. We have already discussed Niebuhr's criticism of scientism in Chapter Three and the significance of his rejection of scientism for his own political thought has been well analyzed by Kenneth Thompson in his article "The Political Philosophy of Reinhold Niebuhr."[49] We might therefore happily leave this matter alone, except for the fact that the first full-scale attack on Niebuhr's political philosophy has come from this quarter. We refer to Holtan P. Odegard's book, *Sin and Science: Reinhold Niebuhr as Political Theologian.*

For the most part, Niebuhr's thought can hardly be recognized in this book, the presentation of it is so wooden, distorted, turned upside down. But what is perfectly clear in the book is this: the dogmatic assumption that the stuff of politics is to be approached, and controlled, in the same manner as a problem in natural science. It is from this perspective that he attacks Niebuhr and elaborates his own "positive" and "rational" approach. This will be evident by taking just a few typical samples of his "criticism" of Niebuhr and his own idea as to how we ought to deal with the "problem" of power.

Mr. Odegard does not like Niebuhr's understanding of the structure of democracy as embodying "the principle of resistance to government within the principle of government itself." This concept of democracy is apparently very bad for at least three remarkable reasons. In the first place it is not logical and therefore it is not "a useful directive of thought. It is, moreover, an ossified concept kept effectively impervious to improvement by the non-logical character which it shares with all paradox and which separates it from the world of practical action."[50] Niebuhr's understanding of the structure of democracy is not only non-logical, it stupidly assumes that the impulse to freedom and the necessity for order and authority are sometimes in conflict! If Niebuhr were only scientifically up to date and could cast off the "chains of dogma" and the acknowledgment of such outmoded things as "sin," a man as bright as he would recognize that "Opposition of freedom to authority, or freedom to order, is one of the fallacious attitudes men have fallen into while floundering around trying to adjust to and understand the relatively new situation of social fluidity."[51] And since Niebuhr is not only admitted to be bright, but indeed "one of the exceptionally brilliant men of our time," he might even be led to the insight that "If organized inquiry, the method of operative perfectible knowledge, is accepted as authoritative, there is a possibility of organically uniting freedom and authority, freedom and order, in a way attuned to the fluctuating times."[52] But this is not all: Niebuhr's understanding of the self, informed as it unfortunately is by his religious perspective, actually views the individual as capable of transcending the group or society and thus as one who gains "a vantage point from which to oppose society."[53] This is deplorable. Niebuhr simply does not understand that "Any . . . transactive approach to the problems of men would deny the actuality of conflict between the individual and society. Individuals are the product of transaction; they are created *with*in the crucible of social arrangements."[54] It does not even occur to Odegard that it is precisely because Niebuhr understands this so well that he has been motivated to reveal not only the limitations but the perils involved in the "scientific" approach to political realities!

It seems that the basic trouble with Niebuhr is that he thinks that there are some problems that are never solved. The statement that "democracy is a method of finding proximate solutions for insoluble problems" means only one thing to Mr. Odegard: Niebuhr is no theorist. "A theorist," Odegard informs us, "is a thinker who, when he finds that his problems are 'insoluble,' questions the problems and tries to reformulate them so that they can be solved."[55] Just how one is to "reformulate" such "problems" as those attending the Cold War so that they can be "solved" Odegard nowhere suggests!

The catalogue of Niebuhr's sins is indeed formidable. The following is but a small sample: Niebuhr lacks a proper "faith in human nature";[56] he is everywhere bound by his view of man's sinfulness which is his fundamental error; his understanding of tolerance "is rendered inoperative by reason of its dependence upon sin";[57] he is altogether naïve about the meaning of Catholic authoritarianism;[58] he "has forgotten the tremendous contribution of 'secularism' to civic and religious freedom";[59] his pessimism is akin to that of Ortega y Gasset, Mosca, and the neo-Machiavellians;[60] he has lost nerve and resigned himself "to the decision that oligarchical rule is actually inevitable."[61] To be sure, not everything in Niebuhr is wrong-headed. He has some good insights and often makes useful suggestions. Moreover, Niebuhr is saved "from carrying his own predilections to their most violent extremes."[62] This happy fact is due in part to "his earlier training in ethical philosophies."[63] But then a frightening image crosses Mr. Odegard's mind. What will be the results when his formulations take root "in the minds of less sophisticated people" and especially those who confront him "in their formative years"?[64] There ought to be an answer for the handling of that one in Mr. Odegard's own assumptions.

One of Niebuhr's greatest defects is that he lacks a proper "scientific" concept of power. All his ideas of power are outmoded. He thinks of power as force, coercive force, and thus engages himself in discussion of such things as the balance of power, all of which reveals that he "has not essentially advanced thinking about power beyond the outposts of Number 10 of the *Federalist Papers.*" [65] All this is very bad. The trouble is that Niebuhr and most statesmen do not see the "problem of coercive power" as a true problem. "Indeed, it is not a true problem for him because he thinks it cannot finally be solved. It permits only of transitory balancing feats." [66]

What is needed, Mr. Odegard assures us, is to get rid of such dated notions of power as "coercive force," acquire a "functional" view of power and then we could go to work to solve the "problem" of power. First, we redefine "power" and then we redefine the "task." Here is Odegard's redefinition of power; the reader must judge for himself what it means.

> He [i.e. Niebuhr] does not understand that the problem is to find a way of making power functional in a fluid society, to develop a method whereby power can again be effective when applied in the context of fluid customs. Power is an amalgam of the desires and values of people. By each of our desires or values we participate in the creation of power. Power is not a force but a composite field or structure. It is to be controlled not by weighing and counterweighing on the macroscopic level, but by reorganization of desires and value patterns. [67]

One is tempted to ask just how this definition would have struck the Hungarians in the autumn of 1956. Having redefined power, Odegard can now define the task before us.

> Actually our problem is to eliminate coercive power, to make power functional in terms of an authority appropriate to the present day, to remake power so that it is no longer a force to be balanced by force or checked by restraint, but a legitimate and essential part of the social structure, working *within* a nexus of authority. [68]

**He continues:**

> Power as force can only be frustrated or sacrificed. Power that is functional knows neither of these; there is simply no sense in speaking of frustrating or sacrificing it; there is no occasion, no need. The fact is that power can be one-sided and still not overweening if it is functionally integrated with a growing and self-correcting authority.[69]

It is unnecessary either to analyze or to comment on such obvious nonsense. It will suffice to observe that these statements contain, in about as crude fashion as can be conceived, every illusion and dogmatism with which Niebuhr has ever accused the "scientific" approach of confusing the field of social analysis. The main illusions with which Niebuhr has charged this approach are: (1) the notion that its approach is presuppositionless; (2) the illusions attending its failure to deal with the great facts of social reality—note, for example, Odegard's avoidance of the very meaning of political and military power; (3) the illusion that the social observer is not involved in the reality he observes; (4) the illusions consequent upon a failure to acknowledge the complexity of historical causation; and (5) the illusion that science is "the profoundest, because it is the latest, fruit of culture."[70] The dubious dogmas that inform and strengthen these illusions are: (1) the idea of the perfectability of man and (2) the notion that man is to be understood and controlled as a piece of nature. It does not even occur to Mr. Odegard to ask by whose power we are supposed "to eliminate coercive power," or just who is to determine the character of "an authority appropriate to the present day." Presumably if we all just give ourselves to the development of "methods" for progressively finding more satisfactory values or of "making power functional" and "a self-improving authoritative method," we will all become by our own resources and methods (above all, never forget the methods!) perfected children for whom "power" has ceased to be "coercive" because it has been redefined, and all "authority" is automatically "self-correcting" because it has become "functional"! In

Odegard's view "science" must simply be opposed to "sin"—and common sense.

One can dismiss Odegard's statements as the harmless illusions of a political babe in arms. But what cannot be so readily dismissed is the relationship between such illusions about man and history and the philosophy of totalitarianism.[71]

## 4. NIEBUHR'S "CONSERVATISM" AND "PRAGMATISM"

To bring the character of Niebuhr's political realism into clear focus, we need to observe not only his rejection of "moralistic" and "scientific" approaches to political reality; we must note also the significance of such labels as "conservatism" and "pragmatism" for his thought. Niebuhr has always been a "progressive" thinker, a thoroughly liberal spirit. But in recent years especially, the terms "conservatism" and "pragmatism" have been increasingly used to indicate his political orientation. We need to ask what these terms mean, and what they do not mean, when applied to Niebuhr.

There are two aspects or virtues of historic conservatism which Niebuhr has increasingly appropriated and emphasized. These are, "its ability to gauge factors of power in social and international relations which liberals tended to obscure; and to trust the organic processes of social cohesion rather than the abstract schemes which liberals were inclined to advance."[72] In this respect the instability of the abstract rationalism of the French Enlightenment offers an instructive contrast with the wisdom and stability achieved by the organic development of British democracy.[73]

It is this concern that informs Niebuhr's increasing references to the wisdom of Edmund Burke. It is Burke's understanding of "the dramatic quality of history and the uniqueness of its various occasions",[74] his rejection of "the abstract dogmas of the idealists because he had discerned the wisdom in the organic developments of history,"[75] and his consequent emphasis upon "historical rather than abstract modes of social engineering"[76] that appeal to Niebuhr

Niebuhr's estimate of Winston Churchill as "the best exemplar of true conservatism in our day,"[77] is even more interesting and instructive. Niebuhr did not always judge Churchill so highly. In 1934 he spoke of Churchill as "the perfect symbol of the inertia of nature in politics."[78] Later, he sees Churchill as above all the one in whom "class interests had not obscured the basic realities of the imperial struggle."[79] Churchill becomes the great example of the manner in which good and evil are intimately intertwined. "How shall we judge the great statesman who gives a nation its victorious courage by articulating its only partly conscious and implicit resources of fortitude; and who mixes the most obvious forms of personal and collective pride and arrogance with this heroic fortitude? If he had been a more timid man, a more cautious soul, he would not have sinned so greatly, but neither would he have wrought so nobly."[80] It was the same Churchill who after the war clearly recognized and gauged the peril of Russian imperialism, but it was also he who, in a day of American anti-communist hysteria sought to persuade them of the necessity of co-existence. At this time Niebuhr remarked, "He has proved his greatness before. But he gives the final proof of his greatness by his present demonstration that a statesman must be prudent as well as firm; that he must count the costs of a battle as well as be resolute in a battle thrust upon him."[81] Churchill's unique endowments will everywhere be acknowledged. But his greatness cannot be abstracted from the peculiar genius and tradition of his people. He not only shaped the spirit of his people in their "finest hour," he is also the product of the peculiar achievements of British culture. British culture and tradition have succeeded in securing a remarkable blending of aristocratic and democratic ideas, the organic character of its life and institutions with the libertarian impulses of its middle class and the equalitarian impulses of its working class, and the flexibility and demands of English parliamentary government. "Thus the Churchill story," remarks Niebuhr, "gives us the most vivid picture of the creative interaction between a great personality and a nation, and confounds the theories of both those who interpret history in terms of the influence of its great personalities and those who minimize the power of personality and try to interpret it as the product of 'social forces.' Here we have a living and vivid display of the way personality and tradition interact in a healthy free society."[82]

Whatever the secret of his success, Churchill certainly embodied all the qualities that distinguish the great statesman. He ever had a clear eye on the national interest and a great capacity accurately to estimate the realities of power; he was resolute in struggle and prudent in his efforts to avoid overt conflict. But joined with this realism was an incomparable capacity to articulate and shape the values of a great people whom he understood and loved—values which undergirded, but also transcended, the interests of his nation. Niebuhr has expressed this nicely, "The only statesman of our age who fully mastered the art of relating morally ambiguous strategy to high moral aims, without emptying the cause of its moral content, was Churchill. That accounts for his peculiar eminence. Almost everyone else fell into moral cynicism in the pursuit of strategy or into moral sentimentality through the separation of the moral cause from strategy."[83]

It is clear that one can use the label of conservatism for Niebuhr only with great care. If by conservatism is meant merely an interest in the preservation of the *status quo* then that, as he himself has put it, "would be anathema for anyone who had drawn inspiration from the Old Testament prophets."[84] Thus if we are to use the label for Niebuhr, it must be sharply distinguished from what is generally known in America as conservatism. American conservatism, Niebuhr has said, is really "not conservative at all in the traditional sense"; it is really only a decadent liberalism intent upon resisting innovation and defending the *status quo*.[85] For this reason also Niebuhr is in no way to be associated with the conservatism of scholars like Kenneth Kirk, who, he remarks, having "discovered the realism of an Edmund Burke always tend to mix this realism with an uncritical acceptance of inequality, conformity, and the current balance or equilibrium of power in any social scene." [86]

His criticism of traditional liberalism is centered in its defective anthropology. "They seem to insist that it is necessary to have illusions about human nature in order to be a good apostle of liberty, equality, and justice." [87] The consequence is that liberalism all too frequently has failed to estimate the power of self-interest either in the foe or in ourselves, depreciated the significance of organic processes in the attainment of justice, or had its energies drained off in the construction of abstract schemes irrelevant to the demands and necessities of the concrete situation. On the other hand, the realism of conservatism has frequently, indeed usually, been used as an instrument for the sanctifying of the inequalities and injustices of the *status quo*. The problem "is how to generate the wisdom of true conservatism without losing the humane virtues which the liberal movement developed." [88]

When Niebuhr's so-called conservatism is seen in this light, then we will not waste our breath talking about the "new development" or "conservative conversion" in his thought. Will Herberg has seen the continuity of Niebuhr's thought at this point more clearly than most. Herberg writes:

> Nor should we be surprised to see his earlier "prophetic" radicalism culminate in the "new conservatism"; there is an inner connection between the two, and no real reversal is involved. For the "prophetic" radicalism implied a radical relativization of all political programs, institutions, and movements, and therefore a thoroughgoing rejection of every form of political rationalism. Add to this a renewed emphasis on the historic continuities of social life, and Niebuhr's brand of "conservatism" emerges. [89]

If those words sum up what is meant by Niebuhr's "conservatism," they also indicate the character of his "Christian pragmatism." His approach to political and social issues is pragmatic in the sense that there is no political or economic system possessing the status of an absolute. There is no "Christian" social system. He is a pragmatist in the sense that he insists upon the freedom and flexibility necessary to attack any social question in the uniqueness of its historical context. But Niebuhr is a normative thinker, and the prefix "Christian" is necessary for the understanding of the character of his pragmatic approach. What does Niebuhr mean by a Christian pragmatism? "One can answer that question very simply," he says, "by the assertion that Christian pragmatism is merely the application of Christian freedom and a sense of responsibility to complex issues of economics and politics, with the firm resolve that inherited dogmas and generalizations will not be accepted, no matter how revered or venerable if they do not contribute to the establishment of justice in a given situation."[90]

The inner connection between Niebuhr's prophetic radicalism and his contemporary pragmatism is clear. All social programs are relativized in the light of the absolute claim of the gospel. A social system must be judged by the norms of love and justice and not from the standpoint of the claims and promises of an alternative social system. It must, however, be acknowledged that Niebuhr did not always see this with consistent clarity and vigor. Arthur Schlesinger, Jr., and Kenneth Thompson have both shown how the remnants of Niebuhr's abstract social idealism blinded him to the creative aspects of the pragmatic revolution of Roosevelt's New Deal.[91] The validity of this criticism can be seen simply by noting his slowly changing estimates of Roosevelt and his achievements. As late as 1938, Niebuhr could write, "Roosevelt is to be preferred to his foes, even to the point of supporting him for a third term in order to prevent reaction from coming into power and throwing the whole nation into confusion. Nevertheless his program reveals how impossible it is to heal the ills of modern capitalism within the presuppositions of capitalism itself."[92] Shortly after this, Niebuhr came to a fresh appreciation of the piecemeal, pragmatic reform of Roosevelt. This change occurred in the context of his gratitude for Roosevelt's foreign policy in the face of Nazism, and Niebuhr's own increasing revulsion from the philosophy of the total solution of a consistent socialism. At the time of Roosevelt's death, Niebuhr hailed his administration as having reached "a new level of maturity" both in foreign and domestic policy.[93]

This pragmatism has issued from the inconclusive contest and the dissolution of the dogmas of the political right and the political left. But for Niebuhr that is far from being the whole story. No one who knows the inward development of his thought can describe it simply in "reactive" terms. On the contrary: it emerges out of the elaboration of his theological understanding of the self, freedom, and history, as this was wrought out in concrete engagement with the realities of our world.

> Christian thought must not pretend that what we have described as its growing pragmatism has not been influenced by this general history in Western thought and life. But we must also recognize that what has been wrought out has actually been a view of life and the establishment of justice in a community which could have been elaborated originally if we had had a clear biblical insight into the nature of history, the freedom of man, and the corruption of sin in that freedom, and had therefore realized that history cannot be equated with nature; nor can the political judgments which we make about our and each other's interests be equated with the judgments which a scientist makes about natural phenomena. In other words the process we have described has been the gradual extrication of our thought from the baneful effects of heresies about man and God which have infected it ever since the French Enlightenment.[94]

In addition to being a remarkable summary of the headlines of his political thought, that passage ought to leave us in no doubt about the Christian nature and rootage of Niebuhr's pragmatism. Pragmatism is not an ultimate principle for Niebuhr. He remains a normative thinker. But the norm inheres in no social program or political system. The norm is the *agape* of the Cross which reveals both the responsibility under which we live and the depth and pervasiveness of human self-interest. It demands that we make responsible decisions between political alternatives and at the same time frees us from the illusion that our choices and causes represent the appearance of pure good in history. Thus freed from the bondage and illusions of "isms," and remaining under the criticism of the transcendent norm of love, it is our task at all times by using and developing adequate political structures to establish justice within the framework of freedom. This is the approach of the Christian pragmatist.


## 5. THE CHRISTIAN DIMENSION IN NIEBUHR'S POLITICAL REALISM

All this serves to indicate the character of Niebuhr's political realism. He has had a close relationship with, and exercised a deep influence upon the realist school of American politics associated with such thinkers as Hans Morgenthau, Kenneth Thompson, C.B. Marshall, George Kennan, Dorothy Fosdick, Adlai Stevenson, and others. The indebtedness of such political thinkers to Niebuhr has been widely and gratefully acknowledged. One such acknowledgment may be noted here. Writing of this school, Thompson remarked, "Undoubtedly it is not without significance that these authorities admittedly owe an important intellectual debt to the Protestant theologian, Reinhold Niebuhr, who as early as 1932 in *Moral Man and Immoral Society* elaborated a realistic theory of international politics. Not long ago Kennan in surveying the growth of interest among the small group of responsible theorists, identified Niebuhr as the precursor of the so-called realists or, in Kennan's words, 'the father of us all.' Morgenthau's first volume, *Scientific Man vs. Power Politics,* which remains in some ways more fundamental to his philosophy than all his subsequent writings, bears the imprint of Niebuhr's influence more than that of any other American scholar. Marshall, Halle, and Fosdick have not been hesitant in acknowledging their debt to Niebuhr."[95] Niebuhr's forthright rejection of "moralistic" or "scientific" schemes that bear no relationship to the contingent realities of particular situations; his devastating attack upon those who would substitute the formulation of humanitarian goals or principles for the am-

biguities of day by day statesmanship; his clear recognition of the
national interest as a primary fact in international politics; his
sturdy refusal to seek for an island of purity in history; his critique
of that portion of the American heritage which believes in simple
answers to political problems, with its tendency to regard power
politics as a temporary phenomenon to be solved by vigorous
"crusades"—all this clearly places him within the "realist" school
of politics.

Nevertheless, just as Niebuhr's pragmatism must be distinguished as "Christian pragmatism", so must also his realism. No
one is more conscious than he of the problems and difficulties involved in relating an absolute, transcendent norm to the contingencies of particular political situations; but it has been his task,
and is the measure of his greatness, that he has not on that account
abandoned the attempt. The very possibility of a Christian ethic
is at stake in the attempt.

Niebuhr is a realist, but he is a Christian realist, that is he seeks
to inquire into the political behavior of the realist who knows
that he still lives and acts under a norm that transcends the realities with which he must responsibly deal. To locate and describe
the character of this boundary line, against those who would completely separate the realms of politics and religion or those who
would too simply identify them, has constituted a large portion of
his task. But he has sought to do more: he has endeavored to show
wherein the vantage point of Christian faith illuminates the task
of the political realist. "Christian realism," Thompson acknowledges with Niebuhr specifically in mind, "by illuminating the misery
and grandeur of man can be a textbook for the diplomatist." [96]

We may distinguish four closely related ways in which Niebuhr
sees the norm and perspective of Christian faith connecting with
political realism in significant and saving fashion. First, it can prevent the realist from conceiving the national interest too narrowly.
For example, if we define the national interest in too exclusively
military terms we will neglect or injure those mutualities between
nations upon the health of which the national interest most cer-

tainly depends. Full awareness of the norm of love, under which nations as well as individuals stand, can help to keep us from a self-defeating pursuit of a conception of the national interest that is divorced from the needs of those with whom our destiny is intertwined. "Nations are, on the whole, not generous. A wise self-interest is usually the limit of their moral achievements; though it is worth noting that nations do not achieve a wise self-interest if generous impulses do not help to drive them beyond the limits of a too narrow self-interest."[97]

Secondly, Christian faith will prod us to find that point of coincidence between the interests of the nation and values which transcend those interests. The capacity to find those points is always the mark of real statesmanship, and the peculiar demand of our time. "The weakness of the realists is that they usually do not go far enough in meeting new problems and situations. They are so conscious of the resistance in history to new ventures; and are so impressed by the force of the perennial problems of politics, which manifest themselves on each new level of history, that they are inclined to discount both the necessity and the possibility of new political achievements."[98] The statesman cannot pursue policies that jeopardize the national interest; but his task is to recognize that since all nations live under a common peril as well as under one ultimate norm, he must pursue those policies which transcend, as they fulfill, the national interest.

Thirdly, the Christian perspective can help the realist from falling into a moral cynicism to which his very virtues tempt him. Moral cynicism does not arise from a clear recognition of the fact that we must come to terms with the brutal facts of existence, it arises from our investing them with normative character. It is this concern that prompted Niebuhr's criticism of George Kennan's *American Diplomacy, 1900–1950.* He fully agrees with Kennan's indictment of our "moralistic-legalistic" approach, our confidence in "grand schemes," our too easy assumptions that we can determine future events, our inclination to think that the interests of other nations can be readily co-ordinated to ours, because ours are moral. But Kennan's solution does not satisfy Niebuhr. "Mr. Kennan's solution for the problem of our pretentious idealism is a return to the concept of 'national interest.' He thinks that this concept should guide our foreign policy on the ground that we must not pretend to know more than what is good for us. This modesty is important. But egotism is not the cure for an abstract and pretentious idealism. Preoccupation with national interest can quickly degenerate into moral cynicism even if it is originally prompted by moral modesty."[99]

In the fourth place, moral cynicism passes quickly into its apparent opposite, moral pretension. Nations may assert that they cannot act beyond their own interests, but once they act, and especially when they fight, it is always for more universal values like democracy, justice, civilization, or God. The national interest thus assumes idolatrous proportions. Only a faith that illuminates the evil and self-interest in the cause of our devotion can moderate the moral pretension of conflicting contestants.[100] It is primarily this that Thompson means when he says that "Christian realism by illuminating the misery and grandeur of man can be a textbook for the diplomatist." In such ways as these Niebuhr's "Christian realism" and "political realism" meet and interpenetrate each other.

In order to round out this discussion of Niebuhr's political philosophy, it will be instructive to inquire into the kind of criticisms he has made and the positions he has adopted respecting American foreign policy since the war. To a brief survey of this we now turn.

## 6. POST-WAR AMERICAN FOREIGN POLICY

The overwhelming political fact of our era has been the sudden vaulting of America into the position of leadership of the free world. Because she possesses unquestioned hegemony in the West, the task of learning quickly the art of exercising authority among the

nations has been thrust upon her. In this position the most necessary, as well as the most difficult task has been to learn the anatomy of authority. What are the sources or ingredients of authority
in international relations?

### a. THE ANATOMY OF AUTHORITY

The first source of authority is power. A nation lacking power
lacks the decisive base for the exercise of authority. The sweet
reasonableness of Peru does not avail in a crisis. Politics is not primarily a matter of mind meeting mind but a matter of interest
encountering other interests. Power breeds responsibility, the responsibility of exercising leadership. The essence of leadership is
not the abdication of power but the responsible and prudent exercise of power. The basis of authority is always power.

But the nation that possesses power and relies exclusively on
its might, not having assessed the limits of power, will soon learn
that the possession of power adds up to something less than authority. Authority is composed of *both* power and prestige. This has
been a constant theme in Niebuhr's occasional writings across the
past decade. "Power, though it is the initial element in establishing leadership, cannot maintain itself very long if prestige is not
added as a source of authority. When prestige is lacking, the addition of power does not remedy the defect." [101] And again, at the
time of the struggle in Vietnam,

> No doubt military action must frequently be the *ultima ratio* in a
> struggle with a foe. We saved the whole situation by prompt military
> action in Korea. But the contemporary situation in Vietnam should
> certainly instruct us on the limits of military power in the cold
> war. . . . Military power is, in short, ineffective when it lacks a
> moral and political base.[102]

Power, indeed military power, is the *ultima ratio* of international
relations, but by itself it is less than authority.

Niebuhr has designated prestige as the second great component
of authority. Of what is prestige composed? There have been

many sources of prestige upon which rulers and nations in the past have been able to draw. Niebuhr sees only two of these as significantly available for a modern hegemenous nation. These are a *reputation for justice based on achievement and a reputation for prudence in the exercise of power*.[103] If prestige derived from this reputation is lacking, power is something less than authority. Authority is derived from not only the power to force compliance but also from the power derived from the faculty of eliciting consent and trust.[104] Nothing is more necessary for the responsible exercise of power than a clear recognition of the limits, as well as the necessity of the power of force in the "managing" of history. The whole ethos of American philosophy and history disposes us to obscure this important fact. This disposition was strongly reinforced by the Republican election campaign of 1952, as they claimed to hold the Democrats responsible for the vast world revolution taking place. In this context Niebuhr again spoke his characteristic word: "Nothing is more dangerous to a powerful nation than the temptation to obscure the limits of power. It will be our undoing if we imagine ourselves the masters of contemporary history."[105]

The possession of great power tempts us to succumb to the two apparently opposite, but intimately related, moods of complacency and heedlessness. America's inordinate power, wealth, and, in the face of communism, her comparative virtue all tempt her to be complacent. But when this is informed by an idealism that does not know the limits of man's wisdom and volition in history, this complacency readily turns into heedlessness which assumes that there are relatively simple solutions to perennial political problems. The need for a fundamental reorientation of the idealism informing our culture has become an urgent political necessity.

Authority is composed of both power and prestige. The possession of great power increases rather than lessens the need for wise and prudent statesmanship. The emergence of the "Anglo-American" alliance as the heart of the free world was thus regarded by Niebuhr as providential, since it provided that combination of power and political experience which alone could provide an adequate basis to meet the issues of the post-war world. Indeed he goes so far as to say that "the world is being held together by American power, frequently deflected, though not always guided, by the wider experience of British statecraft. This is the significance of the 'Anglo-Saxon' alliance at the heart of the free world. It is one of those providential factors in history which no one could have contrived but for which we can only be grateful."[106] We shall later note his interpretation of some of the moments of great strain in this alliance, but it requires no powers of prophecy to see the terms in which it will be set.

The American story since the war has been largely one of winning and losing, of losing and winning, authority among the nations. The heart of the story has been the degree to which she succeeded or failed to combine prestige with power, creative political and economic policies with military strength.

### b. THE MARSHALL PLAN

In any list of those acts of creative American statesmanship that won authority for America, surely the Marshall Plan must be given a very high place. Niebuhr hailed it from the outset, calling it "a kind of turning point in postwar history."[107] Indeed, he had himself, made a similar proposal early in 1943. Looking forward to the role of America after the war he wrote, "America could function in the interest of democracy only if it were ready to give economic support to the continent without seeking to prevent the establishment of systems which sought to combine collective forms of economy with political freedom. That is also the only possibility of preventing the continent from turning to bolshevism . . . ."[108] The Marshall Plan achieved what the Truman doctrine by itself could not achieve.[109] It was a bold and imaginative scheme in which the national self-interest was furthered by an act which met the dire need of others. "In it prudent self-interest was united with concern for others in a fashion which represents the most attainable virtue of nations."[110] To be sure, some Americans are still persuaded that the Marshall Plan was prompted by motives of pure generosity. It was not, and it can be assumed that the point no longer needs arguing. Nations do not act out of sheer generosity. But what is just as important, the spokesmen of nations should never pretend that they do. To do so is to lay the ground for all kinds of resentment. The deciding factor in initiating the Marshall Plan was the conviction that economic aid to Europe would further the political and economic interests of America. The expectation of gratitude ought never to enter the picture in the dealings of nations, because those who receive aid know full well that we consider it to be in our own interests to grant it. Niebuhr saw this clearly. "The European Recovery Program is as necessary for the health of America as for the recovery of the Western world. We should refrain from making undue moral claims for it. We would be well advised, in fact, to strive for modesty in the years to come, and not to expect gratitude from our supposed beneficiaries. Gratitude is a grace beyond the moral competence of nations. It is in any event not as deserved as the supposedly generous nations imagine."[111] In the Marshall Plan, America added prestige to power; the prestige is dimmed when we claim that it was not motivated by concern to further our interests and consolidate our power.

The formation of NATO was an event of central significance in this period. Niebuhr regarded it, not as a departure in our foreign policy, but as "the logical capstone" of a policy which had been developing ever since the end of the war. He saw it as bringing two elements in American policy together—its new-found sense of responsibility for the world community and her special responsibility for leadership of the West. In the effort to maintain preponderant power in the non-communist world, it was the other side of the strategy informing the Marshall Plan.[112]

c. THE KOREAN WAR

The Korean war was a momentous event in the post-war experience of the United States. It served both to clarify and to becloud all the issues facing America as she assumed the responsibilities of her new position in the world. As the struggle wore on, as the casualty lists lengthened, as tragic mistakes were made, and as "victory" did not come in view, it became a highly emotional issue for the American electorate. It was a new kind of experience for the American public, but just therein lies its central importance.

The first thing that must be said is that the Korean war was the first bold and courageous step in collective security. It was of decisive significance. It served notice on the communist world that communist expansion by military means would not be tolerated. It gave clear expression to the fact that lessons had been learned from Munich; it reassured Asian nations that America was not prepared to regard them as expendable.

The Korean war was based on the United Nations. It derived moral meaning from that fact and in turn strengthened the confidence of that body.

It was a limited war; a war fought for limited purposes with limited weapons. The significance of that is difficult to over-estimate; at the same time we must see that the intense unpopularity of this war in America also inheres in this fact. It was a war that must not be lost and must not be won. To take the measure of that is to see the greatness of President Truman's decision. Korea represented a return to an older concept of war, a concept antedating the war of 1914-18. But the whole American experience was against accepting or even understanding this. America's great wars have all been crusades for more or less unlimited purposes; for independence and freedom, to make the world safe for democracy, and for unconditional surrender. To fight a war that must not issue in complete victory was something new and unintelligible. President Truman's wisest decisions could therefore be nothing other than intensely unpopular. Nevertheless, the safety of the whole world hinged—and still does—upon the resolution and the prudence to conduct a limited war for limited purposes. That was, and remains, the central and momentous significance of the Korean war. To be sure, the policy of containment of communism by military means is, in itself, an insufficient policy, especially in Asia. But the recognition of the limitation must, in no way, obscure its necessity.

America gained prestige throughout the world by her prompt action. She almost lost all that she gained when, for a moment, it appeared that she might relax her resolution to keep it a limited war, and forget the limits of power to shape history. This is what was at stake in the debate over General MacArthur.

The achievements of General MacArthur were real and great. He had been a distinguished soldier and his constructive work in Japan after the war must be praised as an almost incredible achievement. But when he viewed the struggle in Korea in too exclusively military terms, when he failed to gauge the limits of military power in combatting communism, when he thought of victory in a limited war in total terms, he became a symbol of American heedlessness and gave the impression that we were more concerned with winning the next world war than with preventing it. When it became apparent that he might not be prepared to accept the restraints put upon him by his government, he became dispensable. Niebuhr's judgment was surely sound when he wrote that "the dismissal of MacArthur without a serious political crisis has not only reassured our European friends about the sanity of our foreign policy but also about the stability of our democratic institutions."[113]

In a dramatic way, the MacArthur debate brought into the clear the issues involved in what we have here called the anatomy of authority. Authority is derived from the basic fact of power along with a clear recognition of the limits of military power. To military power must be added the moral and political wisdom that knows that there are no final solutions to international questions, and the patience to bear the frustrations that attend, not powerlessness, but the limitations of great power. We must learn to distinguish the different dimensions of our struggle with communism, for upon our learning hangs the question of American authority and leadership—and a successful outcome of the struggle. In Niebuhr's words: "The immaturity of American political thought makes it difficult for us to acknowledge the limits of our political and moral authority in various parts of the world, or to distinguish between the military and moral dimensions of our conflict with Communism. If we fail to make such distinctions, the possibility of avoiding an atomic war becomes very minimal. For a policy of countering the expansion of Communism everywhere in the world by military force must make the final conflict inevitable. Fortunately the Senate investigation is having the salutary effect upon the American mind of clarifying distinctions which have been hitherto obscure."[114]

### d. ANTI-AMERICANISM

For anyone concerned with the capacity of America to provide effective leadership, it became necessary, especially in the early 1950's to acknowledge and interpret the wave of anti-Americanism in both Europe and Asia. It is rather difficult for Americans to understand why all the world does not love them. That in itself reveals how unaccustomed Americans are to assuming the role of the hegemenous nation. If it be true, as Niebuhr has said, that "Power and moral leadership are not wholly compatible,"[115] it is even more obvious that power and popularity do not readily go together. It is only to be expected that the power and wealth of America are both envied and resented, and that lands rich in cultural history will express this in terms of condescension to the vulgar, untutored youth who has so recently come into the estate of his fathers. Criticizing America is one of the few luxuries the rest of the world can afford.

Among European nations, it is France in which this sentiment of anti-Americanism has found its most intense expression. Jean Paul Sartre's explosive outburst at the time of the execution of the Rosenbergs may not have been representative, but it no doubt articulated the feelings of some important sections of the French public: "Your country is sick with fear. You are afraid of the Soviets, of the Chinese, of the Europeans. You are afraid of each other and of the shadow of your own bomb. . . . . Some day perhaps men of goodwill will cure you of your fears. Meanwhile do not be astonished if we cry from one end of Europe to the other: 'Watch out. America has the rabies. Cut all ties with her lest we will be bitten in turn and run mad.' "[116] In examining the roots of French anti-Americanism, Niebuhr attempted to assess the significance of America's involvement in German economic recovery and the somewhat hurried efforts at German rearmament, as well as the cultural resentments of France. His conclusion was, however, that the peculiar animus of this sentiment in France was derived primarily from French weaknesses.[117] This led to a significant correspondence between Niebuhr and Roland de Pury, which was later reported on by Arnold Hearn.[118] We need not discuss that here. French sentiment regarding America has been most intense, but the general attitude is one which we must seek to understand, bear, and learn from. For although some of the sentiment is due to resentment of America's position, power, and wealth, much of it we have brought upon ourselves.

In attempting to name a few of the reasons why America so frequently loses prestige, we may begin by saying that she has not yet learned how to talk well. This is not a small matter and it has many different levels. Senators as well as tourists could well heed the common sense spoken by Dorothy Fosdick on this matter.[119] It does no good to talk as though Americans "had a corner on virtue," or that we have "settled all our problems" or that our "standard of living" is the only measure of "success." The truth is so much more appealing than these caricatures. The tendency to make a simple correlation between American virtue and her prosperity is damaging because it is not true, and although we may not know it is untrue all the rest of the world does. That we have not learned to talk well is most evident in the realm of politics. Whenever Americans make a simple identification between devotion to democracy and freedom and the illusions of the philosophy of "laissez-faire," they merely parade their inability to distinguish between the final norms of politics and the characteristic prejudices of a very wealthy nation. Such talk suggests that the only alternative to communism is nineteenth-century capitalism which European nations do not desire and are unable to afford. America has, in practice, passed far beyond this, but we lose prestige when we continue to use the "obsolete and to many of the world's peoples repellent language of the 19th century."[120] The sentiment that America is heedless was further aggravated by such slogans as "massive retaliation," "agonizing reappraisal," and the talk about liberation rather than containment. Perhaps in quieter times they would have created no stir, but spoken at the peak of anti-American feeling, they seemed only to confirm the suspicion that America had no understanding of the limits of power to coerce history. America does *act* better than it talks and there is much consolation in that fact, but a hegemonous nation must learn also to talk well. Our speech is the index to our understanding.

Perhaps nothing proved more catastrophic to American prestige than McCarthyism. The fact that it was the phenomenon rather than the man that concerned other nations ought to prompt us not to speak too confidently about McCarthy*wasm*. The similarity to tyranny was too striking to be missed.[121] So far as American prestige was concerned, McCarthyism justified every misconception and seemed to confirm the fears that under the strain of the long struggle with communism, America might lose her head. As de Pury wrote: "He is but an antic fool, we agree. But he is a fool who has a section of public opinion behind him and who is doing great harm. If you want us not to pay attention to him, it would be well if he lost his power and if Cardinal Spellman did not come to us praising God for his investigations."[122] McCarthy lost his power, but the damage to American prestige has not been so quickly recovered.

Mention must also be made of the American position respecting China. In general this position is regarded by our allies as inflexible and unrealistic, and the arguments advanced for it as insufferably self-righteous. It is not our concern to discuss this complex question here. It will suffice to indicate how two assumptions or habits of thought discredit American prestige. The view so widely expressed a few years ago that Chiang could have been saved if only American aid had been greater, is not only stupid, it is a positive menace to American prestige in Asia. The view that the forces of a mighty social revolution can be stayed by American military power in support of a thoroughly corrupt regime, not only discredits America in the eyes of all Asians, it reveals that we do not understand the limits of power, or the necessity of combatting communism at the political and economic, as well as the military, levels. Power by itself is not authority. Some of the arguments used to justify our refusal to recognize Communist China or to admit her to the United Nations have been almost equally offensive. Leaving aside the question of the advantage that might be gained by fostering the natural clash of interests between China and Russia, the assumption that our allies who do think in these terms are merely revealing a "softness" in their attitude to communism, and that we are the sole custodians of "morality" in international relations, is insufferable. Such a "legalistic-moralistic" approach is regarded as being not only morally presumptuous, but also politically dangerous. The whole question ought to prompt America to review her understanding of "the anatomy of authority."

### e. AMERICA AND ASIA

No area is more crucial in the struggle between communism and the West than Asia. Yet nowhere are the issues so complex, the need for political wisdom and vision greater, and the cultivation of that patience which can accept the frustration of our power more necessary. In this situation we need above all to understand and assess the disadvantages under which we work. Failure to understand these limitations and handicaps can only issue in disaster. It is this dimension of the problem to which Niebuhr has consistently drawn attention.

Democracy labors here under an ideological disadvantage. Asia is not Europe. It has neither Europe's heritage of political freedom, nor her close acquaintance with communist tyranny, nor the delicate balances of power which undergird Western democracy. The most immediately felt need in Asiatic nations is for the technical tools which will enable them to gain viable economies, as they pass from a stage of "feudal" oppression to independence. The danger is that Asia may easily pass from an old, organic collectivism to a communist, technical collectivism presenting itself under the banner of "liberation." Communist diplomacy can thus speak directly to the point of obvious need without bothering about political values which have not been within the common experience, and which took centuries to be developed in the West.

Still another handicap must be acknowledged. The ancient cultures of Asia and the Orient lack the spiritual basis for what we call the "dignity of the individual." Democratic society requires the capacity of the individual to defy society and to relate himself to wider communities while so doing. We have already discussed the vital, though indirect, relationship between democracy and the Christian understanding of man and history. It is difficult to see how this basis could be provided by the pantheism and mysticism of Buddhism and Hinduism, or the humanism of Confucianism. [123]

In this situation, America is saddled with the heritage of Western imperialism and colonialism. It is difficult for America to accept this fact since few nations have talked more about imperialism and none have considered themselves more anti-imperialistic than the United States. For Americans "imperialism" has been a favorite epithet throughout most of their history, to be hurled with special vindictiveness in the direction of the British. But it must now be acknowledged that America derives no special prestige from this fact in Asia. Imperialism takes many different forms and participates in different degrees of evil. Niebuhr once put it cryptically thus: "Imperialism at its worst is the subjugation and exploitation of the national or international community by the powerful. At its best it represents an egoistic corruption of a responsible attitude toward the task of organizing human communities."[124] If we can accept that general description, although we

have not had the same story as the colonial powers of the nineteenth century, and although the fervent disavowal of imperialism
has been part of our official creed, the impulse and reality of
American imperialism ought freely to be acknowledged.

Be that as it may, the evils of imperialism form a very real part
of the difficulties facing Western democracy in Asia and Africa.
The evils are primarily in the spiritual realm. "For arrogance is the
inevitable consequence of the relation of power to weakness. In
this case the arrogance of power reinforced ethnic prejudices; for
the industrial world was 'white' and the non-technical world was
'colored.'[125]

Asia is poor and Asia is colored and she is the battleground between communism and America. In this situation communist
strategy has undergone a significant change. Instead of offering a
revolutionary creed to the "masses," Russia now poses as the friend
and protector of the "colored" nations against the imperialist
powers. By interpreting capitalism as the cause of imperialism and
colonialism, America can without difficulty be cast in the role of
the arch imperialist. Thus Asian poverty is laid at the door of imperialist exploitation, and the justified resentment of the wrongs of
the white man find ample confirmation in the contemporary American scene. Communism by thus adroitly seeking to isolate America
in the colored continents, joins the struggle at the point of the
West's greatest weakness. Thus it is, that in all the untruths of
communist propaganda there is just enough truth for it to be
persuasive.

To interpret the struggle in Asia primarily in military terms is
to give credence to the charge of imperialism. This is not to suggest
that the military factor ought to be minimized. It is simply to emphasize that here, above all, our policy cannot be one of *containment* of communism but of *competition* with communism. Here
all our resources of political wisdom and generous economic aid
will be required if we are to capture the allegiance of revolutionary
leadership. In this respect, American feelings and policies have

been unduly tied to Formosa, South Korea, and the free parts of Indo-China.

The position of India is crucial in Asia. She is the largest of the free nations and possesses by far the greatest moral authority. She is the only real rival to China for hegemony in Asia. We do not like her neutralism, and undoubtedly she has many illusions about communism. But Russia knows that one does not defeat neutralism by lectures on the immorality of such a position, but by appearing as the protector and helper. "It would be ironic," Niebuhr says, "if we refused to help India because her economy was too collectivistic . . . when in fact, India's very freedom and her effort to satisfy the consumer needs of her population make it difficult for her to compete with Red China, which is taking the capital needs of its new industrialism out of the backs of its peasants."[126]

Prestige in Asia cannot be bought by aid nor forced by power. It can be secured only by a real attempt to understand the aspirations, the resentments, and the needs of these rising peoples and the patient, unwearying effort to find the points at which our own interests and their needs coincide.

### f. THE SUEZ CRISIS

We shall conclude our survey of Niebuhr's judgments and positions on recent events and issues by recalling the Suez crisis of the autumn of 1956. Niebuhr wrote a number of articles on this debacle, he felt the issues most keenly, and it is perhaps no exaggeration to say that no post-war event throws into such clear relief so many facets of his political thought.

He did not wait until violence had broken out to begin writing. In the spring of 1956, he was fully alerted to the perils of war in the Middle East and the fact that the rift in the Anglo-American alliance meant that we were rapidly losing control of events.[127] By June he was saying that the only hope of peace "lies in a daring enterprise which will lift the economy of the whole area and relate the nations to each other in a common concern for their natural resources."[128] A year later he returned to this theme, making his plea for American foundations to undertake a stupendous project, involving billions of dollars, to provide for water power development, soil conservation, and industrialization in this area.[129]

We need not here review the complex of events—the move of Israel against Egypt after years of extreme provocation, the action of Britain and France in bombing and invading Egypt to secure the Suez Canal, and the subsequent operations in the United Nations and the Anglo-French withdrawal. To the question "Why did Britain and France do it?" which everyone asked at that time, no doubt many answers can be given. They were exasperated at the failure of America to appreciate the dependence of Europe on oil from the Middle East, the dynamism of the Nasser regime, and the reality and extent of Russian penetration into the area. To this, no doubt, must be added the painful frustration and resentment of nations who realized that after centuries of imperial glory, their power had slipped away. However this may be, one fact stood out with frightening clarity: the Western Alliance lacked a single clear, strong voice to interpret the situation; mutual understanding had disintegrated in vacillating diplomacy, and, as James Reston put it, they "lost control of events." The worst tragedy of all was that this happened during those weeks when the Russian satellite empire was erupting, and we had the spectacle of America, following hard upon "the path of honor," censoring her allies in the United Nations at the moment when Russian armor was beating down the Hungarian revolt.

Before mentioning some of the views expressed by Niebuhr concerning this event, it is necessary to say something else clearly. When Niebuhr and other members of the "school" of pragmatic realism criticized American policy and action, it did not mean that they sought to condone or to justify the British-French action; nor were they simply saying that the United States ought to have supported them. Their concern cut deeper and farther back. Their concern was to inquire into the assumptions and guiding principles of American policy that governed our position at that time, and which had contributed to the whole debacle.

It was an event that divided men usually very close together, an example of which was the division within the Editorial Board of *Christianity and Crisis*. This journal decided to publish a remarkably, perceptive article by Kenneth Thompson (with which Niebuhr wholeheartedly agreed) and which became a springboard for a continuing debate within its pages.[130]

One of the lessons to emerge from the crisis, Thompson pointed out, was that the Western alliance could not be taken for granted. It could not be sustained "without devotion, patience and effort." We have only to recall Niebuhr's views of the significance of the Anglo-American alliance and the meaning and significance of prestige to see how this would be for him a central concern. Britain and France lost prestige by their precipitous action. They lost further prestige through the UN resolution. It was this which made that resolution, to use Niebuhr's word, so "catastrophic." "It destroyed the prestige of our allies and thereby diminished the common fund of prestige of the free world."[131] There is no substitute for the statesmanship that will cement and enrich the Anglo-American alliance.

The main thrust of Thompson's article consisted in his discussion of the differences between the approaches of pragmatic realism and the "legalistic-moralistic approach"—which was so dominant in America during this crisis. He writes: "The American approach is of course not a seamless web. Yet running through much of our foreign relations is the red thread of a sharply rationalistic-legalistic-moralistic approach. . . . We continually view the world through bifocal lenses that see only two alternatives. States are aggressive or peace-loving, policies are internationalist or isolationist and nations are said to be colonial or anti-colonial in their sympathies."[132] He goes on to note that "Peace, anti-colonialism and the United Nations currently are invested with absolute ethical value," that these coincided as regarding the Suez question, but our devotion to peace conflicted with our devotion to anti-colonialism and the United Nations in the Hungarian question. "The endless complexities of international politics play havoc with every

attempt to erect a proximate goal into the ultimate aim of our
foreign relations."[133] We need to learn the lesson that "Peace or
anti-colonialism are both too general and too contingent to be
viable directives of foreign policy."[134] Just what havoc a moralistic
approach can work, he suggests in the following passage.

> For over 200 years the Russians were denied access to the Middle
> East by French and British power. Now by our sweeping opposi-
> tion to the French and British policies on Suez we have substantially
> weakened their power. By weakening them we have weakened our-
> selves. This weakness has created a vacuum into which Soviet in-
> fluence has flowed, threatening not only the interests of the West
> but ultimately those of newly emergent colonial states. Thus a
> heedless anti-colonialism, bereft of awareness of the nature of the
> Soviet threat, is capable of contributing inadvertently to the most
> ruthless colonialism men have known.[135]

Meanwhile, Niebuhr, in a number of articles and editorials, was
leveling similar criticisms at the Administration. "Evidence has
been accumulating for some time that the President has some very
naïve ideas on the relation of power to morality in politics," is the
opening sentence of one such article.[136] America's task does not
call for taking time off from her job of leadership of the free world
to preach moralistic homilies to her allies, and pose as umpire in
the East-West struggle.[137]

Niebuhr found most dismaying the pacifist presuppositions inherent in the numerous speeches disavowing the use of force. To
draw pacifist conclusions from the unthinkable nature of a nuclear
war was to play into the hands of the Soviet and, in this case, to
strengthen Nasser's intransigence.[138]

Equally deplorable was all the glib talk about loyalty to the
United Nations. In this he regarded the Administration as guilty
of accentuating the widespread misconception of the United Nations as a super-government capable of solving world problems.
"Our devout expressions of loyalty to it therefore became but a
screen for our irresponsibility; for the United Nations can do
nothing without the leadership of the Western powers."[139]

In summing up, two things must be said. First, we must reassert that the criticism of realists like Niebuhr, Thompson, and Morgenthau was not designed to condone the British and French action. They regarded that action as reckless, poorly timed, and altogether a wrong procedure. Their indictment is directed at the bankruptcy of American statesmanship that allowed events to get out of control, of being heedless about the meaning of the Western alliance, *and* when events had taken the turn they did, they criticized the criteria by which Britain and France were judged. The latter were clearly mistaken on the grounds of a pragmatic test. But to judge them from moralistic grounds raised to the level of political absolutes was worse than presumptuous; it reinvigorated a dangerous habit of political thought and succeeded in confusing the real issues of the situation.

Secondly, if the criticism offered by Niebuhr and other realists seems to oscillate between contending that at one time America has a too severely military view of power and a moralistic one at others, then what is to be seen *is not the apparent inconsistency of the critics but the fundamental unity of the moralistic and military approaches. Both are fundamentally non-political.* Both overestimate our power, though in different ways. Both are expressions of the "grand simplifiers." Herein is the reason why isolationists and moralists so frequently support each other in concrete issues, and why American policy can move so quickly from the towering moralism of the Suez crisis to the military threats of the Eisenhower doctrine.

We have attempted in this chapter to outline the structure of Niebuhr's political philosophy through a discussion of four major areas—democracy, communism, the character of his political realism, and his views on American foreign policy, with special reference to the "anatomy of authority." At every point it is obvious how his Christian understanding of man and history illuminates and informs his political thought, and how he regards the resources of spirit derived from biblical faith as alone adequate to the strains of the struggle. His norm is truly absolute and transcendent, and this frees him from investing some proximate aim with ultimate value, providing instead a pragmatic flexibility to encounter situations in all their contingency and uniqueness. Nowhere is it more clear that Niebuhr's thought is always controlled by the dialectical relation of *agape* and justice than when he is wrestling with political decisions and policies.

*Seven*

# WAR AND PEACE

No issue has been so central in the experience of our generation as war. Revulsion from war, preparation for war, the prosecution of history's most terrible war, the perilous balance of the "cold war"—such has been the context for those whose days have been set in the past four decades. War has touched every aspect of our experience; it has been, for twentieth-century men, the one universal and inescapable social fact. Consequently, nothing serves to reveal more quickly the structure, content, and relevance of our thought than our attitude to war. This has been, in some respects, especially true of Christian thought. Niebuhr has remarked that it is unfortunate that the debate in Christian circles must always be upon the issue of pacifism.[1] Yet it is inevitable that this should be the case, for the questions of war and peace throw into clear relief not only considerations of strategy but the whole structure of our theological thought, our Christology, our understanding of grace and law, our views of the nature of man and history. In this debate it is never simply a matter of differences in the social views and strategies of Christians; this issue, in our time at least, has always thrown the Christian community into a fundamental struggle over the nature of the gospel itself. Participation in war has always been a profoundly serious question for Christians; and the horrors of modern warfare have made this question a matter of agonizing daily concern for every sensitive spirit. All that we think and believe and love and hope for become passionately and agonizingly focused on this issue.

When we reflect on the social realities and the condition of the theological and political thought of the American churches during the past four decades, it is not surprising that the questions of war and peace have bulked so large in Niebuhr's writing. To follow the development of his thought on this issue, and to see the character of the controversies in which he was engaged with fellow Christians, is to be thrust into the center of the story of American Christianity in our time. Thus, it seems advisable to adopt a more chronological approach in our discussion of this issue.

## 1. NIEBUHR'S EARLY PACIFISM

Niebuhr was once considered a pacifist and was, indeed, for a period the national chairman of the Fellowship of Reconciliation. John Bennett is altogether right, however, in pointing out that Niebuhr was never "in theory consistently an absolute pacifist."[2] It was a position that he never held with clear confidence; all his professions of pacifism were qualified with statements revealing how troubled and dissatisfied he was with the position. Niebuhr's pacifism represents that period in his life when the absolute claims of the Gospel have not been clearly distinguished from the absolutism of his abstract idealism, and when his passion for justice was mixed with the prevailing emotion of revulsion from war.

A few examples will disclose the character of his "troubled pacifism." In 1923 he wrote in his diary that he was *resolved* to be a pacifist. "I am done with this business. I hope I can make that resolution stick."[3] But immediately he is wondering if there is a "more fundamental force" than nausea to maintain the conviction.[4] In an article written in 1927, we see how an abstract idealism informs his pacifism: "I view the antagonisms of nations and insist that in the political situation at least I will follow the law of love. I have sworn off this war business with many of my brethren. I think I see clearly that civilizations are not successfully protected by force and that armaments aggravate fears and fears hatreds. I am therefore a pacifist."[5] But here too he is troubled. He wonders if his pacifist conviction has any real firm rooting. "Would I be as good a pacifist if I belonged to an unsatisfied nation rather than to a satisfied one? Perhaps my pacifism is related to the pacifism of the beast of prey whose maw is crammed."[6] This entire article is a good example of Niebuhr's probing honesty. In 1930 he still thinks that the "judgments of the church on war and peace represent a clear gain over previous generations," but his pacifism remains critical. "Only the day of crisis will reveal . . . whether our present convictions on war and peace are the result of nausea or of a genuine understanding of the moral issues involved in international strife."[7]

Shortly after this, his break with pacifism becomes clear and by 1932 the total inadequacy of the position for a person endeavoring to be politically responsible is a constant theme. The whole issue became focused for him on the question of coercion in the struggle for social justice. The context of his break with pacifism was social and industrial strife rather than international conflict. His use at this time of a Marxian analysis of social ills served only to bring the issue sharply upon the question of coercion.

For a person concerned with the plight of the socially disinherited and the struggle to secure a more equal justice, the position of absolute pacifism became clearly untenable. Religious idealists who opposed the strike activities of organized labor because they regarded them as a violation of the law of love revealed that they were not only politically irrelevant but also morally confused. It meant that in the name of love, injustice was to be preferred to the resistance necessary for the attainment of a higher justice.[8]

Coercion is necessary for the attainment of justice. Those who possess irresponsible power will not be persuaded to sacrifice it through moral and rational exhortations. To be sure, the use of coercion carries with it the danger that its users will become the locus of a new injustice, but that peril in no way lessens the necessity. Acknowledgment of this meant, for Niebuhr, an end to his pacifism. Violence is not in itself evil, therefore it cannot be ruled out on *a priori* grounds. Before long he would acknowledge: "With Augustine we must realize that the peace of the world is gained by strife." [9] A responsible relation to the political order is incompatible with an absolute pacifism.

Although the social order and the "class struggle" form the decisive context for Niebuhr's break with pacifism, his realistic appraisal of the perils of the international situation so unusual in those days of optimism, ought not to be overlooked. As early as 1931 he was estimating the peril to peace in German anger over the Versailles treaty and "the Hitler movement." [10] In 1933, he appealed to the American churches and government to let Germany know how America regarded its anti-Semitism and to find ways of relief for the Jews.[11] In 1934 in *Reflections on the End of an Era,* he wrote, "Another world war seems practically inevitable. But it is not at all certain when it will come." But before he completed the book he was persuaded that "a new war in Europe is only a matter of years."[12] Much of the pacifism of the 1930's was an expression of the confident dogmas of historical progress and human perfectability; Niebuhr was blinkered by no such illusions and so was able to "discern the signs of the times."

John Bennett's remark that the pacifist issue represents "a kind of watershed" in Niebuhr's thought is to be taken in all seriousness. It was a struggle of immense significance for the development and toughening of his thought. For this controversy involved before it was over (if it is over) the whole range of his theological and political thought. To his critique of pacifism we now turn.

## 2. CRITIQUE AND CONTROVERSY

Niebuhr regards most pacifism as not only a deplorable political strategy but as a pernicious heresy. Pacifists are right in their recognition that love is the law of life. Their heresy consists in their reduction of Christianity to this law. The result is that the "good news" is reduced to a "challenge" and a gospel of "we must

try harder." The whole power of the gospel inheres in the fact
that it deals with the condition of men, all men not just some men,
who inevitably violate the law of their own essential nature. At
the precise moment in history when the Reformation understanding of man's sin and the justifying grace of God could illumine
every fact of our collective existence, modern pacifists proclaimed
a Renaissance faith in man. The moralism of American pacifism in
the 1930's was informed by a piety that substituted Jesus the Hero
for the Christ of historic faith, faith in man's goodness for wonder
at God's mercy, the dogma of progress for the doctrine of the
atonement.[13]

Niebuhr has consistently distinguished between two types of
pacifism. He has always held a firm respect for that type of sectarian perfectionism represented by certain Mennonite groups.
This is not "heretical" and performs a valuable service to the community in reminding us that our norms of relative justice are all
tentative and that all our efforts to achieve and maintain a tolerable
justice and order stand under the criticism of *agape*. The pacifism
of such groups is able to perform this service insofar as it does not
claim that its pacifism is a strategy for the solution of political
strife. Such groups disavowed the political task and contented
themselves with setting up a symbol of the Kingdom of God in the
life of individuals and small communities. Most American pacifism was of quite another sort. It regarded the Cross as a social
strategy, as a method for overcoming political and international
conflict. The "way of Jesus" was projected as a success story. It was
against this kind of pacifism that Niebuhr struggled.

Such a pacifism not only turned the Christology and anthropology of biblical faith upside down, it diluted the command of
love it everywhere proclaimed. This was done by changing the
ethic of non-resistance so unambiguously proclaimed in the Sermon on the Mount into an ethic of non-violent resistance. For many
Americans Gandhi, with his rather successful resistance of British
"imperialism," became the grand exemplar of the Christian "way,"
the "strategy" of love, the "politics of the Cross." The Sermon on

the Mount became a counsel of prudence. Through this distortion of the New Testament ethic of non-resistance, pacifism presented itself as at one and the same time a political method and a religious absolute, and thereby compounded political naïveté with heresy at every crucial point.

In the concrete situation, such pacifism issues in two things: it gives the advantage to tyranny, and in the name of love it issues in a perverse lovelessness for the victims of tyranny.[14]

The crux of the whole issue lies in the profound failure of such pacifism to understand the relationship between love and justice. Love is an over-arching command confronting us in every situation and relation of life. It is not a "neat formula to use in situations of violence." Nor is justice merely an inferior, worldly norm; it is love finding embodiment in worldly structures. Love demands not only sacrifice but also social responsibility.[15]

If we are to understand the character and the tenacity of American pacifism in the 1930's we must observe two other deeply ingrained habits of thought—the view that somehow one could act in history without guilt, and the manner in which war was isolated and abstractly viewed as a "system."

This is everywhere evident, but we may focus it on the "open letters" of Niebuhr and the distinguished Canadian churchman and pacifist, Richard Roberts, published at a time when Canada but not the United States was at war. Roberts wrote: "No doubt, in every war, one side is more in the wrong than the other. But the *process* of war is the same on both sides." And again, "I detest Hitlerism and all its works. But the judgment to be made as between the parties at war is not the only judgment called for from Christian men today. There is a judgment to be passed upon the whole business of war, and of *this* war, as *War* over against the revealed righteousness of God."[16] Niebuhr replies by discussing the sectarian perfectionism out of which pacifism has grown and then turns the argument on Roberts: "You are willing to slightly favor the Allies against Hitler, but you are not willing to allow such a discrimination to result in an action in favor of one side against the other. To allow such an action is to involve yourself in sin. Your difficulty is that you want to live in history without sinning. There is no such possibility in history."[17] All historical action is involved in guilt. Our task is not to demand guiltlessness of a party in a strife, nor to imagine that neutrality is innocence, but to make significant discriminations between less and worse evils; and when we act upon that discrimination to be contritely aware of the guilt in our relatively just action, and of the resource of divine mercy that alone can cover the hurt of what we must do to be responsible.

It is impossible to understand the crusading zeal of American pacifism unless we see how war is abstracted from the rest of historical reality and viewed as an entity in itself. When Niebuhr, in his youth, resolved to be a pacifist, he said he had sworn off this "war business." The same concept ruled Roberts's convictions in 1940. It was the "*process* of war," "war as War" that had to be judged and opposed. War was the real evil, the enemy that had to be "fought." Nazi Germany was no doubt an evil and threatening power, but it was not *the* evil, it was not the most serious threat to civilization. The real threat to civilization was war. The slogan "Nothing is so evil as war" was widely and passionately believed, a perfect example of the tyranny of an idea. Neither the zeal—nor the blindness—of the pacifism of these years can be understood until we see how war was abstracted from the rest of reality to where it could be named as *the* evil, and then viewed as something to be "renounced," "disavowed," "sworn off," a "system" to be fought against and once for all "removed." It was a problem to be mastered by men of reason and an evil to be conquered by men of goodwill.

Such a viewpoint involved an entire philosophy of life, an integrated view of the nature of man, evil, and history. This must be seen if we are to understand the tenacity of this pacifism, the vigor of its arguments, and the fact that for so many the coming of war shook, but did not really collapse, the position. To oppose such a position was not merely to have a different viewpoint on a social question, it was to attack an entire life philosophy, to strike its representatives in the center of their beings, in the vital philosophy which pervaded, sustained, and gave meaning to the whole of life. But if this *is* seen we can apprehend the passion, bitterness, and real seriousness of the debate. In a word, what was at issue in the pacifist debate was a whole understanding of the Christian gospel and the nature of historical and political reality. This is why the pacifist struggle was of such signal importance in the development and clarification of Niebuhr's thought.

The times were urgent and the stakes were high. The culture of the great democracies was so vapid as to have allowed them to slip to the very brink of disaster. The London *Times,* for example, hailed the capitulation of Munich as a triumph of reason over force with these words, "at the moment when the current racing toward the precipice seemed irresistible, it was the leadership of the British Prime Minister that showed how immense were the forces ranged on the side of reason against violence."[18]

It was a time when all the resources of the Christian faith for illuminating the nature of historical reality were urgently needed. And in that hour the moralism and pacifism of the churches but further confounded the confusion. Never, Niebuhr felt, had the churches of America been "upon a lower level of spiritual insight and moral sensitivity than in this tragic age of world conflict."[19] "If modern churches were to symbolize their true faith they would take the crucifix from their altars and substitute the three little monkeys who counsel men to 'speak no evil, hear no evil, see no evil.' "[20]

Into this situation came Frank Buchman with his simple solution for the problems of the world. It was, thought Niebuhr, the final and most pathetic fruit of the heritage of liberal moralism, and perhaps no movement received from him such undisguised contempt. "Of the tragic character of either the religious or the political problem of man the Oxford Groupers have not the slightest inkling. They seem really to believe that selfishness flourishes on earth because unselfishness has not had the prestige of being pro-

claimed in international conferences, of being advocated by prominent statesmen and given a blessing by Miss Mae West." [21]

In church circles, the pacifist debate reached its peak during
the period from Munich to Pearl Harbor. It was, as we have said,
an encounter between two incompatible interpretations of Christianity and history. This may be shown by a quick glance at the
controversy between Niebuhr and *The Christian Century*.

Out of a huge quantity of material we select as typical an article
by E. F. Tittle written in the fall of 1938. The article has three main
points: (1) Military resistance of the dictators is a bad thing because war is cruel and solves nothing. (2) Economic boycott would
likewise be bad because such action might lead to war. (3) "A third
answer is that military aggression can be stopped only by a valiant,
persistent attempt to do justly, love mercy and to walk humbly
with God." [22] He then supports the Van Zeeland Report calling for
a World Economic conference. In like vein, A. W. Palmer suggested that the Church should call its own world economic conference, an idea which was supported editorially. Niebuhr replied
to Tittle's article with the inevitable query: "Is it really 'Christian,'
is it God's will, never to call the bluff of a bully for fear that you
might be involved in violence? Then we had better prepare for the
complete victory of the barbarism which is spreading over
Europe." [23]

The notion that a conference of good and reasonable men might
still save the situation, was embraced as late as May 1940 by C. C.
Morrison. In an editorial entitled "What Can America Do for
Peace?" he proposes the calling of a conference of neutrals who are
referred to as—note the phrasing—the "custodians of the civilization
which the war is destroying." He then named the little countries
not yet overrun. Niebuhr replied in a Letter to the Editor, "Has it
not occurred to you that most of them are shivering little mice
waiting for the cat to pounce upon them . . . ?" [24] By the time this
was published, the event had occurred, so Morrison was forced
to acknowledge this in the same issue. His reply is simply incredible. The only thing wrong with his proposal was that it came too

late! "Our proposal may have come too late for this war. It is in
good time, however, for the next war." One shudders, even in the
retrospect of years, at the smug complacency of that line. The
*Blitzkrieg* did not even puncture the philosophy informing this
pacifism. In a sermon preached in Rockefeller Memorial Chapel on
June 2, 1940, Morrison continued to beat his pacifist breast, but
now with the rhythm of isolationism. "How much longer must the
hell of fire burn in Europe before we learn that all our talk of
defending civilization by war is irrational? How could civilization
be more utterly destroyed than by modern war? To prepare America for a gratuitous entrance into this scene because, forsooth,
Great Britain may be about to fall, is to act like a silly moth drawn
into a flame or like a dumb sheep following other sheep to the
slaughter." [25] Pacifism had indeed become a counsel of prudence!

War was the evil. On that basis, it was inevitable that this "political" pacifism fell, at every crucial point, into advocating the peace
of tyranny. Many defended the views of Colonel Lindbergh and
opposed Lend Lease. "No matter how they twist and turn," Niebuhr
wrote, "the protagonists of a political, rather than a religious, pacifism end with the acceptance and justification of, and connivance
with, tyranny. They proclaim that slavery is better than war. I beg
leave to doubt it and to challenge the whole system of sentimen-
talized Christianity which prompts good men to arrive at this
perverse conclusion." [26] One of the reasons for the establishment
of the journal *Christianity and Crisis* was to provide a medium
through which the challenge could be effectively made.[27]

While *The Christian Century* kept appealing to the President
to be more circumspect in his neutrality, Niebuhr was calling for
the repeal of the Neutrality Act. "We demand the immediate repeal of the Neutrality Act because it is one of the most immoral
laws that was ever spread upon a federal statute book." [28] The
essence of morality is the acceptance of responsibility. It is a
soberly reasoned article. But Morrison—less than a month before
Pearl Harbor—countered with a flaming attack. War is the evil,
therefore it is nonsense to say that neutrality is immoral. Of

Niebuhr's article he wrote: "We can only say that when the Christian writings of this war period are brought forth for post-war analysis and judgment, it will surely be cause for regret that a document of this sort will have to be exhibited." [29] It is not necessary to make the obvious comment! Increasingly, political pacifism, informed by Christian perfectionism was forced, by the course of history, to embrace the sorry program of isolationism and the "America First" Committee, which bore no relationship to any sort of religious idealism. Such was the logic of the whole position. [30]

It ought to be made clear that Niebuhr did not advocate America making a declaration of war. He made it clear from the outset, in scores of articles, that such action was indeed what was demanded if she were to be really responsible. But he realized very well that ideals are limited by geography. America's vital interests were not yet imperiled, or rather, not obviously enough imperiled for the Administration to be able to unite the nation behind such a declaration of war. That America both would, and should, enter the war was a conviction from the beginning; the question was a strategic one of when. That question was, of course, resolved by the Japanese attack. "History had overtaken us while we were still debating whether or not we should assume the obligations toward which history pointed." [31]

We have emphasized that the zeal and character of American pacifism cannot be understood until we see that it isolated war as a "system" and regarded it as the prime evil against which men were called to crusade. Nor did the fact of involvement in war collapse this type of thought for many. They had hated war, had "fought" against it, and they had lost. But what many could not see was that their very approach contributed to making war inevitable. Such was the tyranny of an abstract religious idealism.

## 3. MESSAGE DURING THE WAR

Through all the dreary years and months preceding American entrance into the war, Niebuhr had had to inveigh against a moralism that failed to make the kind of historical distinctions upon which freedom and health depend; now it became as necessary to speak against the kind of moralism that viewed the war as a holy crusade. The deep resources of Christian faith are not plumbed until we learn to love the enemy while we fight him with all our strength; to resist to the utmost an evil without hatred or bitterness.

To love an enemy does not mean that we are emotionally attached to him; he is a real enemy. "To love our enemies cannot mean that we must connive with their injustice. It does mean that beyond all moral distinctions of history we must know ourselves one with our enemies not only in the bonds of a common humanity but also in the bonds of a common guilt by which that humanity has become corrupted. The Christian faith must persuade us to be humble rather than self-righteous in carrying out our historic tasks. It is this humility which is the source of pity and forgiveness." [32] Just as a one-dimensional moralism had previously to be opposed because it could not discern our historical responsibilities, so now it must be warned against its tendency to obscure the meaning of the common guilt.

As the war progressed, Niebuhr increasingly emphasized the awful responsibility for positive reconstruction to which the victors would fall heir. He never shared the illusions of pacifists and the generally tender-minded that such a powerful foe could be defeated without involving us in the tragic necessities of total war. The defeat of tyranny would, in itself, give the war a negative justification. But in order to give the war its positive meaning, we must see beyond the immediate issues, pressing as they were. For this task, to quote the title of an article, "Airplanes Are Not Enough." [33] Moreover, to empty our cause of its moral content could only serve to arm the enemy with the morale of pure despair.

Necessities are no less necessities because they are tragic; but an awareness of the tragic nature of necessity is productive of a healing spirit,[34] and of the understanding that "only the Divine mercy is adequate for the infinite pathos of human existence."[35]

Such recognition of the ambiguous nature of good and evil could in no way absolve us from making discriminate judgments in the day of victory, but to know that such judgments themselves stand under a divine judgment is the precondition of reconciliation and indeed of political wisdom. "Vengeance is mine, I will repay, saith the Lord."[36] Failure to heed that injunction means that the judgment of God is obscured by the judgment of the victors, who being judges in their own case are inevitably tempted to vainglory.

The significance of Niebuhr's understanding of justice as grounded in and as an embodiment of *agape*, and yet as always transcended by *agape*, is nowhere more vividly displayed than in the question of the punishment of the enemy. The abstract concepts of a moral or legalistic justice are altogether ill-fitted to deal with such a situation. Religious profundity and political wisdom both arise from an understanding of the complex relation between *agape* and justice.

> Nowhere is the difference between a pure moralism and the reverence and humility of true Christian faith more apparent than in the problem of punishing a foe. Morality demands "justice." But religious faith recognizes that there are crimes too terrible to be punished by the hand of man; and there are punishments in history more terrible than any crime deserves, so that the God of history is both more terrible and more merciful than any of our nicely calculated schemes of punishment and justice.
>
> There is a greater affinity between the forgiveness which faith requires and the prudence which political realities require than there is between either and the "justice" which is demanded by pure morals. There is always something abstract about justice. It tries to measure what can not be measured. For neither the dimension of a great sin, nor the guiltiness of those who are implicated in it can be exactly measured; at least not by creatures who are unable to look into the secret of the heart. But political prudence adjusts itself to the complicated realities of the human community

as Christian forgiveness grows out of an understanding of the dimension of good and evil, of mercy and wrath which transcend the realities of history.[37]

## 4. WORLD GOVERNMENT

Many factors have conspired to make proposals for World Government a topic of widespread discussion in our time. The ancient heritage of religious and moral universalism has converged with the new universalism achieved by modern technology. However, the potential world community has announced itself through the medium of two world wars, with the result that the impetus of fear of world destruction has been added to that of moral and technical universalism. This is clearly expressed in the slogan "one world or none." Coupled with these forces is still another, the heritage of the simple solution informed by rationalistic moralism.[38]

Niebuhr has been consistently and sharply critical of all such proposals. They rest upon assumptions riddled with many fallacies, which can, however, be reduced to two. These fallacious assumptions are that governments can be created by fiat and that governments are capable of creating community.

*Governments are not simply created by fiat.* "A small community is as primordial as the individual. No group of individuals has ever created either government or community out of whole cloth."[39] Americans are particularly inclined to believe that governments can be so created because more than other nations they were influenced by the theory of social contract. But even the American Constitution had, as its purpose, the establishment of a "more perfect union." A previous communal union had been established in battle. The constitution stood at the end rather than the beginning of the process. It is further to be remembered that a civil war was fought to preserve this "more perfect union." The experience of the thirteen colonies is in no way an analogy for the present world situation. Vital, organic social processes and cohesions undergird every communal authority unless that authority is tyrannically imposed. If such a community does not exist, authority for it cannot be created simply by constitutional instruments. The world community to erect such an authority simply does not exist.

We have to deal not only with the fact that governments are not simply created by fiat; we have to deal with the fact of existing sovereign nations. The task of securing the abridgement, let alone the abnegation, of sovereignty is much more difficult than world federalists suppose. In fact, no such *explicit* abnegation has ever occurred. Moreover, the general fear of world anarchy which, it is argued, ought to motivate nations to abnegate their sovereignty is not nearly so potent as the fear of a concrete foe which motivates nations to increase the strength of their *particular* center of power.

There is some recognition of these realities when it is frequently admitted by proponents of World Government, that Russia could probably not be persuaded to abnegate her sovereignty.[40] But there the whole proposal breaks down. They are then reduced either to clutching the illusion that if we established such a government without Russia, it would prove to be so attractive that she would be happy to have a minority voice in it, or to solidify in the name of "one world" the existing division of the world by having a non-communist world government arrayed against the Russian empire. Something like that is perhaps conceivable, but then it would not be based upon "law" but on the extension of NATO power.

*Governments cannot by themselves create community.* The community, in at least inchoate form, is prior to its laws, and the authority of government is primarily the authority of the community itself.[41] Government does not create, but regularizes the integration that takes place through common experience.

To be sure, the international community is not totally lacking in social tissue; there is an increasing measure of economic interdependence, there is the recognition of the real possibility of mutual annihilation, and there is the moral force derived from the sense of obligation that enlightened men have toward the total human community. But these resources are indeed scant when measured against the forces of particularity. As Niebuhr has said, "To call attention to this fact does not mean that all striving for a higher and wider integration of the world community is vain. That task must and will engage the conscience of mankind for ages to come. But the edifice of government which we build will be sound and useful if its height is proportionate to the strength of the materials from which it is constructed." [42]

World government is not among the real alternatives facing us. We are confronted with only two real alternatives; (1) Global destruction through atomic war and (2) an indefinite period in which atomic conflict is precariously avoided and in which the organic processes of world community are given time and opportunity to develop. Instead of having our energies drained off in the construction of irrelevant schemes, concern for building the world community would be better served by a philosophy that knows that life is a better unifier than law, and that community, like political justice, is achieved "not merely by destroying, but also by deflecting, beguiling and harnessing residual self-interest and by finding the greatest possible concurrence between self-interest and the general welfare." [43]

Within these limitations the United Nations serves a most important function. It cannot itself prevent war; nor is there any chance of its growing into a world government. But in addition to the immensely valuable work performed by its various groups, commissions, and organizations, the United Nations performs a signal service in the interests of peace. "On the one hand, it is a minimal bridge across the chasm between Russia and the West. On the other hand, it furnishes the meeting ground for the free nations, the aegis for its various *ad hoc* arrangements for defensive communities; and an assembly of peoples in which world opinion serves to check the policies of the most powerful nations in the alliance." [44] Given the realities of conflict and peril in our world, this service of keeping the lines of communication open is of incalculable significance.

The United Nations can make this contribution the better if it is not expected to do what it is ill-fitted to do. The United Nations cannot fulfill the role of traditional diplomacy. Microphone diplomacy is bad diplomacy—in fact it becomes histrionics. It is inevitable that the positions of the disputants become inflexible. There is no substitute for careful, confidential, professional diplomacy.

The Christian churches, especially in America, are clearly devoted to the principle of the United Nations. This devotion is right and good, but there is a peril in it to which Niebuhr has properly drawn our attention. Loyalty to the principle of the United Nations can easily become an abstract substitute for "concern for those acts of daily fidelity through which an international community comes into being." Niebuhr continues, "We ought therefore, as churches, emphasize not so much the abstract principle of international responsibility as we ought to bring Christian resources to bear upon the tremendous problem of a great and rich nation, relating itself tolerably to a weak and impoverished world."[45] This warning needs to be sounded and it constitutes a concrete example of what is meant by a reorientation of American idealism.

## 5. THE BOMB

We are a frightened generation. The harnessing of atomic energy and the conquest of space are achievements which would have thrilled former generations with visions of the conquest of man, but they have created for us an entirely different vision, and filled the world with fear. In that contrast lies much of the spiritual history of modern man.

War now possesses a new dimension, the dimension of total annihilation. Confronted with that fact, can we now, as previously, say that the slogan "Nothing is so evil as war" is a false slogan?

We are faced with a profound dilemma. Our task is to find the perilous way between atomic warfare and capitulation to tyranny. The "Bomb" has not altered the total situation. What it has done is reveal with fresh vividness the ambiguity of all historic decisions, of how frightfully insecure is the basis of our human security. No one has seen this more clearly, nor expressed it more eloquently than Churchill when he said, "Security is the sturdy child of terror and survival the twin brother of annihilation." Admittedly, the prospect of atomic war has given the pacifist position a new plausibility, and there are voices which regard this atomic peril as being so great that we ought to minimize, in comparison, the peril of tyranny.

This position must, I think, be rejected for a number of reasons. First, it assumes that nations can simply renounce the power of their defense and thus invite destruction. There is no evidence whatever that nations possess this capacity. It contains further an assumption about man which is untenable. Man cannot win freedom by renouncing his freedom to destroy, he can win freedom only by mastering that freedom. The freedom to create cannot be extricated from the freedom to destroy as such a pacifism assumes. The predicament of man cannot be so simply solved; the path in which we must walk is more tortuous.

Our century has been filled with proposals and negotiations for disarmament, and it has been a dismal story. These proposals have never produced disarmament. When we have disarmed it was not because of negotiations, but out of complacent illusions of security which produced disastrous consequences. In the present situation, the fundamental error is simply that disarmament proposals put the cart before the horse. Niebuhr put this succinctly at the time Mr. Stassen was pursuing his negotiations. There is, said Niebuhr, "an *a priori* reason for predicting the ultimate failure of the negotiations. It is that international tensions are not mitigated by disarmament, but disarmament is made possible by the relaxation of tensions."[46]

The question of a balanced defense program is much more to the point. The capacity of the two great powers to wage an all-out nuclear war may deter the outbreak of the "ultimate war." But the capacity to deter the expansion of communism is dependent upon the capacity to wage a limited war with "conventional" weapons. Failure to do this would only make the "ultimate war" increasingly inevitable.[47] The theologian has no competence to discuss the details of such questions of strategy, but he has something to say to the "all or nothing" psychology.

The new dimension of war underlines the importance of finding methods of peaceful change. It has not altered the basic situation, but it has made this need compellingly urgent. Wise, patient, and prudent statesmanship is no longer simply desirable, it has become an utter necessity. The church can best contribute to the development of such statesmanship by leaving aside its predilection for grand and simple solutions, by counseling against all movements that make for hysteria, by illuminating with its knowledge of man's grandeur and misery the nature of historical reality, and by the development of those resources of spirit that will enable us with patience, steadiness, and understanding to confront the perils, within and without, with which we are beset. For the peril in which we live will not be conquered in a decade or in a century. Man now knows that he lives under the shadow of such perilous power forevermore.

*Eight*

# ECONOMICS

Niebuhr is no economist in the narrow and more technical sense of the term. He has sustained no specialized study in this area. But insofar as economics is a branch of moral and political philosophy, it has been very much in the center of his thought. His passion for social justice first expressed itself in his concern for the desperate plight of the economically impoverished in the late 'twenties and 'thirties and in a basic criticism of the economic structure of society. Nor has the improvement in the lot of the worker in recent years or the changes in his own economic and political philosophy blunted his recognition of the immense significance of the realities of economic life for a just and functioning society. His outlook has remained rigorously whole. Unlike many of his contemporaries, the incredible wealth of post-war America has not provided the occasion for him to retreat into a consideration of Christian faith in an individualistic or exclusively personal manner.

Niebuhr's present thought in this area can best be understood if it is first seen in the light of his earlier struggle. That context is the intellectual struggle in the days of the Great Depression to find a vantage point from which to make an effective Christian criticism whereby the economic and social realities of the day could be livingly engaged, without falling into the inanities of conventional religion on the one hand and without embracing the illusions and dogmatism of Marxism on the other. It was an immensely difficult task. His present position, however, is not to be understood without some consideration of the insights won, and the mistakes made, in an attempt undertaken with such honesty and restless self-criticism.

The character of this struggle can be most briefly indicated by noting his profound dissatisfaction with the inadequacy and irrelevance of conventional religion and by considering his so-called Christian Marxism.

## 1. NIEBUHR'S CRITIQUE OF CONVENTIONAL RELIGION AND HIS CHRISTIAN MARXISM

Confronted with a profound economic breakdown involving untold suffering in large sections of society, conventional religion assumed that the profundity of Christian criticism and love were contained in the message of stewardship which usually did not extend beyond exhortations to philanthropy.[1] Charity has been the favorite substitute of conventional religion for justice. The Christian Church has always had difficulty relating its norm of *agape* to the struggles to secure a balance of power in the social order, and this historic difficulty has been further compounded by the individualism and simple perfectionism of America's revivalist heritage. This was vividly brought home to Niebuhr when, as a member of a church committee, he was invited to investigate an outbreak of industrial violence occasioned by a strike of miners in Harlan County, Kentucky. Commenting on the fact that the church was "pretty unqualifiedly on the side of the operators," Niebuhr adds:

> Since the conscience of the Christian church has been confused by the tendency to substitute charity for justice through all the ages, one ought not be too severe on the ministers and Christian people of Pineville. One of the best ministers in Pineville refuted my analysis of this problem in the traditional Christian manner. I insisted that whenever the love ideal of Christianity degenerates into pure philanthropy without regard for the difficult task of achieving social justice, it becomes a cloak behind which social

injustice hides itself. He answered by accusing me of "putting the cart before the horse." Only the Christian spirit of love, he declared, could achieve justice. Since we were told that in a revival meeting in all the churches which preceded our visit by several weeks practically everyone in town had been brought to "salvation," I naturally wondered just what one should think of the "fruits of the spirit" which the history of the town had recently revealed![2]

Philanthropists are invariably more popular than social prophets. And when in hard times the philanthropist can boast that his generosity takes the form of providing security and justice for his workers, then he becomes a hero. Thus Henry Ford, with his claim that an adequate wage was the basis of his philanthropy, became the hero of America. Niebuhr has acknowledged that in attacking this boast his "first interest was not so much to challenge the reigning laissez-faire philosophy of the community as to 'debunk' the moral pretensions of Henry Ford,"[3] but it helped nevertheless to lead him to a profounder consideration of the limitations of the prevailing economic philosophy. But certainly he debunked the pretensions of Ford! In two devastating articles, "How Philanthropic Is Henry Ford?" and "Ford's Five-Day Week Shrinks," he showed the emptiness of the claim by disclosing what the annual wage of the majority of workers was and by a humane, detailed description of the plight of representative families and the desperate need for unemployment insurance. Clearly the situation revealed not only the hollowness of Ford's boast, but also the hopeless inadequacy of "a social philosophy not advanced beyond the doctrinaire individualism of the nineteenth century. . . ."[4]

If the individualism of conventional religion was inimical to the concern for social justice, it soon became clear to Niebuhr that the sentimentalism and pacifism informing so much of the social gospel approach was likewise inadequate. A far more realistic understanding of the nature of power relations was necessary if the realities of the social order were to be clearly grasped and if Christian faith was to make any contribution to the social question. It is in the light of this that Niebuhr's "Christian Marxism" ought to be considered.

It is not our concern here to trace the influence of Marxist thought in Niebuhr's intellectual pilgrimage or to measure its intensity at various stages. That has been done by professors Bennett, Schlesinger, and Thompson.[5] Niebuhr frequently—especially in 1934—referred to himself as a Christian Marxist. Our concern is to say as plainly as possible what his Christian Marxism was and what it was not.

The first thing to say is that it was largely a polemical instrument, a resource of social analysis which appeared most strong at the points where liberalism seemed most defective. "The intellectual attraction of Marxism," remarks R. H. Crossman, "was that it exploded liberal fallacies—which were real fallacies."[6] The dogma of progress, the notion that power politics was a transitory phenomenon, the idea that social injustice could be resolved by appeals to love, reason, and the operations of the free market—these illusions and many more were challenged by the Marxian analysis. It was perhaps inevitable that the illusions of liberalism made the truth in Marxism appear more completely true than it was. Nevertheless there were very few in those days who combined his passion for social justice with such a clear recognition of the serious limitations of Marxism as did Niebuhr. He referred to himself as a Christian Marxist, he appropriated its insights into the nature of the class struggle and the ideological corruption of our idealism, but he was never beguiled by the most basic assumptions of Marxism.

From the beginning, Niebuhr deplored the dangerous utopianism in Marxist thought. "The hope that the internal enemies will all be destroyed and that the new society will create only men who will be in perfect accord with the collective will of society, and will not seek personal advantage in the social process, is romantic in its interpretation of the possibilities of human nature and in its mystical glorification of the anticipated automatic mutuality in the communist society."[7] Two years later—in 1934—he would assert even more pointedly of such radicalism, "Its utopianism makes it incapable of recognizing the relativities in its moral attitudes and the possibilities of new tyrannies and injustices in its policies." [8] Marxist utopianism, like its liberal counterpart, had no room for the experience of grace. [9] Nor was he ever beguiled by the Marxist pretension to be an authoritative philosophy of history because of its supposed scientific character. This he simply consigned to the "category of religious overbeliefs rather than that of scientific truths." [10] Its confident faith, he remarked elsewhere, "that good will grow out of disaster, belongs definitely to the category of mythology rather than science." [11] Such illusions only served to blind it politically. Although the full horror of a political movement claiming to possess a total human solution only gradually came home to him, Niebuhr was never anything but critical of such assumptions and aware of the social dangers inherent in them.

What then can we say of the positive impact of Marxism on his thought in the 'thirties? This influence can be divided into two categories: (a) those insights first derived from Marxism as opposed to the illusions of liberalism which, having been rethought in his own philosophy, remain as important elements in the structure of his thought and (b) certain aspects of the Marxian analysis which he retained for a time and eventually cast off.

In the first group we must place his emphasis upon the social character of human existence. The Christian must learn to take the economic and political structures of society seriously, rejecting the notion that all will be well if only good and pious men are at the helm. The insight into the ideological character of our thought and action made a permanent deposit in Niebuhr's thought. There is an important difference, however: Niebuhr's understanding of ideology is much more radical than the communist, who sees it everywhere except in himself, whereas Niebuhr extends it to the "ideology of conscience." The view that justice is dependent upon the destruction of radical disproportions of power remains central in Niebuhr as we have repeatedly seen. But whereas communism compounds this insight with such illusions about the nature of "revolutionary men" that it issues in a monolithic concentration of political and economic power, Niebuhr uses it for the purpose of equilibriating power within a democratic framework.

In the second category, that is, ideas he retained for a period and eventually cast off, must be placed the Marxist analysis of capitalism. The Fellowship of Socialist Christians in its original statement of principles declared that it was "committed to the belief that the social ownership of the natural resources and the basic means of production is a primary requisite of justice in a technical age." The conviction was justified, as Niebuhr himself has recently reminded us, by the fairly orthodox Marxist analysis that "capitalism in its inevitable contracting phase subordinates the needs of the masses to the preservation and enhancement of a steadily narrowing class of owners."[12] Although critical of the dogma of progress associated with most socialist thought, Niebuhr still spoke in 1936 of the "logic of history" and asserted that "socialism is the next step forward."[13] Likewise in 1938 he writes that capitalism "is incompatible with the necessities of a technical civilization. Social ownership of the means of production is and has become a primary requisite of social health in a technical age."[14] He clearly recognizes, however, that ownership is not the only form of power achieved through property, and we find him at the same time critical of the unexamined Marxism informing much of John Mac-Murray's thought.[15] Socialism, like Marxism, was never unequivocally espoused but there can be no doubt that its analysis of capitalism, and consequently the necessity for socialist planning, remained in his thought for a period after he had rigorously rejected Marxist philosophy.

What was the significance of this fact? We have already noted that it was this which prevented him from coming to an appreciation of Roosevelt's pragmatic New Deal revolution. The abstract character of socialist analysis controlled his thought at this point at a time when he had otherwise cut himself free from abstract programs and blueprints. Speaking of the Fellowship of

Socialist Christians and its successor the Frontier Fellowship, Niebuhr writes:

> The fellowship partly challenged and partly shared the dogmas of socialism and the presuppositions of the "social gospel" tradition in modern Christianity. The worst that can be said about the fellowship, including its editorial voice, *Christianity and Society*, and the man who wrote most of the editorials (including this one) was that the fellowship was born in the thirties, and that the journal began publication almost synchronously with the New Deal, and that we all judged the beginning of this very significant pragmatic social revolution (which changed the whole face of America and its conscience) from the standpoint of an abstract idealism which we professed to abhor.[16]

In these days of almost hysterical conservatism, it may be worth emphasizing that it was the "abstract idealism" rather than the "left wing" character of his thought that Niebuhr deplores. The abstract character of American, as well as Marxist, idealism continued to inform the periphery of his thought after he had broken through it in the center. His clear recognition of this is an aspect of the increasing concreteness of his approach to political and economic questions. Seen in this light the aptness of Kenneth Thompson's observation is clear: "Perhaps no other error in Niebuhr's thinking has influenced so profoundly the development of the last stage of his philosophy."[17]

## 2. ECONOMIC PHILOSOPHY

The intellectual struggle to find a vantage point free from the illusions of the warring bourgeois and Marxist creeds has had its influence on the manner in which Niebuhr approaches the question of economic philosophy. He almost invariably approaches the question historically, through a critique of classical liberal economics, the Marxian revolt against its errors and consequent injustices, and the even greater injustices resulting from the errors and miscalculations contained in the revolt. Since in each case the errors and illusions are rooted in defective views of man and history, the debate has served to illuminate anew and to draw out the meaning and relevance of the Christian understanding in remarkably fresh ways. Indeed it is just this which gives Niebuhr's (usually brief) summaries of this debate in Western culture their distinctive character. His historical sketching is conventional enough, but what is unusual is the precision with which he brings the perspective of Christian understanding to illuminate the deeper meanings of the struggle.

The substance of Niebuhr's writing on the question can be gained from a single essay entitled "The Christian Faith and the Economic Life of Liberal Society," published in *Goals of Economic Life*. This book is one of the series on ethics and economic life produced by a study committee of The Federal Council of Churches.

He begins this essay by acknowledging that "It was the great achievement of classical economic liberalism to gain recognition of the doctrine that the vast system of mutual services which constitute the life of economic society could best be maintained by relying on the 'self-interest' of men rather than their 'benevolence' or on moral suasion, and by freeing economic activities from irrelevant and frequently undue restrictive political controls."[18] It is to be noted that Niebuhr here acknowledges the necessity and the legitimacy of the concept of self-interest. But liberalism accompanied this emancipation of economic life with a very dubious theory. That theory was that justice would issue automatically from a free play of all competitive vitalities. Disbalances of power would be checked by the operations of the "free market." History shortly proved this confidence to be misplaced; self-regulating competition failed dismally to produce the justice it promised.

Niebuhr believes that the errors and miscalculations of this theory may be reduced to two primary ones. The first is that it is oblivious to the meaning and nature of power. This failure properly to assess the meaning of economic power, and how injustice inevitably flows from such disbalances of economic power, quickly revealed the illusion in the assumption of an identity between the individual and general interest. "Power, in the thought of the typically bourgeois man, is political."[19] The early bourgeois man sought to reduce power to a minimum because it represented the advantage of the aristocracy over him; the contemporary bourgeois also seeks to reduce it to a minimum because it represents the democratic attempt to bring disproportions of economic power under communal control.

Thus is the perpetual debate in Western culture focused. There is a profound truth in liberal economics. Benefits of freedom and initiative have resulted from the bourgeois revolution which understood the meaning of "relying upon" and "using" self-interest. The question of debate is how these benefits may be retained without the community suffering the injustices and convulsions attending the error that justice would flow automatically from the "free market." There is no question but that Niebuhr sees it as a prime task of government to redress the inequalities occasioned by disproportionate economic power without concentrating within itself a monopoly of both political and economic power. To be sure, this is a very general statement, allowing for various degrees of government regulation between the extremes of non-interference and complete control. That is as it should be, inasmuch as there is no standard by which the demands of justice can be precisely measured, while that fact in no way obviates the necessity to act as the concrete occasion demands. Niebuhr has given pointed expression to this view in his "debate" with Kenneth Boulding.

> With reference to the feeling of Professor Boulding that interference with the inequalities of a market economy proceeds capriciously without any defined standard of equality or inequality, one might observe that there are naturally no possibilities of arriving at explicit agreements in any society about the degree of inequality which is necessary for the proper performance of different functions or for the maintenance of social incentives, or how much equality is necessary to meet the requirements of justice. But it is significant that any unregulated enterprise or relationship in human life will tend to produce more inequality than is morally justified or scarcely

acceptable. This tendency is due to a simple fact. If there are no restraints upon human desires, any center of power in human society will be inclined to appropriate more privilege to itself than its social function requires. Therefore, no matter how inexact are the equalities and inequalities which emerge from a political interference with a market economy, they are probably closer to the requirements of justice than those of a completely unregulated economy. They have been established, not by nice calculations of "natural law," but by tensions and contests of power which are a legitimate part of a democratic society. They serve the general ends of justice because the equality of political power (inherent in the rights of universal suffrage) has been used to level undue inequalities in the economic sphere."[20]

The second primary error of the liberal theory was its economic rationalism, "which tended to equate every form of self-interest with economic interest."[21] The consequence of this defective anthropology has been that the bourgeois world has been rather consistently surprised by the demonic power of other forms of self-interest, pride, and ambition not accounted for in this rationalism. "It understands neither the traditional ethnic and cultural loyalties which qualify a consistent economic rationalism; nor the deep and complex motives in the human psyche which express themselves in the desire for 'power and glory.' "[22] All the conflicts that gather up the resentments, ambitions, and ideals of classes and nations which constitute the stuff of politics are obscured by this approach.

Instead of the justice promised by the theory, the fluctuations of the market created such misery for the industrial workers that this entire story is necessary to explain the rise of Marxism. But the errors of the Marxian revolt have issued in even more grievous consequences. In Marxist thought, political power is the subservient tool of economic power. The locus of economic power is the ownership of property. Thus it is assumed that the destruction of the possession of property will destroy not only the source of evil oppression but also the center of human self-interest. By locating both economic power and the source of self-interest in the ownership of property, thereby obscuring the meaning of managerial power, the oligarchs of communist society can suppose themselves to have interests identical with those of the proletariat in whose name they govern. Thus by a defective view of man and the dynamics of history, a diabolical concentration of political and economic power can proclaim itself as a movement for the liberation of man.

The debate over "freedom" and "planning" has been the very stuff of modern history. It has been an inconclusive debate and must remain so. "It is inconclusive because only the most grievous extremes of the two warring creeds have been refuted by experience, while the wisest communities have mixed the two creeds in varying proportions."[23] There is no neat solution to the problem of maintaining freedom and achieving justice in a technical society. Inordinate power, whether economic or political, must be checked, but we must proceed pragmatically, from case to case and point to point. What is required is to be freed from the dogmas of both Adam Smith and Karl Marx, so that we can possess that flexibility to encounter the demands of concrete situations knowing that both freedom and justice are preconditions of social health.[24]

It will be useful, in rounding out this aspect of our discussion to see how this general position is applied to the question of property.

## 3. PROPERTY

A sympathetic Catholic critic, James V. Schall, S.J., has complained, that among other things, Niebuhr lacks a theory of property. "Niebuhr's major failure in discussing property," he writes, "can be stated simply: he never wonders whether property has a positive function of its nature. Surely it is wise to recognize that property creates power and that power can be abused. But property, like power, can also be a protection against the state by enabling men to resist the state. Socialists always fail to recognize this."[25] Schall goes on to say, "The problems of modern insecurity and rootlessness are not unrelated to a lack of tangible property."[26] Put in this way Schall's criticism can hardly be sustained. Niebuhr clearly recognizes the positive function of property both as a source of personal security and as a defensive instrument. One example will suffice, in which he expresses himself almost in the same words as Schall: "The social wisdom of regarding property as a relatively effective institution of social peace and justice can not be challenged. It is a 'remedy for sin' in the sense that it gives the person power to defend himself against the inclination of others to take advantage of him. It endows him with instruments for the proper performance of his function and grants him a measure of security in an insecure world."[27]

Niebuhr is fully aware of the positive function of property, but the social realities of the modern age are such that we must be careful not to exalt this positive and "natural" purpose of property into an *absolute* right. This is the nub of his criticism of the Catholic theory of property. "Catholic property philosophy," he writes, "is consistent but nevertheless inadequate for the problems of our day. It recognizes that property is a legitimate form of security in one of its aspects; but it has no answer for the problem when property becomes inherently so powerful that it becomes a threat to security and justice."[28] Both Catholicism and orthodox Protestantism have tended to make the right of property much too absolute, a fact which has compounded the difficulties of securing justice in an age when the dynamic forces of economic power make for the acquisition of an inordinate degree of property by the few. The recognition of the early Christians that property could readily be a source of injustice as well as a defense against the inordinate claims of others, Niebuhr regards as much truer and relevant to our age than the more unqualified views of later Catholic theory.[29]

Bourgeois ideas of property contain two closely related errors. The first is due to the excessive individualism of middle-class philosophy. Moreover, this philosophy became regnant just at that point in history when highly collective forms of commercial and industrial wealth emerged. Thus to emphasize its "private" character possessed by the "inalienable right" of a "natural law" merely heightened the contrast between this claim and the social function of such property.[30]

The second error lies in the "prevailing presupposition of liberal thought that property represents primarily an ordinate and defensive power to be used against the inclination of others to take advantage of the self."[31] This is one of its functions, of course, but when it is itself strong it becomes an instrument of injustice. That has happened with such immense social and political consequences in the modern era that to emphasize anything but the morally ambiguous character of property can only lead to disaster.

Despite their contrasting views on property, Marxism and liberalism make the same mistake concerning it. Neither recognizes it as an instrument that can be used against the general interest. "Liberalism makes this mistake in regard to private property and Marxism makes it in regard to socialized property."[32] Both illusions are rooted in a fatuous conception of human nature.

The debate over the property issue must be continuous in any healthy society. Here again, this can be most fruitfully pursued if we can rid ourselves of the illusions and dogmas of both extremes, and if we can keep vigorous the democratic structure that both presupposes and facilitates the clash of opposing ideas and interests. The following summary statement by Niebuhr possesses relevance to this end:

> The obvious facts about property which both liberal and Marxist theories have obscured are: that all property is power; that some forms of economic power are intrinsically more ordinate than others and therefore more defensive, but that no sharp line can be drawn between what is ordinate and what is inordinate; that property is not the only form of economic power and that the destruction of private property does not therefor guarantee the equalization of economic power in a community; that inordinate power tempts its holders to abuse it, which means to use it for their own ends; that the economic, as well as the political, process requires the best possible distribution of power for the sake of justice and the best possible management of this equilibrium for the sake of order.[33]

The closing words of that statement referring to the distribution of power in a community lead us now to note Niebuhr's view of the role of labor and labor unions in the task of securing justice in a democratic society.

## 4. LABOR IN A DEMOCRACY AND DEMOCRACY IN LABOR UNIONS

No factor has been more important in the transformation of the American social scene and the character of its present problems than the rise and power of labor unions. The fact that Niebuhr did not anticipate this rapid development is perhaps the greatest single reason why he retained the socialist analysis of capitalism at a time when he had become a vigorous critic of its wider philosophy.

> It was the great and irresponsible power of the Ford Motor Company of two decades ago which persuaded the present writer to embrace the socialist creed. The "speedup" seemed too heartless and the "layoffs" so capricious. The social facts prompted me to coin a slogan which seemed very telling to me at that time, though it would not convince me now. "Private property," I said, "should no longer be private when it is no longer private"—that is, it should not be private in law when its power is not private in fact. Yet, in the course of history, this private and essentially arbitrary power was changed not so much by law as by a challenging social force, the rising, and now established, labor movement. My doctrinaire idealism did not anticipate this historical development so characteristic of the whole course of Western history. The labor movement alone is not responsible for all the shifts in the equilibria of power by which relative justice has been established, but it is certainly symbolic of the pragmatic approach to the issues of justice in a technical civilization.[34]

The efforts of labor to secure proximate goals of justice by equilibriating economic power has been a far greater contribution to the health of society than the dogmas of the total solution or any blueprints for utopia.

Labor has waged a long and difficult struggle but its position in the national life is now assured. Niebuhr has gone so far as to say that "the nation, as such, has accepted the principle of collective bargaining as almost as necessary a prerequisite of justice in a technical society as universal suffrage is a prerequisite of political justice."[35] That may be true in Washington but the adoption by a number of states of "Right To Work" laws, which have as their design the crushing of the union shop, reminds us of the strength of the pre-industrial philosophy of individualism in certain regions. Niebuhr has been most forthright in his attack on the "Right To Work" laws. Regardless of what may be the problems posed by the power of unions, and the abuse of that power, they are not to be solved by a return to the philosophy and practice of earlier times. "Dave Beck, the potent and ambitious head of the Teamsters, has certainly disabused anyone who thought that unions were dedicated angels of justice. But we do not cure problems of a technical society by eliminating the power of one of the partners of labor and management, who jointly contribute to the balance of power through which justice is achieved. Nor do we contribute anything by assuring some lonely workman of the right to find employment alone without the 'falderal' of unionism."[36]

Justice is dependent upon equilibriating power. We must not allow the egotism or the corruption of union leadership to detract us from this grand point. "There were sentimental purists," Niebuhr once remarked, "who used to declare when Lewis founded the C.I.O. that no decent person had a right to support him because he was an egotistic, ambitious, demogogic politician. They were wrong because the cause for which Lewis stood transcended the defects of his personality. That cause was the organization of the unskilled workers in our mass production industries, a cause which was a *sine qua non* in the attainment of social justice in a technical society."[37]

The recent scandals concerning union leadership must not

prompt us to obscure the necessity of strong unions for a healthy society, but they point up the absence of, and the necessity for, democracy in the labor movement. Here, as everywhere, democracy demands an adequate structure and a resource of moral purpose. Both of these have been defective in the labor movement. The structure of most unions permits the investment of undue power in the executive. This defect can be remedied, in part at least, by legislation. The changing of the "moral climate" will be much more difficult, but not less important for the democratic functioning of the unions as well as for the health of the wider community. We enter here again that area of the relationship between self-interest and norms and standards that transcend self-interest. Labor is an interest group, legitimately so, but if its interests in the securing of higher wages and better working conditions, are conceived too narrowly and pursued with scant regard to the "means" or without reference to wider values, its tactics will prove in the long run self-defeating and wreak havoc on the general welfare.[38]

Democratic safeguards against corruption within unions is an important, but not, Niebuhr thinks, the most important problem posed by the "bigness" of labor in the present situation. The most important problem in the present post-individualistic era, he contends, is twofold. The first is the problem of securing discriminate rather than indiscriminate justice for the skilled worker.[39] This issue is especially acute where the old industrial unions have engulfed skilled craftsmen. Thus Niebuhr suggests that if Hoffa is a symbol of the problem of corruption, Mike Quill of the Transport Workers Union is a symbol of this more basic and far-reaching issue.[40] The second aspect of the problem is to protect the community against the irresponsible use of power by the "quasi-sovereign satrapies" of big business and big labor. We live in a radically changed situation, and if it is not yet altogether clear where the battle lines are being drawn, it is well to recognize that they are not where they were yesterday.

## 5. RELIGION AND A TECHNICAL CIVILIZATION

What positive contribution can be made by a prophetic Christian faith to issues arising in the realm of economic life? In answering that question we may distinguish three main areas in which Niebuhr has focused his thought—the resources and insights Christianity can bring to bear in the struggle to secure economic justice, the perspective it provides in the problem of relating a wealthy America to a poor world, and the vantage point if offers for confronting the peculiar moral and religious problems attending a technical civilization and an economy of abundance. In general, the first task of Christian faith is to illuminate the nature of historical reality. It will call all programs to recognize how the freedom and destructive power of man, his dignity and misery, are inextricably united. It will insist on the creative capacity of man to shape communities and social harmonies and at the same time the constant temptation of men to use this creative capacity for selfish ends. Its knowledge of values transcending self-interest will make us resolute in the struggle, and its knowledge of the ideological taint corrupting even our best causes will serve to mitigate the severity of the struggle. All this Niebuhr constantly focuses in terms of the dialectical relation of love and justice.

The crux of the question in economic philosophy concerns what Niebuhr calls the legitimacy and necessity of "using" or "harnessing" self-interest. We have previously noted that he regards this as "the creative idea of classical economic theory." But self-interest is assuredly not the norm for economic life any more than it is for other areas of human existence. It is not normative, but it is a reality which must be properly recognized, and if rightly "harnessed" can serve the cause of justice. No one would accuse Niebuhr of sentimentally overlooking the demonic possibilities in man's self-interest. The sentimentalist is he who thinks it can be simply suppressed. The task is that of securing political and economic structures, and a cultural ethos that acknowledges the creative role of self-interest while at the same time remaining fully aware of the peril to social health when it is not "harnessed." Niebuhr sees two main reasons why self-interest must be harnessed rather than suppressed. In the first place, "It is too powerful and persistent to be simply suppressed or transmuted. Even if individual life could rise to pure disinterestedness so that no human mind would give the self, in which it is incarnate, an undue advantage, yet it would not be possible for collective man to rise to such a height. The institution of the family would alone prevent a simple substitution of 'motives of service' for 'motives of profit'. . . . . For the self as 'breadwinner' will seek to serve his family by seeking gain for his toil."[41] The second reason for allowing self-interest a measure of free play is "that there is no one in society good or wise enough finally to determine how the individual's capacities had best be used for the common good, or his labor rewarded, or the possibilities of useful toil, to which he may be prompted by his own initiative, be anticipated."[42]

If self-interest may not for these reasons be simply suppressed, no more can it be allowed to go unrestrained. The reason for this is that human needs, desires, and ambitions are without natural limit. "The Christian faith," Niebuhr stresses, "can make no greater contribution to the organization of man's common life than its interpretation of the root of this inordinacy."[43] It has been precisely the faulty anthropology of both liberalism and Marxism which lies at the basis of the conflict of modern history. The Christian Church has therefore no more relevant task than to illuminate the political and social struggle by clearly proclaiming its understanding of man in both the radicality of his freedom and self-corruption.

It has been the peculiar power of Niebuhr as an apologist to be able to put the Christian understanding without burdening his message with traditional theological terminology. The following passage—a typical paragraph—reveals, nevertheless, how his theology informs every line.

Thus the errors of both those who abjure every effort to control human enterprise and those who would bring it completely under a plan rest upon false estimates of the desires and ambitions of men which furnish the stuff of human history. The self-interest of men must be used, rather than merely controlled, not only because it is too variable and unpredictable to be simply controlled but also because the corruption of self-interest among the oligarchs, who would control it, is actuated by ambitions and power lusts, more dangerous than is dreamed of in either philosophy. On the other hand, the self-interest of men, when uncontrolled, does not simply create a nice harmony of competitive striving. That is why the healthier modern societies constantly experiment with social strategies in which neither creed is followed slavishly.[44]

One of the greatest difficulties in bringing the insight of biblical faith to bear upon the issues of communal life is provided by the sentimentalism, utilitarianism, and individualism of conventional religion. The prophet is necessarily first of all a critic of the prevailing cult. We have noted how, at the outset of his public career, Niebuhr had to attack the notion that philanthropy rather than justice was the main social concern of the Christian. America is even more generally religious now than it was then, but that only serves to make the prophet's task both more necessary and more difficult. [45]

There is a great deal of irony in this situation. History has discredited the secular utopian illusions which constituted for many a few decades ago, a substitute faith. The contemporary religious revival is, in part, occasioned by this discrediting. Yet it thrives by offering even simpler solutions to complex problems than they! The irony deepens when we reflect on the fact that no critic more persuasively succeeded in puncturing secular illusions than the theologian Reinhold Niebuhr. This ironic situation points clearly to one great fact: if the insight and healing resources of biblical faith are to be savingly brought to bear upon social issues, then the first need is for religious America to encounter afresh the majesty of the historic, vertebrate Christian faith. The "secularists"

have listened to Niebuhr and they have learned; the time has come
for the "religious" to take up and read.

We have already, in Chapter Six, discussed the important problem of how a wealthy America can relate itself to a poor world in
such a way as to establish some real mutuality. Here it is necessary
to stress only two things. America's economic position in the world
is such that the need to keep her own economy healthy and
buoyant is one that transcends the self-interest of Americans. The
theologian has no contribution to make as to how this is to be
achieved. But to relate ourselves to a poor world in such a way
that our wealth is not simply odious to others, demands a perspective upon American achievement and good fortune best provided in the Christian faith. Here let it be strongly reasserted that
no utilitarian culture faith and no individualistic-pietistic-revival-
ism can save us from the perennial temptation to make a simple
correlation between our success and our virtue, our power and
our wisdom.

A technical civilization produces moral and religious problems
of its own which can be met only by a profound faith that knows
well the fragmentary character of human existence. Much has
been written about the manner in which our vast urban centers
in which men are no longer organically related to each other
threatens to destroy the personal; the problem of viewing assembly line work as a vocation; of the emptiness that ensues when
leisure is confused with "amusements," and of how the habit of
measuring quantitatively obscures the mystery of human existence
and robs life of both its beauty and its terror. The tendency of
a technical civilization to issue in cultural vulgarity, superficiality,
and futility does constitute a major challenge to religious faith
in our time.

As a first step we do well to consider the relation between economic efficiency and cultural vitality. It serves no purpose to damn
economic efficiency and productivity or to make a simple correlation between the wealth of a nation and its vulgarity. Such criticism is cheap, even if it sometimes comes from cultured Europe.

"Human culture depends in fact upon the ability of an economy to establish margins of welfare beyond the satisfaction of primary needs." [46] But there are, Niebuhr emphasizes, two reasons why this relation is subject to a law of diminishing returns. The first is a fact we have previously discussed—that human needs have no natural limits. Human needs and desires are essentially indeterminate. "The second reason for the law of diminishing returns in the relation of efficiency to culture is the fact that technical efficiency is more effective in providing the basis for cultural and spiritual values than in contributing to its heights." [47] Mass communication is a case in point.

The "conquest of nature" achieved by a technical civilization is a gift to be accepted with gratitude. Our task is to recognize the spiritual possibilities within it, clearly acknowledge its limitations, and be sensitively aware of its great temptations. The Christian faith is peculiarly fitted to meet this situation. It affirms the significance of man's earthly life and its material goods, but it ever insists "that the final pinnacle of meaning transcends all possibilities of history." [48] In this day of "The Organization Man" no perspective is more necessary.

A technical civilization produces increasing hours of leisure. This raises most acutely the question of meaningful activity and its relation to a faith in the meaningfulness of life. An economy of abundance obscures but does not obviate the perilous insecurity of human existence. In this situation nothing is so relevant as a faith which knows that life is insecure not just because we live in the Atomic Era, but because human existence as such is utterly and permanently insecure. Man's final limits remain the same regardless of whether his culture is "advanced" or "primitive."

A technical civilization is always tempted to confuse means and ends, secondary and ultimate questions. No culture faith can turn this temptation aside. But the final and most important relation of Christian faith to the problems of a technical culture lies right here. A faith nurtured in the Bible that knows in every moment the fragmentariness of all our achievements, the inveterate tendency of the human heart to idolatry, that keeps ever before us the mystery of life and death, such a faith alone can sharpen our discrimination between means and ends by shattering our complacency with intimations of the beauty and the terror of things Eternal.

*Nine*

# RACE

Racial conflict is, next to war, the most acute social problem of our time. It is a world-wide problem complicating the major political struggle of the age, and in certain regions, like South Africa, the personal tragedy, misery, and degradation involved are beyond all reckoning. The question of racial tensions, dogmas, and resentments have an immense import for the shaping of foreign policy and the conduct of diplomacy, but for Americans the racial issue must be viewed primarily as the major domestic problem of this generation. A profound revolution in race relations involving incalculable cultural consequences is taking place in America. No one can foresee all that is entailed, but everyone senses that it contains within it a dynamic that will have a far-reaching impact upon the total culture. This revolution is as heavy with change as it is big with promise, and when we do not react to it with hysteria we still grope toward its meaning with uncertainty. It is a mighty issue: to come to grips with it is to wrestle with one of the most explosive and stubborn of all social problems, and at the same time to find ourselves revealed to ourselves, to have a light flashed into the hidden recesses of our pride.

The centrality of the racial question has not escaped Niebuhr although one must read the articles as well as the books to see the significance it possesses in his thought and total writing. His attitude and approach have been clear and consistent across the years. His thought on this issue has gained the expected depth and precision but there have been no shifts such as occurred in his economic philosophy and his attitude to the question of war.[1] He has frequently given pointed expression to the centrality of this question. "Racial conflict has become the most vicious of all forms of social conflict in this nation. And the racial tensions will become worse long before they will become better."[2] That was written twelve years before the events of Little Rock. "Race pride," he says bluntly, "is revealed today to be man's primary collective sin." Consequently, he continues, "issues of racial justice" constitute that "area of human relations" having "the first charge on the Christian conscience."[3]

There is no question but that the racial issue is central to Niebuhr's concern. This is not to suggest, however, that he has given himself to a detailed study of the anthropological or sociological dimensions of the issue. He has, of course, availed himself of such studies, but he has not sustained the same kind of inquiry in this area that he has in political philosophy. Nevertheless, his writings on the race question constitute an unusually good illustration of the character and structure of his social thought. All the motifs and leading concepts that we have met with earlier are knit together when Niebuhr discusses race. The majesty and the limits of law, the relation between equality and liberty in a free society, the dynamics of group behavior, the manner in which pride, fear, and insecurity are compounded in collective life, the necessity to undercut the illusions of a too rationalistic or sentimental approach and to reveal the deeper dimensions of the problem, illuminating criticisms of conventional religion, the necessity of a reorientation of our idealism and a fresh exploration of the resources of grace in the gospel—these themes are so woven together as to provide both a significant perspective on the problem of race and a clear illustration of the structure of Niebuhr's thought.

Our discussion in this chapter is limited to the question of Negro-White relations in America for two reasons: this is the burning issue of our age and it best illustrates the character of Niebuhr's thought. To be sure, Niebuhr has written a fair amount on relations with the Jewish people and the relation between Judaism and Christianity. He has a profound admiration for the

Jewish people and an unusually keen appreciation for their sense of social and civic responsibility. However, to enter into a discussion of Niebuhr's understanding of the relation between Judaism and Christianity, or the place of Israel in the modern world, would lead us far beyond the scope of this inquiry.[4] Consequently, we shall confine the present discussion to Niebuhr's views on racial conflict, as that finds expression in the Negro-White tensions of the American scene.

## 1. THE THEOLOGICAL DIMENSIONS OF THE CONFLICT

It is as theologian that Niebuhr makes his distinctive contribution to the understanding and meeting of the present racial conflict. That is to say, his theological perspective provides him with an insight into the depths and the dynamics of racism, an insight into the depths of the resources of grace, and a profound understanding of the manner in which grace can be appropriated. This is not to suggest that he theologizes in a vacuum or discusses the race question abstractly. On the contrary, it is simply to say that here, as in other areas, both the depths of the problem and of the gospel are seen as they are brought into living engagement. In what way does the theological perspective illumine the problem? What, if any, can be the contribution of the theologian to this issue?

The Christian understanding of man ought to lead us to see this conflict in its full seriousness. Americans passionately believe in, and rather loudly profess, the "American creed of equality and freedom," but white Americans have never practiced this creed toward their colored fellow citizens. Therein lies the "American Dilemma" to use the phrase made famous by Gunnar Myrdal's great treatise. But there is more to the matter than the obvious chasm between "creed" and "deed." Waldo Beach has put the question sharply:

It is not just negative inertia and caution which lie behind racial discrimination, but the positive counterfaiths which produce them. The "conflicting valuations" turn out to be a warfare of the gods in the soul of man. Ultimately the racial problem is not one of hypocrisy but of idolatry, not of cultural lag but of conflicting faiths.[5]

Ultimately the problem is one of idolatry. That is the key to Niebuhr's writing on racial pride and it has been his peculiar achievement to analyze and describe with unmatched accuracy and richness the complex dynamics of the idolatrous spirit particularly as it operates collectively.

No one, least of all Niebuhr, would underestimate the significance of the results of anthropological and sociological studies for the destruction of the dogmas of racism. Bigotry feeds on ignorance and enlightenment is the ally of tolerance and justice. Niebuhr's concern is to insist that it is insufficient—especially for the Christian—simply to point to the fact that "there are no pure races" and no "inferior races." It is necessary and worth while to refute false ideas. But the real problem lies deeper. We must get at the root of the predisposition of one group to accept false ideas or stereotypes of other groups. "The predisposition to think ill of a divergent group is a dark and terrible abyss of evil in the soul of man. If it is robbed of implausible rationalizations, it is quite capable of inventing more plausible ones."[6] Race bigotry is bolstered by ignorance but is itself more than ignorance.

The anthropologists, sociologists, and psychologists have done a remarkable job in analyzing the complex combinations of economic, cultural, social, and psychological ingredients of race prejudice.[7] Such analyses must be carefully studied and used. The racial question is not a safe area for the Christian to commit the error of theologism. Nevertheless, it is the task of the theologian to insist that the root dynamics of the issue have not been completely understood when we have comprehended a combination of *specific* social and psychological factors productive of arrogance and insecurity. He must go on to show how "the particular forms of pride and arrogance in man are prompted by a general predisposition to pride and arrogance, and how this general predisposition is man's abortive effort to hide his general insecurity. Race bigotry is, in short, one form of original sin."[8] If we are really to come to grips with the dynamics of this issue either in society or in the private deeps of our own souls, then we need to know the full stature of human freedom and the radicality of its self-corruption.

The question, at bottom, is one of idolatry, of man's "partly conscious and partly unconscious effort to make himself, his race and his culture God."[9] We come to grips with the roots of racial pride only when we know ourselves to be under the judgment of Him who sees into the secrets of the heart and who alone is able to tear away the tissue of our self-deception. For this reason, as Niebuhr says, "Race bigotry . . . must be broken by repentance and not merely by enlightenment."[10] This must not be said glibly. Awareness of the judgment of God can lead to despair as well as to a repentance to new life; and to be judged by God's law and not healed by His grace is to create a condition which exaggerates rather than mitigates our fury and our pride. To take the full measure of that fact is to stake out the mission of the Church in this situation. No greater task or opportunity confronts the Church in this situation than to bring the searchlight of the Gospel to bear upon the sin of race pride and the dynamics of group guilt, by being that community within the wider community that knows and appropriates the healing resources of grace.

The problem of racial conflict brings us up hard against the question of the moral capacity of collective man. Racial pride is a concomitant of collective life. To lose sight of that fact is to obscure the stubbornness of the issue and to be deceived into an inadequate strategy in dealing with it.

Group pride, of which racism is one of the most vicious expressions, is not merely some "vestigial remnant of barbarism" that will readily disappear with education. "Group pride is the sinful corruption of group consciousness."[11] We must take the full measure of that fact. Race bigotry stems from the corruption of a good, and it is precisely that which gives it its demonic power. Contempt for another group is the pathetic expression of respect for our own group. Thus "white" refers to more than color. It designates a whole complex of cultural values and traditions, and racism becomes the instrument by which such acknowledged values are maintained. That is the power of idolatry. It is the worship of a value, a finite value to be sure, but a value nonetheless. "White" arrogance is the corruption of respect for its own cultural values and the desire to maintain its cultural solidarity.

Every group generates a collective survival impulse. This is never simply, or even primarily, a matter of physical survival. It seems almost inevitable that dominant groups—particularly when they feel threatened—make their own standards "the final norms of existence and . . . judge others for failure to conform to them."[12] Thus the "real crime of any minority group is that it diverges from the dominant type; most of the accusations leveled at these groups are rationalizations of the prejudice aroused by this divergence. The particular crime of the Negroes is that they diverge too obviously from type. They are black."[13] Integration is seen therefore as a threat to the survival of both the cultural values of a long tradition and the pride we have in them.

Niebuhr stresses the theological dimensions of racism and the fact that racial pride is a corruption of group consciousness to emphasize the stubbornness of the issue and the necessity for a many sided strategy. He has frequently, however, given the impression that he regards the race problem as insoluble. The following is not an untypical remark: "There are, in other words, no solutions for the race problem on any level if it is not realized that there is no absolute solution for this problem."[14] Niebuhr is not always as careful in his phrasing as he might be with the result that it is good to have Liston Pope reply: "Sin is perennial but it is not a social problem. It emerges into many diverse social problems, each of which may in itself be capable of final solution or of transformation beyond recognition."[15] That Niebuhr occasionally writes sentences which tend to identify the historical manifestation with the

perennial sin of man is to be readily acknowledged. But his meaning remains at all times clear. First, that in dealing with such a
problem as race prejudice we must take the full measure of the
depth of man's "fallen state" else we will be led by superficial
diagnosis into a strategy that fails to assess the stubbornness of the
problem.[16] Secondly, failure to take the measure of the fact that
race prejudice is a corruption of group consciousness, a concomitant of collective life, and failure to make the necessary distinctions between the life and behavior of individuals and groups are
equally disastrous. It will prompt Christians especially to pervert
the meaning of love by emptying it of justice and thus excuse themselves from dealing with the contest of power necessary for the
establishment of justice. In short, such failure in thought will obscure the necessity for developing strategies relevant to collective
life.

Group pride is perennial although racism may not be the perennial historical manifestation of it. It is the power of group pride
to which Niebuhr is explicitly pointing when he says that there is
"no absolute solution for this problem." Indeed he says this in the
very next sentence. "There is no absolute solution in the sense that
it is not possible to purge man completely of the sinful concomitant
of group pride in his collective life."[17] We may sometimes quarrel
with the phrasing but we can never escape his meaning.

No single strategy is sufficient to approach a problem of such
proportions. Racism feeds on ignorance, therefore it must be met
by the enlightenment of scientific inquiry; it has its ultimate root
in idolatry, which can be broken only by the repentance induced
by confrontation with the gracious, sovereign God; it is a group
phenomenon, therefore it must be restrained by legislation and
corrected by the moral majesty of law. This brings us to a consideration of one of the major themes in Niebuhr's discussion of
the race issue, the majesty and limits of law.

## 2. THE MAJESTY AND LIMITS OF LAW

In Chapter Six we discussed at some length the authority of government as a compound of force and prestige. The same ingredients constitute the majesty of law. If either element is lacking or if they are improperly related, law loses its majesty. Moral prestige, by itself, is unable to avail in a critical situation where the life and customs of groups are involved; force without prestige can win a temporary victory but lacking the majesty of accepted authority, its victory is the precarious tenure of tyranny. It is this delicate relationship between force and prestige that makes statecraft, as Niebuhr never tires of insisting, an art rather than a science.

The racial tension which broke out into the open at Little Rock in the autumn of 1957 provided a vivid illustration of the relationship between force and prestige in the majesty of law. No president has talked more in general about morality than President Eisenhower; and yet it would appear that failure promptly to bring the full moral prestige of the presidential office to bear upon the crisis was not unrelated to the necessity of later having to resort to force to uphold the majesty of the law.[18]

The majesty of law is obscured as well as upheld when it is necessary to resort to armed force. But there is real majesty in the law respecting desegregation. That is so not only because it is the ruling of the Supreme Court of the realm, but also because this particular ruling deals with one of the fundamental preconditions of democratic society—equality.

Equality is not an ultimate principle; but it is one of the two regulative principles of justice. Indeed one of the far-reaching effects of the Supreme Court decision has been to make us all aware of the great moral resource we possess in the Constitution in its insistence upon this fact.[19] Equality "exists," as Sidney Hook has so powerfully argued, "*first* in the field of human rights."[20]

The other forms of equality such as political, educational, and social equality are desired by Negroes "in order to enforce recognition of their human rights, which they believe they have even when they lack political equality."[21]

In similar fashion, George Kelsey has pointed out that if the familiar phrase "equality of opportunity" is to be anything other than a fiction then it must not be viewed externally but only in terms of the equality of persons. "For horses," Kelsey writes, "equality of opportunity is probably definable wholly in terms of feeding, pasturage, grooming, and conditions of the stable. But for men, it must include the things of the mind and spirit. These latter factors will not be made available unless a society is committed to equality and mutuality of persons. This is obviously a point at which the churches should long since have led the way in race relations."[22] The Supreme Court has said more clearly than any other public organ, that equality of opportunity cannot be understood apart from equality of person. In this clear recognition of the spiritual and psychological dimensions of equality, the Supreme Court has indeed made us aware, to return to Niebuhr's phrase, "of the great moral resource we possess in our Constitution in its insistence upon equality as a regulative principle of justice."

The significance of law in the proclaiming and securing of the fundamental human equality of persons is immediately relevant at still another level of the struggle for racial justice. There are, of course, cultural differences between those who have had the opportunities attending full citizenship and those who have been deprived. Moreover, the fears of parents who think that an integrated education would result in a real lowering of their own children's education must be taken into account and given sympathetic consideration. Niebuhr frequently acknowledges this fear and certainly gives it due consideration. But the root of the problem is not here. The root of the matter is the affirmation of the basic equality, and hence potentiality, of men. When that is affirmed, the future is open. That is fundamental. "Therefore," Niebuhr remarks discussing the South African situation, "justice means essentially that the hope of the future be not cut off. When that hope is destroyed, every present injustice becomes insufferable to the victims and destroys the humanity of the perpetrators because they are forced to indulge in every kind of self-deception to justify their cruelty to their own conscience."[23] The sin of South Africa, as he remarks elsewhere, "was in closing the doors of hope."[24] Human equality was denied instead of being enshrined in law. But when the majesty of law stands behind the affirmation of equality, hope, without which no man is truly human, becomes vigorously alive.

There is majesty in law. Law has the power to raise the standards of communities. Not a little of our civic virtue is derived from the restraints of law. But law has its limits as well as its majesty. Law, if it is too far in advance of the mores of the community can only prompt revolt. This is not in any way to underrate its positive significance. Equality is not secured without a power struggle and the firm securing of it in law. Nor is it to obscure the fact that values at stake in a struggle of power, and even violently contended for, gradually come to be accepted. It is merely to emphasize that the majesty of law is derived from prestige as much as from force, and only when it possesses the prestige indicated by its acceptance by a majority of the community is the law itself enforceable in spirit as well as letter. Without that, the core of resistance becomes hardened, striking out in hysteria and despair.

If the majesty of a law enshrining a fundamental human right is not to be impaired, through want of prestige, then the moral and spiritual vitalities and valuations must ever be freshly empowered and sharpened. This is central to the concern and mission of the church.

## 3.  SEGREGATION  AND  THE  CHURCH

It is painfully clear that there is no institution in America more segregated than the Church. Or to look at the matter from another perspective, there is no point at which the Church is so thoroughly secularized as in its racial practice and ideology. It is well to begin by acknowledging the propriety of the indictment voiced by Waldo Beach: "Quantitatively measured, the churches enjoy a phenomenal prestige, but qualitatively they fail so lamentably to be the consciences of the communities in which they stand that their dismissal by social scientists as 'functions of culture' seems amply justified by the evidence."[25]

If one insists, as Niebuhr does, that the roots of racism are such that they "must be broken by repentance and not merely by enlightenment," then—in addition to an acknowledgment that there is not much evidence for this in the churches—he must make a probe into the reasons for such a dismal failure on the part of conventional religion. Niebuhr does not fail to do this. He is churchman and theologian and the main thrust of his writing on race is directed toward the theological and social ineptitude of conventional religion as it confronts this issue. To get the full force of his critique we must bear in mind the total structure of his theology and social analysis. However, the main directions of his criticism can be briefly indicated by noting his criticism of the technique and theology of popular revivalism, the prevailing concept of the church, and the manner in which central Christian concepts have become perverted.

## 4. NIEBUHR'S CRITIQUE OF CONVENTIONAL RELIGION IN THE CONTEXT OF THE RACE ISSUE

Revivalism has played a most important role in the history of American Christianity, especially in that area of our country where the racial conflict is most acute. Any critique of the reasons for the failure of conventional religion in that area can well begin with the question of why revivalism has been ineffective in challenging collective evil. It is particularly appropriate in our time also because there can be no doubt that the religious hero of America in the Eisenhower era has been Billy Graham.

It is quite a commentary on the state of contemporary religion that few writings of Niebuhr have produced such a flurry as the little pieces he has devoted to discussing Billy Graham and the current revival of religion. Niebuhr's critical questions [26] prior to Graham's New York appearance sparked a curious discussion among Church leaders, and his gentle remarks on Graham in *Life* brought forth a large response which Niebuhr acknowledged and analyzed in his article "After Comment: The Deluge." [27] The impression appears to be rather widespread that Niebuhr "doesn't like Graham." It would be useful in approaching Niebuhr's critique of revivalism to see just what his attitude is.

Niebuhr regards Graham with considerable personal respect. "Graham is a world traveller," he writes, "and a very perceptive observer of the world scene with its many collective problems. His instincts are genuine and his sense of justice well developed." [28] If anyone could embody the cause of justice in the revival message it would be he. But it is right here, even in the strongest representative of the tradition, that we see the irrelevance of revivalist Christianity to issues of collective evil.

Revivalism has failed significantly to challenge collective evil or to illuminate collective problems, in the first instance because of its technique. Revivalism must simplify the issues in order to create the "crisis" which leads to conversion. To do this, attention is focused upon the transgression of some *accepted* norm, and the individualization of the sin. "Collective sins are therefore not within the range of a revival." [29] "The moral transgressions that are embedded in the customs of the community, the sins that we do, not 'one by one,' but with the approval of our community, are not such effective means of creating the sense of crisis upon which the revivalist depends. If the 'sinner' is to be convicted of involvement in some collective sin, it is necessary to appeal not only to the emotions but to the mind; that is, it is necessary rationally to analyze the social situation, conformity to which means the violation of the love commandment. This is true even in such an uncomplicated problem as the issue of desegregation."[30] With the inadequacy of the technique goes an inadequate grasp and presentation of the message of the Gospel in this pietistic fundamentalism. We need not go into that here; the whole of Niebuhr's thought stands as a critique of it. It will be sufficient to quote one sentence giving his summary judgment: "Pietistic fundamentalism combines the naïveté of literalism with the simplicity of the old liberalism."[31]

The doctrine of the Church is the point at which the defect both in theology and practice becomes most vivid. The fact that this has been a generally neglected area in American theology does not help the situation. A fundamental concept of revivalist evangelicalism is fellowship. But a fellowship that is not ever conscious of the fact that its togetherness is a gift of grace to equally unworthy people, easily degenerates into a "chumminess" based upon this or that attractive quality, not least of all upon ethnic particularity. Niebuhr always puts his finger on this point. "This actual 'chumminess' of the local congregation has invalidated the universal principle at the heart of the gospel. Particular brotherhood, ethnically based, has invalidated the universal brotherhood implicit in the Christian ethic."[32] It simply must be acknowledged with Waldo Beach that "congeniality, not *agape*, is its cement."[33] And further, "No headway can be made in the process of integration of local churches without a profound conversion of the laity to awareness that the church is not a club but the body of Christ in the world, a house of prayer for all."[34]

Roman Catholicism brings two advantages to the problem which may have had some significance for their comparative success in facing the issue. The hierarchical structure of the church and its long tradition of demanding and expecting obedience enables "the bishops and priests to set standards even in defiance of lay opinion."[35] This structure is, of course, a resource instead of an impossible hurdle only when and where the hierarchy is progressive on the race issue.

The second advantage is the sacramental character of the Roman Catholic fellowship. It is not easy to be exclusive at the altar. One might have expected that this would be a great resource also for Episcopalians. This, however, would not yet appear to be the case; according to one Episcopal reporter, this church shows all the tendencies toward the congregational "clubbiness" of the others.[36]

To begin to assess the power of the pressures making for this, we must estimate how the requirements of institutional self-preservation, expansion, and competition all dictate policies and practices acceptable to the general public. Faced with these demands, nothing is more feared than controversy and division. This is not peculiar to the Southern churches in the present difficult situation, but is characteristic of American Protestantism in general. Indeed, it would appear that fear of division through controversy over fundamental theological and social issues is one of the marks distinguishing denominational life. "The denomination," as Sidney E. Mead in a most penetrating article has observed, "unlike the traditional forms of the Church, is not primarily confessional, and it is certainly not territorial. Rather it is purposive . . . . It is . . . a voluntary association of like-hearted and like-minded individuals, who are united on the basis of common beliefs for the purpose of accomplishing tangible and defined objectives."[37] Bitter debate over an issue like integration might very readily interfere with the attainment of defined objectives, and thus strike at the very heart of the denomination's self-understanding. The full dimension of the question about the meaning of the Church in the racial issue will not be faced until we wrestle with such questions as to whether our understanding of the denomination can bear the full meaning of the word Church.

To be sure, the present situation is raising this question in the sharpest manner possible. No "objective" has been more central in the life of American denominations than the missionary enterprise. Both the pietism and the voluntaryism of our tradition have contributed to that. Blake Smith, reporting the situation in the

Southern Baptist Churches, has seen and expressed this with great clarity. "The one thing that unites us and makes us a fellowship is that we are utterly committed to the Great Commission. This is the heartbeat of our denomination."[38] But the continued practice of segregation transforms this great commitment into a stark question mark. Smith continues:

> The race issue is forcing us to an ultimate decision. Either we abandon segregation both in principle and practice or we must abandon our passion for world evangelism. If we abandon evangelism nothing remains to justify our existence as a denomination. Any other basis of unity carries within it the seeds of disunity.[39]

The situation forces us all upon the elemental question of the nature of the Church, and the meaning and source of renewal. Renewal is the gift of God given to the Church whenever and wherever she accepts to be renewed. As Calvin remarked, in his Commentary on Micah, the story of the Church is the story of many resurrections and a new miracle is repeated again and again when, at the point of desperation brought about by complacency and idolatry, the Church turns anew to the Lord of the Church in repentant trust.

Such "turning" is the precondition of the exercising of the prophetic task of the Church. That task involves a rigorous theological analysis of the roots of racism.[40] Or as Niebuhr puts it: "If, for instance, the church were to make a rigorous religious analysis of the motives that underlie the white man's pride and fear, if it allowed the Word of God to be sharper than a two-edged sword, . . . it might help white people to see to what degree the very hysteria of their attack upon the Negro is the evidence of an uneasy conscience."[41] Such analysis would show how all the basic affirmations of Christian faith are perverted by our idolatry. It would show how our racism perverts the affirmation that we are made in the image of God from its meaning that we are called and designated to image a particular relation with Him, into something we possess. The doctrine of sin is turned into a social legalism and justification by faith is emptied of its meaning. The Kingdom of God which means union and communion is turned into its opposite—separation and segregation. Two segregated souls do not meet in God.

Perhaps most of all the Church needs to center on the perversion of the heart of the Gospel, the meaning of love, because of the power of self-deception in this perversion. The white racist always contends that he both "understands" and "loves" the Negro, and in a way he does love, but it is a profoundly perverted love. Waldo Beach has given this pointed description.

> The respectable, cultured form of racial pride is exactly this pater-
> nalistic love, the concern of the superior for the inferior. The Negro
> neighbor is "loved," is cared for. Thus, in the eyes of the paternalist
> and churchman the law of Christ is fulfilled in his own behavior.
> His very kindness is an aid to self-deceit. He is blinded to the
> corruption at the heart of paternalistic love: that the neighbor is
> loved, not by reference to God the Creator, but by reference to the
> sinful order of white superiority and Negro inferiority.[42]

What has happened can be put in a sentence. Love has been separated from justice and reduced to a sentiment, thus providing a sanctified cloak for injustice; justice has been separated from love, and thus made static in concept has become the bulwark for the injustice of custom.

Niebuhr is undoubtedly right when he says that it would "be well for the church to make fewer ideal demands upon the community for a while and center upon this problem in its own life."[43] For upon the reality of the religious encounter between two great ethnic groups and the divine justice and mercy hinges the health of American society and the destiny of its churches.

We live in an age when the fundamental human questions are being asked with fresh intense urgency. What is man? What is the meaning of life, or does it have any meaning? What is the source of healing for the cleavages that rend our society and go down into the deeps of our being? Who or what is God? But such questioning

—such a crisis in meaning—has its context in a profound and frightening social dislocation. The questions are asked out of the full range of our social relations. It is imperative therefore that theology, if it is to discharge its responsibility, if it is to speak words of clarification and healing in this tortured time, must take the social dimension of man's existence with utmost seriousness. The theologian must learn to know the world as well as the faith from within and to explore the boundary lines of their most vital engagements. The age demands of Christians that peculiar quality of mind and spirit, that certainty of faith, which enables us to leave our pre-established fortresses and in the midst of the world to learn both to listen and to speak. Such has been the achievement of Reinhold Niebuhr.

NOTES AND INDEX

KEY TO ABBREVIATIONS

*Books*

BT: Beyond Tragedy
CLCD: The Children of Light and the Children of Darkness
CPP: Christianity and Power Politics
CRPP: Christian Realism and Political Problems
CRSW: The Contribution of Religion to Social Work
DCNR: Does Civilization Need Religion?
DST: Discerning the Signs of the Times
FH: Faith and History
IAH: The Irony of American History
ICE: An Interpretation of Christian Ethics
LJ: Love and Justice (edited by D. B. Robertson)
LLT: Reinhold Niebuhr: His Religious, Social and Political Thought
    (Edited by C. W. Kegley and R. W. Bretall) The Library of Living
    Theology, vol. 2.
LNTC: Leaves From the Notebook of A Tamed Cynic
MMIS: Moral Man and Immoral Society
NDM: The Nature and Destiny of Man, 2 vols.
PSA: Pious and Secular America
REE: Reflections on the End of an Era
SDH: The Self and the Dramas of History

*Journals*

CC: Christianity and Crisis
CS: Christianity and Society
NL: The New Leader
RR: Radical Religion

# Notes

## INTRODUCTION

1. NDM, vol. 2, p. 204.
2. Odegard, Holtan, P., *Sin and Science; Reinhold Niebuhr as Political Theologian*, The Antioch Press, 1956, p. 12.
3. ibid. p. 21.
4. ibid. p. 166.
5. Hofmann, Hans, *The Theology of Reinhold Niebuhr*, Charles Scribner's Sons, New York, 1956, p. 247.
6. Oates, W.J. Introduction to *Basic Writings of Saint Augustine*, Random House, New York, 1948, vol. 1, p. xii.

## One THE NORM OF LOVE

1. Lehmann, Paul "The Christology of Reinhold Niebuhr," LLT, p. 275f.
2. NDM, vol. 1, p. 16.
3. Letter to the Editor. *The Christian Century*, March 15, 1933, p. 362.
4. ibid.
5. ibid. p. 364.
6. Williams, D.D., *God's Grace and Man's Hope*, New York, Harper & Brothers, 1949, p. 32.
7. ibid. pp. 36,37,38.
8. ibid. p. 79.
9. ibid. p. 75.
10. ibid. p. 78.
11. Williams, D.D., "Niebuhr and Liberalism," in LLT, vol. 2, p. 210.
12. "Reply to Interpretation and Criticism," LLT, vol. 2, p. 442.
13. FH, p. 185.
14. MMIS, p. 265.
15. NDM, vol. 2, p. 69.
16. CRPP, p. 141.
17. FH, p. 177.
18. Review of Fromm's *Man For Himself* in CS, Spring, 1948, pp. 27-8.
19. See, for example, CRPP, p. 16of.
20. NDM, vol. 2, p. 82.
21. ibid. p. 86.
22. ibid. p. 88.
23. Williams, D.D., *God's Grace and Man's Hope*, op. cit. p. 75.
24. Ramsey, Paul, "Love and Law," in LLT, p. 113.
25. NDM, vol. 2. p. 88.

26. ibid. p. 89.
27. Lehmann, Paul, "The Christology of Reinhold Niebuhr" in LLT, p. 254.
28. NDM, vol. 1, p. 15.
29. SDH, p. 232.
30. NDM, vol. 1, p. 265.
31. ibid. p. 272.
32. ibid. p. 270.
33. FH, p. 174.
34. FH, p. 174.
35. NDM, vol. 1, p. 286.
36. ibid. p. 279.
37. ibid. p. 288.
38. ibid.
39. ibid. p. 271.
40. ibid. p. 289.
41. Calvin, J., *Institutes* 3:2:42.
42. NDM, vol. 1, p. 292.
43. ibid. p. 293.
44. ibid. p. 294.
45. "Ten Years That Shook My World," *The Christian Century*, Apr. 26, 1939, p. 545.
46. See "The Two Sources of Western Culture" in Fuller, E. (ed.), *The Christian Idea of Education*, Yale University Press, 1957.

### *Two* LOVE AND JUSTICE

1. Schlesinger, Arthur Jr., "Reinhold Niebuhr's Role in Political Thought," LLT, p. 149.
2. ICE, p. 9.
3. Brunner, E., "Reinhold Niebuhr's Work as a Christian Thinker," LLT, p. 30.
4. ibid.
5. NDM, vol. 1, p. 295.
6. ibid. p. 285.
7. ICE, p. 140.
8. NDM, vol. 1, p. 295.
9. ibid.
10. "Christian Faith and the Common Life," Oxford Conference book of the same title, Willett, Clark and Co, 1938, p. 72.
11. MMIS, p. 258.
12. "Moralists and Politics," *The Christian Century* (July 6, 1932), p. 858.
13. NDM, vol. 2, p. 248.
14. ibid.
15. ibid. p. 252.
16. ibid. p. 256.
17. LLT, p. 30.
18. Bennett, J.C., "Reinhold Niebuhr's Social Ethics," in LLT, p. 59.
19. Strauss, Leo, *Natural Rights and History*, The University of Chicago Press, 1953, pp. 4–5. Attention should also be drawn to the illuminating discussion of this book by Will Herberg and John H. Hallowell in *The*

*Christian Scholar* (Sept. 4, 1954).

20. FH, p. 180.
21. ibid. p. 183.
22. See Niebuhr's essay "A Protestant Looks at Catholics" in *Catholicism in America*, Harcourt, Brace and Co., New York, 1953.
23. NDM, vol. 1, p. 221.
24. Niebuhr, R., "Christian Faith and Natural Law," in *Theology*, Feb. 1940, p. 87.
25. ibid. p. 89.
26. LLT, p. 431f.
27. Brunner, E., *Justice and the Social Order*, Harper and Brothers, New York, 1945, p. 89.
28. NDM, vol. 2, p. 197.
29. Brunner, E., op. cit. p. 116.
30. ibid. p. 128.
31. ibid. pp. 128,129.
32. ibid. p. 130.
33. ibid.
34. ibid.
35. ibid.
36. ibid. p. 261.
37. Brunner, E., *Christianity and Civilization*, vol. 1, Scribners, New York, 1948, p. 116.
38. Brunner, E., *The Divine Imperative*, Lutterworth Press, London, 1937, p. 233.
39. ibid.
40. CRPP, p. 167.
41. Ramsey, Paul, *Basic Christian Ethics*, Scribners, New York, 1950, p. 3.
42. See, for example, "Religion and the New Germany" in *The Christian Century* (June 28, 1933). Also Niebuhr's "Comments on E.G. Homrighausen's article 'Barthianism and the Kingdom'" in *The Christian Century* (July 15, 1931).
43. "Karl Barth and Democracy," RR, vol. 4, no. 1. (Winter 1938), p. 4f.
44. ibid. p. 5.
45. "We Are Men and Not God," *The Christian Century*, Oct. 27, 1948, p. 1139.
46. ibid. p. 1140.
47. ibid. p. 1139.
48. Barth, K., "Continental vs. Anglo-Saxon Theology," *The Christian Century*, Feb. 16, 1949, p. 203.
49. "An Answer to Karl Barth," *The Christian Century*, Feb. 23, 1949, p. 236.
50. ibid.
51. See also CRPP, chap. 2.
52. Niebuhr, R., Review of Barth's *Against the Stream* in CS, vol. 19, no. 3, (Autumn 1954), p. 29.
53. ibid. See also Niebuhr's thrust at the position of this book in his article "Theological and Political Thought in the Western World" in *The Ecumenical Review*, vol. 9, no. 3 (April 1957), pp. 260–61.
54. Jan. 23, 1957, p. 108f.
55. ibid. p. 109.
56. ibid.

57. ICE, p. 172.
58. ibid. p. 178f.
59. "Reply to G.G. Atkins" (Letter to the Editor) *The Christian Century*, April 10, 1935, p. 370.
60. "Moralistic Preaching" in *The Christian Century*, July 15, 1936, p. 986.
61. "Christian Moralism in America," RR, vol. 5, no. 1, p. 19.
62. ibid.
63. "Moralistic Preaching," op. cit. p. 986.
64. Morrison, C.C., "Is Christianity Practicable?", *The Christian Century*, June 21, 1933, p. 807.
65. Ferguson, John (ed.). *Studies in Christian Social Commitment*, London, Independent Press Ltd., 1954, p. 69.
66. ibid.
67. ibid.
68. NDM, vol. 1, p. 298.
69. *Christian Faith and the Common Life*, op. cit. p. 92.
70. "The Christian Perspective on the World Crisis," CC, vol. 4, no. 7, p. 3.
71. See above p. 26f.
72. NDM, vol. 2, p. 248.
73. MMIS, p. 30f.
74. "The Rationalist Rearguard," in CS (Spring 1940), vol. 5, no. 2, p. 5.
75. BT, p. 186. See also REE, pp. 233–4, where Niebuhr gives a "parable" of the general effect of moral sentiment upon established social relations in the story of the relation between a generous housewife and her charwoman.
76. CPP, p. 26.
77. "Power and Justice," CS, vol. 8, no. 1 (Winter 1942), p. 10.
78. "Christian Faith and Social Action" in Hutchison, J.A. (ed.), *Christian Faith and Social Action*, New York, Scribners, 1953, p. 241.
79. ICE, p. 108.
80. NDM, vol. 2, p. 254.
81. FH, p. 189f.
82. "Christian Faith and the Common Life," op. cit. p. 85.
83. SDH, p. 151.
84. ibid. p. 151f.

### Three LOVE, JUSTICE AND THE SELF

1. SDH, p. 144.
2. "The Two Sources of Western Culture," in Fuller, E. (ed.), *The Christian Idea of Education*, op. cit. p. 238.
3. SDH, p. 77.
4. ibid. p. 78.
5. ibid. p. 4.
6. ibid. p. 6f.
7. ibid. p. 12.
8. See SDH, chap. 6.
9. ibid. p. 26.
10. ibid. p. 30.
11. ibid.

12. ibid. p. 31.
13. ibid.
14. ibid. p. 32.
15. ibid. p. 33.
16. ibid.
17. ibid.
18. ibid. p. 63.
19. ibid. p. 64.
20. ibid.
21. ibid. p. 84f.
22. NDM, vol. 1, p. 54.
23. ibid. p. 55.
24. "Sex Standards in America," CC, vol. 8, no. 9 (May 24, 1948), p. 65.
25. "Sex and Religion in the Kinsey Report," CC., vol. 13, no. 18 (Nov. 2, 1953), p. 139.
26. NDM, vol. 1, p. 75.
27. For Niebuhr's discussion of the Romantic Protest against Rationalism, see ibid. chap. 2.
28. NDM, vol. 1, p. 40.
29. ibid. p. 82f.
30. LLT, p. 17.
31. CRPP, p. 6.
32. ibid. pp. 182–3.
33. "The Tyranny of Science," in *Theology Today*, vol. 10, no. 4 (January 1954), p. 465.
34. ibid. p. 471.
35. SDH, p. 128.
36. CRPP, p. 199.
37. In *Science*, January 14, 1949.
38. "The Wisdom of the World," in CS, vol. 14, no. 2 (Spring 1949), p. 4.
39. CRPP, p. 3.
40. "The Tyranny of Science," op. cit. p. 471.
41. "Intellectual Biography" in LLT, p. 18.
42. ibid. p. 21.
43. ibid. p. 20.
44. "Reply to Interpretation and Criticism" in ibid. p. 433.
45. "Reinhold Niebuhr's Doctrine of Knowledge," ibid. p. 40.
46. ibid. p. 432f.
47. ibid. p. 433.
48. CRPP, p. 184.
49. ibid. p. 202.
50. CRPP, p. 9.
51. NDM, vol. 1, p. 182.
52. ibid.
53. ibid. p. 185.
54. NDM, vol. 1, pp. 180–81.
55. ibid. p. 252.
56. ibid. p. 186.
57. ibid. p. 17.
58. ibid.
59. DST, p. 38.

60. BT, p. 290.
61. SDH, p. 237.
62. BT, p. 302.
63. SDH, p. 238.
64. Herberg, Will, *Judaism and Modern Man,* Farrar, Strauss and Young, New York, 1951, p. 229.
65. This address was published, along with the addresses by Perry Miller, Robert L. Calhoun, and Nathan M. Pusey, by Doubleday & Co; 1954. The booklet is edited by H. P. VanDusen.
66. ibid. pp. 63–4.
67. SDH, p. 163.
68. CLCD, p. 53.
69. CRPP, p. 18.
70. ibid. p. 26.
71. SDH, p. 42.
72. CRPP, p. 11f.

<br>

*Four* LOVE, JUSTICE AND HISTORY

1. FH, p. 55.
2. SDH, p. 44.
3. FH, p. 20.
4. ibid. p. 19.
5. ibid.
6. ibid. p. 19f.
7. SDH, p. 45.
8. See ibid. chap. 11.
9. *In Modern Age,* vol. 1, no. 1 (Summer 1957), pp. 103–7.
10. Freund, Ludwig, op. cit. p. 104.
11. FH, p. 117.
12. ibid. p. 118.
13. NDM, vol. 2, p. 4f.
14. FH, p. 14f.
15. ibid. p. 16.
16. ibid. p. 38.
17. ibid. p. 37.
18. ibid. p. 64.
19. ibid. p. 1f.
20. ibid. p. 32.
21. Quoted in Shinn, R., "The Christian Gospel and History" in Hutchison, J.A. (ed.), *Christian Faith and Social Action,* op. cit. p. 24.
22. See Herberg, W., *Judaism and Modern Man,* op. cit. p. 201.
23. NDM, vol. 2, p. 160.
24. For detailed discussion of this see *Faith and History,* chaps. v and vi.
25. CRPP, p. 49.
26. Niebuhr, R., "Two Forms of Utopianism," CS, vol. 12, no. 4 (Autumn 1947), p. 6. For a fuller discussion of the character of this distinction, and its place in history, see *Faith and History,* pp. 206–13.
27. CPP, p. 112f.
28. FH, p. 4.

29. ibid. p. 196.
30. Niebuhr, R., "The Pope's Domesticated God," *The Christian Century*, January 8, 1950, p. 74.
31. NDM, vol. 2, p. 135.
32. ibid. p. 145.
33. ibid. p. 203.
34. ibid. p. 202f.
35. FH, p. 203.
36. J. Bennett, "Reinhold Niebuhr's Social Ethics" in LLT, op. cit. p. 62.
37. CPP, p. 51.
38. NDM, vol. 2, p. 190.
39. ibid. p. 193.
40. CPP, p. 58.
41. See, for example, NDM, vol. 2, p. 194 and FH, p. 199.
42. In his *Heritage of the Reformation*, Beacon Press, Boston, 1950. chap. 1.
43. ibid. p. 11.
44. There is one point where Niebuhr appears to acknowledge the truth of this criticism. In a review of Bishop Bergraav's *Man and State*, Niebuhr says, "It has long been a favored indictment of Lutheran thought in the realm of politics that it is incapable of discriminate judgments. We have frequently been told that this defect inheres in German rather than Lutheran thought *per se;* and that the Scandinavian Lutherans have always been superior to the German in their political discriminations. This book would seem to be a proof of such a thesis. It is at any rate an impressive and illuminating treatise on Christian political ethics." CS, vol. 16, no. 3, (Summer 1951), p. 28.
45. NDM, vol. 2, p. 176.
46. FH, p. 113f.
47. ibid. p. 125.
48. ibid. p. 132.
49. ibid. p. 114.
50. ibid. p. 103.
51. ibid.
52. NDM, vol. 2, p. 27.
53. ibid.
54. ibid. p. 51.
55. NDM, vol. 1, p. 148. Compare the interesting note in LNTC under the date of 1926. "We had a communion service tonight (Good Friday) and I preached on the text 'We preach Christ crucified, to the Jews a stumbling block and to the Gentiles foolishness, but to them that are called the power of God and the wisdom of God.' I don't think I ever felt greater joy in preaching a sermon. How experience and life change our perspectives! It was only a few years ago that I did not know what to make of the cross; at least I made no more of it than to recognize it as a historic fact which proved the necessity of paying a high price for our ideals. Now I see it as a symbol of ultimate reality." (LNTC, p. 85).
56. FH, p. 143.
57. BT, p. 168.
58. FH, p. 144.
59. Niebuhr's indictment of liberal theology is essentially this, that liberalism in sacrificing the essential positions of Christian faith was unable to pro-

vide a resource and perspective for understanding the tragic history of our time. "In seeking to persuade the modern mind that Christianity is respectable and intelligent, the liberals sacrificed most of the essential positions. Christ was transmuted into the good man Jesus, who could charm all men to become good as he was. The classic Christology of the God-man was repudiated, though innumerable reservations sought to hide the repudiation. It was not recognized that this absurd doctrine of the God-man Christ contains the whole essence of the Christian faith—its belief that God transcends history and yet makes himself known in history; that history measured by Christ is tragic and ends tragically for it crucifies Christ; that only God is able to resolve the conflict between what man is and what he ought to be, a conflict in which all men stand; that God cannot do this by simply wiping out history and transmuting it into eternity, but by redeeming history, but that the redemption of history involves more than persuading man to follow the law of God. It involves God's taking upon himself the inevitable violation of that law." ("Ten Years That Shook My World" in *The Christian Century*, April 26, 1939, p. 544).

60. FH, p. 145.
61. NDM, vol. 2, p. 55.
62. ibid.
63. ibid. p. 67.
64. LLT, p. 437.
65. NDM, vol. 2, p. 125.
66. ibid. p. 125f.
67. ibid. p. 212.
68. ibid. p. 289.
69. ibid. p. 316f.
70. ibid. p. 319.
71. BT, p. 21.
72. NDM, vol. 2, p. 292.
73. ibid.
74. ibid. p. 295.
75. FH, p. 152. The whole of chap. 10 in *Faith and History* deals with this question.
76. ibid. p. 152.
77. See FH, p. 154.
78. ibid.
79. ibid. p. 163.
80. ibid. p. 165.
81. ibid.
82. ibid. p. 167.
83. Löwith, Karl, *Meaning in History*, University of Chicago Press, 1949, p. 192f.
84. Löwith, Karl, "History and Christianity" in LLT, p. 289.
85. "Reply to Interpretation and Chiticism," ibid. pp. 439–40.
86. BT, p. 279.
87. ibid. p. 284.
88. In a biting editorial under the heading "An Ineffectual Sermon on Love," prompted by a speech at an isolationist meeting held under religious auspices at the moment Hitler was overrunning Europe, Niebuhr writes,

"How blindly these apostles of love seek to make a success story out of the Cross. And what foolishness they make of the Cross. Only their foolishness is not the foolishness of God which is wiser that the wisdom of men. It is just foolishness. They think they can rob human life and history of its tragic note by just a little more moral admonition." CC, vol. 1, no. 22 (December 15, 1941), p. 2.

### *Five* THE RESOURCES OF LOVE FOR A RESPONSIBLE SOCIETY

1. This article appeared in *The New Christian Advocate*, vol. 1, no. 9 (June 1957.
2. ibid. p. 17.
3. ibid. p. 14.
4. The quotation is "The ethic of Jesus does not deal at all with the immediate moral problem of every human life—the problem of arranging some kind of armistice between various contending factions and forces." (*An Interpretation of Christian Ethics*, p. 39).
5. The quotation is that the ethic of Jesus "does not establish a connection with the horizontal points of a political or social ethic. . . ." The reference given by Stokes is CLCD, p. 39. It does not appear there. The quotation is from ICE, p. 39.
6. NDM, vol. 2, p. 45.
7. Stokes, M.B., op. cit. p. 15. Emphasis mine.
8. ibid. p. 17.
9. CRSW, p. 90.
10. DST, p. 16.
11. ibid. p. 18.
12. ICE, p. 223.
13. NDM, p. 217, vol. 2.
14. DST, p. 29.
15. "When Will Christians Stop Fooling Themselves?" *The Christian Century*, May 16, 1934, p. 659.
16. CLCD, p. 151f.
17. See, for example, his article "Christian Faith and Political Controversy" in CC, vol. 12. no. 13 (July 21, 1952).
18. "Anglo-Saxon Destiny and Responsibility," CC, vol. 3, no. 16 (Oct. 4, 1943), p. 3.
19. See "The Peril of Complacency in Our Nation," CC, vol. 14, no. 1 (Feb. 8, 1954).
20. ibid. p. 2.
21. "Religiosity and the Christian Faith," CC, vol. 14, no. 24, (January 24, 1955), p. 185f.

A few other pieces dealing with this theme may be noted, e.g. *Editorial Notes* in CC, vol. 16, no. 5 (April 2, 1956), in which Niebuhr discusses the televised "prayer breakfast" held in Washington at which President Eisenhower was present and for which Conrad Hilton acted as host. *Piety and Politics* in CS, vol. 18, no. 3 (Summer 1953) should be noted. From somewhat earlier years see *Culture Religions* in RR, vol. 3, no. 3 (Summer 1938), in which he remarks: "Every culture religion is . . . a form of idolatry in which God has become domesticated into a tame icon of the family hearth who sanctifies and guarantees the 'highest values' of this culture. He ceases to be a judge and redeemer" (p. 9). Also his biting, but still relevant criticism in *Religion and Patent Medicine* in RR, vol. 3, no. 2 (Spring 1938): "These paens of praise for religion as a panacea, in which the modern pulpit abounds are a nice indication of the decay of religion. When men are truly religious they worship God, are convicted of sin by his holiness, prompted to charity and justice by his commandments and by gratitude for his mercy and encouraged to live joyfully in a world full of evil. But when they are not truly religious they talk about religion as if it were a nice cure for something or other, perhaps a spiritual 'Carter's Little Liver Pill' " (p. 5f.).

22. See "Does the Church Pray?" in CC, vol. 2, no. 10 (June 15, 1942).
23. "Prayer and a Global Civilization," CC, vol. 4, no. 15 (Sept. 18, 1944), p. 1.
24. ibid.
25. In Hutchison, J.A., (ed.), *Christian Faith and Social Action* op. cit. p. 236.
26. NDM, vol. 2, p. 217.
27. ibid. p. 219; see also CLCD, p. 137.
28. ibid. p. 221.
29. ibid. p. 243.
30. ibid.
31. Niebuhr, R., "Ten Years That Shook My World," *Christian Century*, April 26, 1939.
32. IAH, p. 166.
33. ibid.
34. ibid. p. 166f.
35. ibid. p. viii.
36. ibid. p. 11.
37. ibid. p. 24.
38. ibid. p. 42.
39. ibid. p. 74.
40. ibid. p. 160.
41. ibid. p. 106.
42. ibid. p. 108.
43. ibid. p. 133.
44. ibid. p. 168.
45. NDM, vol. 2, p. 284.
46. REE, p. 296.
47. "Christian Otherworldliness," CS, vol. 9. no. 1 (Winter 1943), p. 12; see also "In the Battle and Above It," CS, vol. 7., no. 4 (Autumn 1942).
48. "Can We Avoid Catastrophe?", *The Christian Century*, May 26, 1948, p. 506; see also "Providence and Historical Confusion," CS, vol. 11, no. 3 (Summer 1946).
49. "Our Chances for Peace," CC, vol. 7, no. 2 (Feb. 17, 1947), p. 2. Some of Niebuhr's most important articles since the war are centered in this theme. See "Utilitarian Christianity and the World Crisis," CC, vol. 10, no. 9 (May 29, 1950); "The Theme of Evanston," CC, vol. 14, no. 14 (August 9, 1954).
50. Wolf, W.J., "Reinhold Niebuhr's Doctrine of Man," LLT, p. 248.
51. Scherer, P., "Reinhold Niebuhr—Preacher," ibid. p. 330.
52. Lehmann, P., "The Christology of Reinhold Niebuhr," ibid. p. 277f.

53. Hofmann, Hans, *The Theology of Reinhold Niebuhr,* op. cit. p. 246.
54. Davies, D. R., *Reinhold Niebuhr: Prophet from America,* The Macmillan Co., New York, 1948., p. 99.
55. FH, p. 238.
56. ibid. p. 242.
57. BT, p. 122.
58. "Sentimental and Shallow Religion," CS, vol. 9, no. 2 (Spring 1944), p. 7.
59. "A Problem of Evangelical Christianity," CC, vol. 6, no. 8 (May 13, 1946), p. 6.
60. "The Reunion of the Church Through the Renewal of the Churches," CC, vol. 7, no. 20 (Nov. 24, 1947), p. 7; see also FH, p. 239.
61. "The Weakness of Common Worship in American Protestantism," CC, vol. XI, no. 9 (May 28, 1951).
62. ibid. p. 70.
63. See "The Reunion of the Church Through the Renewal of the Churches," op. cit.
64. Scherer, Paul, "Reinhold Niebuhr—Preacher" in LLT, chap. 14.
65. CPP, p. 224.
66. FH, p. 240.
67. NDM, vol. 2. p. 224(n).
68. ibid. p. 226(n).
69. "Has the Church Any Authority?", CC, vol. 10, no. 5 (April 3, 1950), p. 36.
70. LLT, p. 437.
71. Lehmann, P., "The Foundation and Pattern of Christian Behavior" in Hutchison, op. cit. p. 101.
72. ibid. p. 112.
73. See CRPP, p. 112. The entire chapter entitled "The Christian Witness in the Social and National Order" is a rich and moving piece of writing.
74. IAH, p. 63.

Six POLITICS

1. CLCD, p xi.
2. ibid. p. 118.
3. NDM, vol. 2, p. 268.
4. Thompson, K., "Beyond National Interest: A Critical Evaluation of Reinhold Niebuhr's Theory of International Politics," *The Review of Politics,* vol. 17, no. 2 (April 19, 1955), pp. 167–88.
5. CLCD, p. 16f.
6. ibid. p. x.
7. ibid. p. 10.
8. ibid. pp. 18,43.
9. See Chapter Five above.
10. CLCD, p. 60.
11. In Chapter Three above.
12. MMIS, p. xi.
13. "Human Nature and Social Change," *The Christian Century,* March 15, 1933, p. 363.
14. See SDH, p. 63 and MMIS, xif.

15. SDH, p. 35.
16. For full discussion of this question see SDH, chap. 8 and CLCD, chap. 2.
17. SDH, p. 223.
18. Buber, M., *Between Man and Man*, The Beacon Press, Boston, Paperback edition, 1955, p. 200.
19. "The False Defense of Christianity," CC, vol. 10, no. 10 (June 12, 1950), p. 73.
20. CLCD, p. 85.
21. For discussion of all this see CRPP, chap. 7. Also "Democracy, Secularism and Christianity" in CC, vol. 13, no. 3 (March 2, 1953); "The Christian Perspective on the World Crisis," CC, vol. 4, no. 7 (May 1, 1944); "The Catholic Hierarchy's Analysis of the Ills Of Our Day," CC, vol. 14, no. 22 (Dec. 27, 1954).
22. This is a favorite phrase of Niebuhr's. See CLCD, p. 75 and CRPP, p. 102.
23. CLCD, p. 122.
24. See above Chapter Five. Also the whole of chap. 4 of CLCD for a detailed discussion of the question of social pluralism.
25. IAH, p. 11.
26. SDH, p. 164.
27. CLCD, p. 178.
28. NDM, vol. 2, p. 266.
29. ibid.
30. Niebuhr's seeming preference for parliamentary government may be noted in the following articles: "Chaos in Congress," CS, vol. 9, no. 1 (Winter 1943); "We Face Inflation," CS, vol. 11, no. 4 (Fall 1946) "Our Constitutional Difficulties" CS vol. 12, no. 1 (Winter 1946). "The Death of the President," CC, vol. 5, no. 7 (April 30, 1945).
31. NDM, vol. 2, p. 267.
32. For Niebuhr in this connection see especially NDM, vol. 2, chap. 9, particularly pp. 269–86. SDH, chap. 20 and the penetrating article "Augustine's Political Realism," chap. 9 of CRPP.
33. NDM, vol. 2, p. 269.
34. In CRPP, chap. 3.
35. ibid. p. 34.
36. ibid. p. 36.
37. "The Tyrant as Symbol of Community," NL, May 21, 1956. See also: "Nikita Khrushchev's Meditation on Josef Stalin," CC, vol. 16, no. 12 (July 9, 1956); "Stalin—Deity to Demon," CC, vol. 16, no. 6 (April 16, 1956); "The Second Geneva," NL, Nov. 28, 1955.
38. CRPP, p. 37.
39. "God's Design and the Present Disorder of Civilization" in vol. 3 of the Amsterdam Series, p. 21. See also IAH, p. 128f.
40. CRPP, p. 40.
41. ibid. p. 41.
42. For example, Kenneth Thompson's complaint on this in LLT, p. 173.
43. "Moralists and Politics," *The Christian Century*, July 6, 1932, p. 857.
44. CRSW, p. 92.
45. MMIS, p. xii.
46. "Peace Through Cultural Co-operation," CC, vol. 9, no. 17 (Oct. 17, 1949), p. 132.

47. "The Good People of Britain," RR, vol. 4, no. 3 (Summer 1939), p. 7. See also "The Hitler-Stalin Pact," RR, vol. 4, no. 4 (Fall 1939), p. 2; and "Christian Moralism in America," RR, vol. 5, no. 1.
48. "Our Responsibilities in 1942," CC, vol. 1, no. 24, p. 1.
49. LLT, chap. 6.
50. Odegard, H.P., *Sin and Science,* The Antioch Press, Yellow Springs, Ohio, 1956, p. 141.
51. ibid. p. 142.
52. ibid.
53. ibid. p. 143.
54. ibid. p. 142.
55. ibid. p. 165.
56. ibid. p. 146.
57. ibid. p. 145.
58. ibid. p. 118.
59. ibid. p. 119.
60. ibid. p. 150.
61. ibid. p. 151.
62. ibid. p. 173.
63. ibid.
64. ibid.
65. ibid. p. 123.
66. ibid. p. 122.
67. ibid. p. 122.
68. ibid. p. 186f.
69. ibid.
70. FH, p. 53.
71. For a good discussion of the relationship between the "scientific approach" to political reality and totalitarianism, see Ludwig Freund, *Politik und Ethik,* Alfred Metzer Verlag, 1955, especially pp. 106ff. For the entire question, see Hans J. Morgenthau, *Scientific Man vs. Power Politics,* The University of Chicago Press, 1946. Both of these works reveal a large indebtedness to Niebuhr.
72. CRPP, p. 66.
73. See "France's 'Liberal' Colonialism: Old Evils, New Slogans," NL, Oct. 24, 1955.
74. SDH, p. 149.
75. ibid. p. 189.
76. CRPP, p. 72; see also "We Need an Edmund Burke," CS, vol. 16, no. 3 (Summer 1951).
77. CRPP, p. 70.
78. REE, p. 118.
79. CPP, p. 121.
80. DST, p. 192.
81. Editorial Notes, CC, vol. 14, no. 13 (July 26, 1954), p. 99; see also SDH, p. 214.
82. "Winston Churchill and Great Britain," CC, vol. 15, no. 7 (May 2, 1955), p. 52.
83. "For Peace We Must Risk War," *Life,* Sept. 20, 1948, p. 39.
84. LLT, p. 434.
85. See CRPP, chap. 5.

86. "Liberalism and Conservatism," CS, vol. 20, no. 1 (Winter 1954–55), p.3.
87. ibid.
88. CRPP, p. 67.
89. "Reinhold Niebuhr: A Symposium," *Union Seminary Quarterly Review,* vol. xi, no. 4 (May 1956), p. 15.
90. "Theology and Political Thought in the Western World," *The Ecumenical Review,* vol. 9, no. 3 (April 1957), p. 253.
91. LLT, chap. 5 and 6.
92. "The Domestic Situation," RR, vol. 3, no. 3 (Summer 1938), p. 4.
93. See "The Death of the President," CC, April 30, 1945.
94. "Theology and Political Thought in the Western World," op. cit. p. 256.
95. Thompson, K., "Beyond National Interest: A Critical Evaluation of Reinhold Niebuhr's Theory of International Politics," *The Review of Politics,* vol. 17, no. 2 (April 1955).
96. Thompson, K., "Prophets and Politics," CC, vol. 15, no. 8 (May 16, 1955), p. 61.
97. "Streaks of Dawn in the Night," CC, vol. 9, no. 21 (Dec. 12, 1949), p 162.
98. "Plans for World Reorganization," CC, vol. 2, no. 17 (Oct. 19, 1942), p. 4.
99. Editorial Notes, CC, vol. 11, no. 18 (Oct. 29, 1951), p. 139.
100. See above, especially Chapter Five.
101. "The Sources of American Prestige," NL, Jan. 31, 1955, p. 7.
102. "The Limits of Military Power," NL, May 30, 1955, p. 16; see also "American Leadership in the Cold War," CC, vol. 14, no. 17 (Oct. 18, 1954).
103. "The Sources of American Prestige," NL, Jan. 31, 1955.
104. Cf. Marshall, C.B., *The Limits of Foreign Policy,* Henry Holt & Co. New York, 1954, p. 89.
105. "The Limits of American Power", CS, vol. 17, no. 4 (Autumn 1952), p. 5.
106. "British Experience and American Power," CC, vol. 16, no. 8 (May 14, 1956), p. 57.
107. Editorial Notes, CC, vol. 7, no. 14 (Aug. 4, 1947), p. 2.
108. "The Peril of Our Foreign Policy," CS, vol. 8, no. 2 (Spring 1943), p. 20.
109. Editorial Notes, CC, vol. 7, no. 13 (July 21, 1947), p. 2.
110. "Hybris," CS, vol. 16, no. 2 (Spring 1951), p. 4; see also, "The Marshall Plan," CC, vol. 7, no. 17 (Oct. 13, 1947).
111. "Streaks of Dawn in the Night," CC, vol. 9, no. 21 (Dec. 12, 1949), p. 162; cf. Dorothy Fosdick, *Common Sense and World Affairs,* Harcourt, Brace and Co., New York, 1955, pp. 104ff.
112. "The North Atlantic Pact," CC, vol. 9, no. 9 (May 30, 1949).
113. "The Peril of War and the Prospects of Peace," CC, vol. 11, no. 17 (Oct. 15, 1951), p. 129; see also "The MacArthur Episode," CS, vol. 16, no. 3 (Summer 1951).
114. "The Two Dimensions of the Struggle," CC, vol. 11, no. 9 (May 28, 1951), p. 66; see also "The Anatomy of American Nationalism," NL, Feb. 28, 1955; and "Frustrations of American Power," NL, Nov. 29, 1954.
115. "As Others See Us," CC, vol. 6, no. 21 (Dec. 6, 1946), p. 5.
116. Quoted by Niebuhr in "The French Do Not Like Us," CS, Winter 1953–54, p. 12.
117. ibid.
118. "Report on a Conversation: Niebuhr and de Pury," CS, Winter 1954–55.
119. *Common Sense and World Affairs,* op. cit. chap. 11.

120. "What Course for the Ship of State?" *Voting Guide*, 1956, p. 30; also "The Resources of Nations," CS, vol. 12, no. 3 (Summer 1947).
121. "Beria and McCarthy," NL, Jan. 4, 1954, p. 4.
122. "Report on a Conversation: Niebuhr and de Pury," op. cit., p. 23.
123. IAH, pp. 124ff; see also Ludwig Freund, *Politik und Ethik* in which he discusses the presuppositions and boundaries of democracy, especially note his use of Niebuhr, p. 101f.
124. "Imperialism and Irresponsibility," CC, vol. 1. no. 2 (Feb. 24, 1941), p. 6.
125. IAH, p. 112f.
126. "Neither Adam Smith nor Karl Marx," NL, Dec. 23, 1957, p. 9.
127. Editorial Notes, CC, vol. 16, no. 5 (April 2, 1956), p. 34f.
128. "Mideast Impasse: Is There a Way Out?", NL, June 4, 1956, p. 10.
129. "New Hopes for Peace in the Middle East," CC, vol. 16, no. 9 (May 28, 1956).
130. "Europe's Crisis and America's Dilemma," CC, vol. 16, no. 23 (Jan. 7, 1957).
131. "The Decline of Britain and France," CC, vol. 17, no. 2 (Feb. 18, 1957), p. 11.
132. Thompson, K., "Europe's Crisis and America's Dilemma," CC, Jan. 7, 1957, p. 184.
133. ibid. p. 185.
134. ibid. p. 186; cf. Louis J. Halle's letter in CC, vol. 17, no. 4 (March 18, 1957), p. 31.
135. ibid. p. 185.
136. "Eisenhower's Theory of Power and Morals," NL, March 11, 1957.
137. See "The Situation in the Middle East," CC, vol. 17, no. 6 (April 15, 1957) and "The Anglo-Saxon Alliance," vol. 17, no. 8 (May 13, 1957).
138. See, for example, "Seven Great Errors of U.S. Foreign Policy," NL, Dec. 24–31, 1956.
139. ibid.

*Seven* WAR AND PEACE

1. "The World Council and the Peace Issue," CC, vol. 10, no. 14 (August 7, 1950), p. 108.
2. LLT, p. 64.
3. LNTC, p. 47.
4. ibid.
5. "Why I Am Not a Christian," *The Christian Century*, Dec. 15, 1927, p. 1482.
6. ibid.
7. "The Preaching of Repentance," *The Christian Century*, April 30, 1930, p. 780.
8. This dilemma is the subject of many articles, but see CRSW, p. 21 and, of course, the whole of MMIS.
9. ICE, p. 61.
10. See "Let Liberal Churches Stop Fooling Themselves," *The Christian Century*, March 25, 1931, p. 402.
11. "Germany Must Be Told," ibid. Aug. 9, 1933.

12. REE, pp. 147 and 247.

13. For example, CPP, chap. 1.

14. See "Individualism and Civilization," CS, vol. 5, no. 4 (Fall 1940), p. 9; see also CPP, chap. 1.

15. See "God Wills Both Justice and Peace," CC, vol. 15, no. 10 (June 13, 1955).

16. Roberts, Richard, "An Open Letter to Niebuhr," CS, vol. 5, no. 2 (Spring 1940), pp. 41 and 43.

17. "An Open Letter to Richard Roberts," CS, vol. 5, no. 3 (Summer 1940), p. 31.

18. Niebuhr wrote a scorching critique of the *Times* on this issue; see "The London Times and the Crisis," RR, vol. 4, no. 1 (Winter 1938) and CPP, pp. 87-9.

19. CPP, p. 33.

20. ibid. p. 34.

21. "Moral Rearmament," RR, vol. 4, no. 4 (Fall 1939), p. 10. For further and more serious criticism see CPP, chap. 12, entitled "Hitler and Buchman,"; also "Buchmanism and World Peace," RR, vol. 3, no. 4 (Fall 1938).

22. Tittle, E.F., "God and the National Policy," *The Christian Century*, Nov. 30, 1938, p. 1464.

23. "The Will of God and the Van Zeeland Report," ibid. Dec. 14, 1938, p. 1550.

24. ibid. May 29, 1940. p. 706.

25. "Isaiah [*sic!*] Speaks to America," *ibid.* July 3, 1940, p. 850. C.B. Marshall has perfectly expressed our feelings as we read the literature of those days: "One reads now the literature and the debates on international affairs in the 1930's almost with a sense of disbelief. What might happen in regard to factors of power elsewhere in the world was to be of no moment to us. Whether nations friendly or hostile to us controlled the seas and the resources of the continents of the bad old hemisphere was deemed inconsequential. In a favored phrase of the day, America was to be a 'pool of sanity'—a sanity presumed to inhere in a complete disregard of the importance of factors of power. America was to sit apart from the world in complete moral self-sufficiency. Others might fight. We would be indifferent to the outcome. The battles over, the victor and the defeated could then lower their buckets and draw up draughts of sanity from our pool to wash away the stains of their transgressions." (*The Limits of Foreign Policy*, op. cit. p. 118).

26. "To Prevent the Triumph of an Intolerable Tyranny," *The Christian Century,* Dec. 18, 1940, p. 1580.

27. "The Christian Faith and the World Crisis," CC, vol. 1, no. 1 (Feb. 10, 1941), p. 4.

28. "Repeal the Neutrality Act," CC, vol. 1, no. 18 (Oct. 20, 1941), p. 1.

29. Morrison, C.C., "Is Neutrality Immoral?", *The Christian Century*, Nov. 12, 1941, p. 1400.

30. "Pacifism and America First," CC, vol. 1, no. 10 (June 16, 1941); see also "National Defense," CS, vol. 5, no. 2 (Spring 1940).

31. "We Are at War," CC, vol. 1, no. 23 (Dec. 29, 1941), p. 2.

32. "Our Responsibilities in 1942," CC., vol. no. 24 (Jan. 12, 1942), p. 1f.;

see also "Love Your Enemies," CS, vol. 7, no. 4 (Aug. 1942); "Restraint and Modesty in the Pulpit," CC, vol. 1, no. 25 (Jan. 26, 1942); "Preaching in War Time," CC, vol. 2, no. 1 (Feb. 9, 1942).

33. CC, vol. 4, no. 1 (Feb. 7, 1944).
34. e.g. "Is the Bombing Necessary?", CC, vol. 4, no. 5 (April 3, 1944).
35. "The End of Total War," CS, vol. 9, no. 4 (Fall 1944), p. 4.
36. A constant theme with Niebuhr in these years; see "Judgment and Forgiveness," CS, vol. 9, no. 3 (Summer 1944); "Anger and Forgiveness," which is chap. 2 of DST.
37. "Justice for the Enemy," CS, vol. 9. no. 4 (Fall 1944), p. 6.
38. Niebuhr has written much on this subject. However, the following chapters contain the meat of all he has had to say: CLCD, chap. 5, "The World Community"; CRPP, chap. 2, "The Illusion of World Government"; SDH, chap. 22, "The Integration of the World Community." Our discussion here is largely based on these chapters.
39. CRPP, p. 18.
40. See "Alternatives to the H-Bomb: A Century of Cold War," NL, August 2, 1954. This article is a devastating criticism of Lewis Mumford's proposals for World Government.
41. CRPP, p. 22ff.
42. ibid. p. 29.
43. CLCD, p. 186.
44. SDH, p. 206.
45. "The Churches and the United Nations," CS, Winter 1952–53, p. 3.
46. "The Dismal Prospects of Disarmament," CC, vol. 17, no. 15 (Sept. 16, 1957), p. 113.
47. See Niebuhr's favorable comments on Henry Kissinger's book, *Nuclear Weapons and Foreign Policy*, in CC, vol. 17, no. 19 (Nov. 11, 1957).

*Eight* ECONOMICS

1. See, for example, "Is Stewardship Ethical?", *The Christian Century*, April 30, 1930.
2. "Religion and Class War in Kentucky," *The Christian Century*, May 18, 1932, p. 638. Niebuhr recalls this experience as late as 1956 in a discussion of the inability of this religious heritage to deal with collective evils. See his "Proposal to Billy Graham," *The Christian Century*, August 8, 1956.
3. LLT, p. 5.
4. "Ford's Five-Day Week Shrinks," *The Christian Century*, June 9, 1927.
5. In LLT, chaps. 3,5, and 6.
6. Crossman, R. (ed.), *The God That Failed*, Bantam Books, p. 5.
7. MMIS, p. 194.
8. REE, p. 273f.
9. ibid. p. 274.
10. MMIS, p. 167.
11. REE, p. 195.
12. See Niebuhr's review of the thought of the Fellowship in Hutchison (ed.), *Christian Faith and Social Action*, op. cit.
13. RR, vol. 1, no. 3 (Spring 1936), p. 27.

14. "Socialist Decision and Christian Conscience," RR, vol. 3, no. 2 (Spring 1938), p. 2.
15. "Christian Socialism," RR, vol. 3, no. 4 (Fall 1938).
16. "Farewell," CS, vol. 21, no. 3 (Summer 1956), p. 3.
17. LLT, p. 160.
18. "The Christian Faith and the Economic Life of Liberal Society," in Ward, A.D. (ed.), *Goals of Economic Life*, Harper, New York, 1953, p. 433.
19. IAH, p. 93.
20. "Coercion, Self-Interest, and Love," in Boulding, K., *The Organizational Revolution*, Harper, New York, 1953, p. 234f.
21. In Ward, op. cit. p. 435.
22. IAH, p. 94.
23. In Ward, op. cit. p. 437.
24. For a scathing criticism of the one-sidedness of the American "dogma" or "ideology" of freedom, see Nieuhr's article "The Cult of Freedom in America" in CC, vol. 9, no. 1 (Feb. 7, 1949). The occasion for this article was the response in reactionary quarters to the Amsterdam Report of the World Council of Churches. See also the chapter entitled "Liberty and Equality" in PSA. for an excellent discussion of these two regulative principles. "The principle of 'equality' is a relevant criterion of criticism for the social hierarchy, and the principle of 'liberty' serves the same purpose for the community's unity. But neither principle could be wholly nor absolutely applied without destroying the community." (PSA, p. 62).
25. Schall, James V., "The Political Theory of Reinhold Niebuhr," *Thought*, Spring 1958, p. 74.
26. ibid. p. 75.
27. FH, p. 191.
28. "The Pope on Property," CS, vol. 9, no. 4 (Fall 1944), p. 8.
29. See, for example, FH, p. 191 and CLCD, p. 91f.
30. CLCD, p. 102.
31. ibid. p. 99.
32. ibid. p. 106.
33. ibid. p. 118.
34. "The Fate of European Socialism," NL, June 20, 1955, p. 8; cf. "Farewell," CS, Summer 1956 and SDH, p. 199.
35. "The 'Right To Work' Laws," CC, vol. 17, no. 4 (March 18, 1957), p. 25.
36. ibid.
37. "Lewis and the C.I.O.," CS, vol. 6, no. 1 (Winter 1940), p. 6f.
38. See "Democracy and the Trade Unions," CC, vol. 17, no. 8 (May 13, 1957) and "Hoffa and the Teamsters," CC, vol. 17, no. 18 (Oct. 28, 1957).
39. "Discriminate Justice in a Technical Society," NL, Jan. 20, 1958, p. 14.
40. See ibid.
41. Ward, op. cit. p. 445f.
42. ibid. p. 446.
43. ibid. p. 445.
44. ibid. p. 447.
45. See PSA, chap. 1.
46. In Ward, op. cit. p. 455.
47. ibid. p. 456.
48. ibid. p. 452.

*Nine* RACE

1. See, for example, "The Confession of a Tired Radical," *The Christian Century*, August 30, 1928. Reprinted in LJ, pp. 120ff.
2. "Christian Faith and the Race Problem," CS, Spring 1945. Reprinted in LJ, pp. 125ff.
3. Editorial Notes, CC, vol. 12, no. 23 (Jan. 5, 1953), p. 178.
4. For the reader concerned with this the following will be of interest: "Jews after the War," an article in two parts in *The Nation*, Feb. 21 and Feb. 28, 1942. This article was republished in LJ, pp. 132-42. "The Relations of Christians and Jews in Western Civilization," chap. 7 of PSA. See also Niebuhr's Introduction to Waldo Frank's *The Jew in Our Day*, Duell, Sloan and Pearce, New York, 1944.
5. Beach, W., "A Theological Analysis of Race Relations," chap. 7 in Paul Ramsey (ed.), *Faith and Ethics: The Theology of H. Richard Niebuhr*, Harper and Brothers, New York 1957, p. 208.
6. "The Christian Faith and the Race Problem," CS, Spring 1945; also LJ, p. 126.
7. This literature is already a shoreless sea but mention might be made of the standard text by G.E. Simpson and J.M. Yinger, *Racial and Cultural Minorities: An Analysis of Prejudice and Discrimination*, Harper and Brothers, New York, 1953.
8. "The Christian Faith and the Race Problem," op. cit. (LJ, p. 127f.).
9. ibid. (LJ, p. 129).
10. ibid. (LJ, p. 128).
11. "The Race Problem," CS, Summer 1942; LJ, p. 130.
12. CLCD, p. 140.
13. ibid. p. 140f.
14. "The Race Problem," CS, Summer, 1942; LJ, p. 130f.
15. "Can Social Problems Be Solved?", in Hutchison, J. (ed.), *Christian Faith and Social Action*, p. 223.
16. "The Race Problem," LJ, p. 132.
17. ibid. p. 131.
18. "Bad Days at Little Rock," CC, vol. 17, no. 17 (Oct. 14, 1947), p. 131.
19. "The Race Problem in America," CC, vol. 15, no. 22 (Dec. 26, 1955).
20. Hook, S., "Democracy and Desegregation," NL, sect. 2, April 21, 1958, p. 11; see the entire article.
21. ibid.
22. Kelsey G., "The Ethico-Cultural Revolution in American Race Relations," *Religion in Life*, Summer 1957, p. 342.
23. "The South African Tragedy," CS vol. 20, no. 2 (Spring 1955), p. 5.
24. "The Supreme Court on Segregation in the Schools," CC, June 14, 1954; or LJ, p. 152.
25. Beach, W., "Storm Warnings from The South," CC, vol. 16, no. 4 (March 19, 1956), p. 30.
26. See Editorial Notes, CC, vol. 16, no. 3 (March 5, 1956).
27. *The Christian Century*, Sept. 4, 1957.

28. "Proposal To Billy Graham," *The Christian Century*, Aug. 8, 1956; LJ, p. 158.
29. ibid.
30. ibid. (LJ, p. 156f.).
31. "After Comment: The Deluge," *The Christian Century*, Sept. 4, 1957, p. 1035. See also "Literalism, Individualism and Billy Graham," *The Christian Century*, May 23, 1956.
32. PSA, p. 82.
33. Beach, W., "The Southern Churches and the Race Question," CC, vol. 18, no. 3 (March 3, 1958), p. 17.
34. ibid.
35. PSA, p. 83.
36. For an excellent discussion of all this see CC, vol. 18, no. 3 (March 3, 1958). The entire issue is given over to reports by well-qualified observers of the situation of the churches in the South. The issue must be reckoned one of the most important to appear in this journal in recent years.
37. Mead, S.E., "Denominationalism—The Shape of Protestantism in America," *Church History*, Dec. 1954, p. 291.
38. CC, vol. 18, no. 3 (March 3, 1958), p. 24.
39. ibid.
40. Attention ought here to be drawn to a few such attempts, e.g. Waldo Beach, "A Theological Analysis of Race Relations" in Ramsey, P. (ed.), *Faith and Ethics: The Theology of H. Richard Niebuhr*, Harper's New York, 1957; G.D. Kelsey, "The Christian Way In Race Relations," in a book bearing the same title edited by W.S. Nelson, Harper, New York, 1948; H. Shelton Smith, "Christian Faith and Racial Valuation," *Theology Today*, July 1945.
41. "The Negro Issue in America," CS, Summer 1944; LJ, p. 144.
42. Beach, W., "A Theological Analysis of Race Relations," in Ramsey, P. (ed.), op. cit. p. 213.
43. "The Negro Issue in America," LJ, p. 145.